SYSTEMATIC THEOLOGY AT THE TABLE

A 90-DAY DISCUSSION GUIDE FOR FAMILIES

BUILT TO STAND PUBLISHING

TABLE OF CONTENTS

INTRODUCTION TO SYSTEMATIC THEOLOGY AT THE TABLE

WELCOME TO YOUR FAMILY'S THEOLOGICAL JOURNEY

Whether you're starting this devotional with excitement, hope, or even honest skepticism, we're glad you're here. Over the next ninety days, your family will explore the foundational truths of the Christian faith—not in a seminary classroom or only from a pulpit, but around your dinner table, in your living room, in the car, and in the ordinary spaces where real life happens.

This guide exists for one simple reason: to help your family grow in knowing Jesus and living out your faith together. Not to turn you into theologians. Not to make you feel like you must have all the answers. Instead, the goal is to create space for honest conversation, for wrestling with hard questions, and for discovering how faith shapes everyday life.

IT'S OKAY IF THIS ISN'T COMPLETED IN 90 DAYS

Let's get this out of the way right away: You don't have to complete this guide in ninety consecutive days. Life is messy. Kids get sick. Schedules get busy. You'll have weeks when you miss several days—or even an entire week. That's not failure. That's simply real life.

This guide is designed to be flexible and grace-filled. Use it at the pace that works best for your family. Some families might do one devotion each day. Others might do three each week. Some might work through it over six months or even a full year. Whatever rhythm helps your family stay consistent without feeling pressured—that's the right rhythm.

Think of this as a journey of faith, not a sprint. The goal isn't to check boxes or finish a challenge. The goal is to build a culture of faith-filled conversation in your home—one discussion at a time, at whatever pace works best for your family.

WHERE AND WHEN TO USE THIS GUIDE

THE DINNER TABLE

The dinner table is the heart of family life. It's where you naturally gather, where conversations flow, where you can slow down together. We designed this guide specifically for that context.

Here's why the dinner table matters:

- Everyone is usually present and relatively free from distractions (ideally).
- It's a natural rhythm that many families already maintain.
- Food naturally invites conversation.
- It's informal enough to encourage honest conversation without making it feel forced.

BUT THE DINNER TABLE ISN'T YOUR ONLY OPTION

If dinner table conversations don't work well for your family, maybe schedules are chaotic, maybe dinners are rushed, or maybe your kids are resistant to lingering at the table, that's okay. Use this guide wherever meaningful conversations naturally happen in your home. Here are a few other places where this devotional can work beautifully.

- The Car
- Bedtime
- Family Meetings
- Breakfast or Coffee
- Sunday After Church

- Snack Time or Afternoon Hang
- Screen-Free Nights
- Weekend Getaways
- One-on-One Time

FLEXIBLE FREQUENCY

You don't have to do one devotion per day. Here are some other rhythms that work:

- 3 times a week → Finish in 30 weeks
- 2 times a week → Finish in 45 weeks (roughly 10 months)
- Once a week → Finish in 90 weeks (roughly 20 months)
- Combination approach → Maybe 3-4 times a week during the school year, 1-2 times during the summer
- Seasonal → Work through one unit per season (10 units, 4 seasons = natural rhythm)

WHAT TO EXPECT IN EACH DEVOTION

Every daily entry follows the same structure, so your family will quickly know what to expect:

Opening Scenario: A relatable, real-life situation that introduces the topic naturally.

Conversation Starter: One open-ended question to get everyone talking before any teaching begins.

Short Teaching: A few paragraphs explaining the theological concept in everyday language (this is for you to read and share, not for your kids to read).

Discussion Prompts: 2–3 questions that move from understanding, to personal response, to lived practice.

Parent Note: Coaching for you (not to read aloud) about how to lead the conversation.

Action Step: One simple, concrete practice to do together that day or week.

One-Sentence Anchor: A memorable truth your family can repeat and remember.

Scripture Reading: 3–5 Bible passages to read together.

TIPS FOR SUCCESS

1. You Don't Need to Be a Theologian
   You're not delivering seminary-level lectures. You're having real family conversations. If a question stumps you, it's perfectly okay to say, "I don't know. Let's look that up," or "That's a great question. Let's think about it together." Honesty and curiosity are far more powerful than having all the answers.

2. Invite Honest Questions and Doubts
   If your kids say, "I don't believe that," or "That doesn't make sense," don't shut them down. Engage with their questions and help them wrestle with the ideas. Faith that can't handle doubts is fragile. Real faith grows when it's explored through honest conversation.

3. Don't Force It
   If a particular devotion doesn't seem to connect with your family, skip it. You don't have to do every devotion in order. If the conversation shifts direction, let it unfold naturally. This is a guide, not a rigid script.

4. Keep It Age-Appropriate
   You have kids of different ages. Adjust the discussion prompts and teaching to match what they can understand. A ten-year-old and a seventeen-year-old will engage with the conversation differently. That's okay. Let them contribute at the level that feels comfortable for them.

5. Make It Conversational, Not a Lecture
   Don't read the "Short Teaching" section word-for-word. Paraphrase it in your own words. Tell stories from your life. Ask authentic questions. Let your kids see you thinking through theology for yourself, not just transmitting it.

6. Be Vulnerable
   Share your own struggles, doubts, and spiritual growth. Let your kids see that faith isn't about having it all figured out. It's about trusting Jesus and walking with Him, even when life feels messy.

7. Follow Up on the Action Step
   The action steps are where theology becomes a lived reality. Don't just suggest them and move on. Take time actually to do them. And the next time you gather, ask: "How did that go? What did you learn?" This helps train your family to apply faith in everyday life.

8. Celebrate What You're Building
   You're not just teaching content. You're creating a family culture where faith is explored, practiced, and lived together. That's extraordinary. Take time to notice it. Thank your kids and celebrate their growth. Let them know this time together matters.

9. Before You Start
   Sit down without your kids and:

   Decide what daily or weekly rhythm works best for your family

   - Pick the time and place that works best for your conversations
   - Read through a few devotions first to get a sense of the tone
   - Pray and ask God to guide your family during these conversations
   - Release the pressure to be perfect

10. When You Gather

    1. Set the tone: "Hey, tonight we're going to talk about [topic]. I want to hear what you think."
    2. Read the opening scenario, or paraphrase it in your own words.
    3. Ask the conversation starter questions and truly listen to their answers.
    4. Share the teaching in your own words, not as a lecture.
    5. Ask the discussion prompts, giving space for genuine answers.
    6. Commit to the action step together.
    7. Close with the anchor statement and scripture reading.

11. After the Conversation
    Follow up to see if the action step was completed

    - Notice growth in your kids' thinking and daily life
    - Adjust the pace and approach based on what works best
    - Keep going, even when it feels like nothing is sticking

The Big Picture

These 90 devotions are organized into 10 units:

1. Who God Is (Who your family is worshiping)
2. Human Identity (Who your family is)
3. Brokenness and Sin (Why your family needs Jesus)
4. Jesus and Redemption (How Jesus saves and transforms)
5. Grace and Salvation (What it means to be saved by grace)
6. The Holy Spirit (How transformation actually happens)
7. Growth and Character (How your family is becoming like Jesus)
8. Community and Church (Why your family needs others)
9. Purpose and Work (How your family finds meaning)
10. Hope and the Future (Where your family is headed)

Each unit builds on the previous one. So even if you don't do all 90 consecutively, try to do them in order. Theology has a logic. Each truth builds on the others.

A FINAL WORD BEFORE YOU BEGIN

You're about to invest something precious, time with your family, talking about what matters most.

You might not see immediate results. Your kids might seem disinterested. The conversations might feel awkward at first. That's normal. Keep going anyway.

What you're building is a foundation. You're teaching your family that faith matters enough to talk about. That theology isn't boring; it is life-changing. That every voice in the family matters. That God is worth talking about.

Over time, it may take longer than you expect. This becomes the culture of your home. Your kids may begin asking faith questions on their own. They may start applying Scripture to their lives. They may even comfort each other with the truth of the gospel. They become disciples who learn to think theologically about everyday life.

That's worth it!

So take a deep breath. Don't worry about doing it perfectly. Gather your family. Ask good questions. Listen well. And trust that God is already at work.

A PRAYER BEFORE YOU START

Pray this as you begin:

Father, as we gather around this table, or in this space, we invite You in. Help us to know You better. Help our family understand Your truth, not only in our minds, but in the way we live each day. Open our hearts. Give us the courage to ask hard questions and the wisdom to listen well. Transform us through Your Word and Your Spirit. Not because we will do this perfectly, but because You are faithful. Amen.

Now, Let's Begin!

UNIT 1

WHO GOD IS

(THEOLOGY PROPER)

DAY 1 WHY OUR VIEW OF GOD SHAPES EVERYTHING

OPENING SCENARIO

It is Tuesday evening, and your daughter has not stopped moving since she got home from school. She has rearranged her backpack three times, rewritten her homework planner, and asked you twice whether her project is good enough. When you gently ask what is going on, she blurts out, "What if I mess up? What if I do not get it right?" Her voice cracks slightly.

Across the table, your son shrugs. God does not really care about homework, he says flatly. But you notice he has been unusually quiet lately, like he is carrying something heavy he does not want to name. Both kids seem to be living in two different worlds, one clinging tightly to control, the other drifting into indifference. *And you realize that the way they think about God shapes how they move through their day.*

CONVERSATION STARTER

Before we go further, let us talk. When you picture God in your mind, what do you imagine? Does he feel close or far away? Do you feel excited about your life, or mostly disappointed?

SHORT TEACHING

Here's the truth we often miss: our view of God shapes almost everything in our lives. If we believe God is harsh and impossible to please, **we'll live in fear and exhaustion**, constantly trying to be good enough. If we think He's distant and uninvolved, we'll drift through life without purpose or hope. If we imagine Him as weak or irrelevant, we'll try to control everything ourselves, only to burn out.

But what if God is actually good? **Not just all-powerful, but kind.** Not just holy, but near. Not just aware of our failures, but devoted to our flourishing. The Bible doesn't start with rules or rituals; it starts with a God who creates, calls things good, and walks with His people. That God doesn't change. He's not moody. He doesn't play favorites. He's not shocked by our struggles or bored by our ordinary days.

When we begin to see God clearly, as He truly is, everything shifts. **Fear turns into trust. Striving turns into rest.** Shame turns into confidence. Our view of God isn't just a theological idea; it is the lens through which we interpret every moment: stress at school, conflict with a friend, disappointment in ourselves, uncertainty about the future.

The question isn't whether our view of God will shape us. It's whether we'll let the true God shape who we are. Or settle for a distorted version pieced together from fear, assumptions, and cultural noise.

DISCUSSION PROMPTS

1. **Understanding:** What are some ways people misunderstand who God really is? (Examples: always angry, uninterested, only cares about big spiritual things, etc.)

2. **Personal Response:** Think about a time this week when you felt worried, frustrated, or unsure. Now imagine if you truly believed that God was good and right there with you in that moment. How might it have felt different?

3. **Lived Practice:** Where in your life right now do you feel like you're white-knuckling control or drifting in indifference? What would it look like to trust God there instead?

PARENT NOTE

This conversation may surface some surprisingly honest and even uncomfortable answers. Kids often reveal that they think of God as a distant boss, an unpredictable judge, or a cosmic vending machine. Don't worry, this is actually a gift. It shows you where the real work of spiritual formation needs to happen.

Your goal tonight isn't to correct every wrong idea or deliver a perfect theology lesson. It's to start the conversation and model curiosity, honesty, and trust. Let them voice their doubts. Affirm their questions. Then gently point them toward Scripture's consistent picture*: a God who is powerful and personal, holy and compassionate, sovereign and good.*

Common misconception to address: Many kids, and even adults, often assume that believing in God's goodness means life will be easy or pain-free. Clarify that God's goodness does not take away hardship. Instead, it means we can trust Him during hard times, because His character never changes and His purposes are loving, even when life is difficult.

ACTION STEP

Tonight, go around the table, and each person finish this sentence:
"One thing I'd like to trust God with this week is…"

Then pray together, keeping it short and simple, asking God to help your family see Him clearly and trust Him more.

ONE-SENTENCE ANCHOR

Our view of God shapes how we face every moment—fear or trust, control or surrender.
"The LORD is good, a stronghold in the day of trouble; he knows those who take refuge in him." — *Nahum 1:7*

SCRIPTURE READING

Psalm 103:8–14
Exodus 34:6–7
James 1:17
John 1:14–18
Romans 8:31–39

DAY 2 GOD'S ATTRIBUTES IN EVERYDAY LANGUAGE

OPENING SCENARIO

Your son is building a Lego set at the kitchen table when his younger sister accidentally knocks half of it to the floor. He explodes. "You never pay attention! You always wreck my stuff!" You step in, asking him to calm down, and he fires back, "Well, isn't God supposed to be just? She should get in trouble."

Later that evening, your daughter whispers to you before bed, "Is God mad at me for knocking over the Legos?" You assure her He's not, but she looks uncertain. "Then does God even care about little things like that, or is He only paying attention to big stuff, like wars and diseases?"

Both kids are grasping for language to describe who God is. One wants justice—the other wonders about attention. And you realize they are actually asking about *God's attributes, even though they don't have the words for it yet.*

CONVERSATION STARTER

Let's start here: If you had to describe God to someone who had never met Him, what words would you use? What is He like?

SHORT TEACHING

The Bible uses specific words to describe who God is, not to make theology complicated, but to help us know Him accurately. These are called God's attributes, and they matter because the God we worship is not a vague feeling or a general idea. **He is real, and He has a character we can trust.**

Let's make it simple. God is good, which means everything He does flows from love and aims toward what is truly best, even when we can't see it yet. He is just, which means He cares deeply about right and wrong and values truth. **Sin and cruelty matter to Him. He doesn't ignore injustice. He is powerful, not just strong, but able to do anything that aligns with His nature.** Nothing is too hard for Him, and nothing catches Him off guard. And He is present, which means He's not watching from a distance like a distracted supervisor. He is near, attentive, and involved in the details of your life.

Here's why this matters at the dinner table, in the carpool line, and during homework meltdowns: these attributes work together. His goodness shapes God's justice. His love guides his power. His presence means His care is personal, not mechanical. You are not serving a God who is sometimes kind and sometimes cruel, sometimes strong and sometimes absent. He is always all of these things, perfectly, at the same time.

When your kids understand God's attributes in everyday language, they stop imagining a God who is moody, unreliable, or indifferent. They begin to trust a God who is steady, faithful, and worthy of their whole hearts.

DISCUSSION PROMPTS

1. **Understanding:** Which of these words, good, just, powerful, or present, is easiest for you to believe about God? Which one feels hardest to believe, and why?

2. **Personal Response:** Think about a time when you felt like God wasn't noticing or didn't care. What would it mean to believe that He was *both powerful and present in that moment?*

3. **Lived Practice:** Think about a time when you felt like God wasn't noticing or didn't care about what was happening. What would it mean to believe that He was both powerful and present with you in that moment?

PARENT NOTE

Attributes can feel abstract, so your job is to make them concrete and relational. Instead of giving a vocabulary lesson, think of this as helping your kids build a mental picture of God they can return to when life gets confusing.

Watch for two common pitfalls: kids who overemphasize God's justice and become anxious rule-followers, and kids who overemphasize God's love and assume He overlooks sin or doesn't care about obedience. The beauty of God's character is that His attributes don't contradict; they complete each other. His justice is loving. His love is truthful. His power is gentle. His presence is holy.

Coaching tip: When your kids bring up attributes in real time, like "Is God mad at me?" or "Why didn't God stop this?" don't rush to fix their theology. Instead, ask a follow-up question: "What do you think that tells us about who God is?" Let them process their thoughts out loud. You are not just teaching content; you are teaching them how to think about God.

ACTION STEP

Tonight, pick one attribute of God and find one place this week where you need to remember it.

Write it on a sticky note and put it somewhere you'll see it every day: the bathroom mirror, the car dashboard, the backpack, or the lunchbox. Let it be a simple, repeated reminder of who God truly is.

ONE-SENTENCE ANCHOR

God is good, just, powerful, and present—and these truths shape how we face every day.
"The LORD is righteous in all his ways and kind in all his works."
— Psalm 145:17

SCRIPTURE READING

Psalm 145:8–9, 17–18
Deuteronomy 32:4
Psalm 139:7–10
Isaiah 40:28–31
1 John 4:8–10

DAY 3

MISUNDERSTANDINGS—DISTANT GOD, HARSH GOD, PASSIVE GOD

OPENING SCENARIO

Sunday morning. You're trying to get everyone out the door for church, and your teenager is dragging his feet again. You finally ask what's wrong, and he mutters, "I just don't see the point. I pray, and nothing happens. I mess up, and nothing happens. It's like God is just not really involved."

Meanwhile, your youngest is in tears because she accidentally lied to you yesterday about finishing her chores, and now she's convinced God is "really, really mad" and might not forgive her. She's been scared to pray ever since.

Two kids. Same household. Same teaching. But one thinks God is too distant to care, and the other thinks He is too harsh to approach. Somewhere in the middle, you're realizing how easy it is to get God wrong and how much damage those misunderstandings can do.

CONVERSATION STARTER

Let's be honest: What's one way you've misunderstood God before—or maybe still do? What made you think that about Him?

SHORT TEACHING

If we're not careful, we'll create a version of God in our minds that bears little resemblance to who He really is. The three most common distortions look like this:

The Distant God feels far away, uninvolved, and maybe even indifferent. He seems to be watching from a distance but not really participating. This version says, "God is busy with bigger things. He doesn't care about your problems." It leads to loneliness, self-reliance, and a faith that feels more like a theory than a real relationship.

The Harsh God is impossible to please, always disappointed, and keeps a record of wrongs. This version says, "You'd better get it right, or else." It produces fear, shame, and exhausting religion, where you are always trying to earn approval you never quite reach.

The Passive God is kind but weak, present but powerless. He means well, but he can't actually do anything. This version says, "God loves you, but He can't really help." It leads to anxiety, because if God isn't in control, then you feel like you have to be.

Here's the problem: **none of these gods is real.** The God of Scripture is not distant. He is Immanuel, God with us. He's not harsh. He is patient, slow to anger, and abounding in steadfast love. And he's not passive. He is the Creator of the universe, sovereign over history, and powerful enough to hold every moment of your life in His hands.

When we believe lies about God, we end up living in fear, shame, or despair. But when we replace those lies with truth, everything changes. We can be honest in prayer because God is near. We can confess sin without fear because God is merciful. We can rest in uncertainty because God is powerful and good.

DISCUSSION PROMPTS

1. **Understanding:** Which of these misunderstandings, distant, harsh, or passive, have you noticed in yourself or others? Where do you think these ideas come from?

2. **Personal Response:** If you've ever felt like God was far away, too strict, or unable to help, what truth from Scripture could remind you of who He really is instead of that lie?

3. **Lived Practice:** This week, when you're tempted to imagine God in one of these distorted ways, pause and ask: "Is this really true? Or is this fear talking?"

PARENT NOTE

Your kids didn't invent these distortions out of nowhere. They absorbed them from culture, from painful experiences, from things other people said, and yes, sometimes from us. If you've ever said or implied, "God's going to be so disappointed in you," or "Just pray harder and it'll work out," you may have accidentally reinforced one of these lies.

This is not about parental guilt. It is about parental awareness. You have the opportunity to correct the narrative now, gently. When your child expresses a distorted view of God, do not shame them for it. Trace it back: "Where did you get that idea?" Then offer a better story, rooted in Scripture.

Watch for this. Kids who grow up with a harsh view of God often become either perfectionistic rule-followers or secret rule-breakers. Kids who grow up with a distant view of God often become spiritually apathetic or self-reliant. Kids who grow up with a passive view of God often become anxious, controlling adults. The stakes are higher than we realize.

ACTION STEP

Together as a family, name one lie about God that you've believed and then replace it with a truth from Scripture. Write both down. Keep the truth. Throw the lie away, literally rip it up, or toss it. Let it be a physical reminder that we don't have to live under false versions of God.

ONE-SENTENCE ANCHOR

When we replace lies about God with truth, fear turns to trust, and shame turns to rest.
"Draw near to God, and he will draw near to you." —James 4:8

SCRIPTURE READING

Psalm 103:8–14
Matthew 28:20
Lamentations 3:22–23
Isaiah 41:10
Romans 8:38–39

DAY 4 IDENTITY UNDER A GOOD GOD—ANXIETY, SECURITY, AND SURRENDER

OPENING SCENARIO

Your daughter comes home from school and immediately starts spiraling. She didn't make the team. Her friend said something weird at lunch. Her quiz grade wasn't what she hoped. Now she's pacing the kitchen, talking too fast, and unable to settle. "What if I'm not good at anything? What if no one really likes me?" You try to reassure her, but she waves you off. "You have to say that. You're my parent." The anxiety isn't really about the quiz or the team; it's deeper. She's questioning whether she's enough, whether she matters, and whether she's secure.

And you realize this is **an identity crisis**. She's trying to build her worth on performance, approval, and control, and it's crumbling under the weight. What she needs isn't another pep talk. She needs to know who she is under a good God.

CONVERSATION STARTER

Let's start here: When do you feel most anxious or insecure? What are you usually worried about in those moments?

SHORT TEACHING

Here's the pattern: when we don't believe God is truly good, we start trying to secure ourselves. We think, "If I can just perform well enough, control enough outcomes, and earn enough approval, then I'll finally be okay." But it never works. There's always another test, another opinion, another thing we can't control. Anxiety becomes the background noise of our lives.

But here's what changes everything: **if God is good, then your identity is already secure.** You are made in His image. You are seen, known, and loved—not because of what you achieve, but because of who He is. Your worth doesn't rise and fall with your grades, friendships, successes, or failures. It is anchored in the God who created you on purpose, calls you His own, and is committed to your good.

This is where surrender comes in. **Surrender isn't giving up or being passive.** It is letting go of the exhausting job of holding your life together by sheer force. It's saying, "God, I can't control all of this. But You are good, You are powerful, and You are present. So I am going to trust You with it."

When your identity is rooted in a good God, anxiety doesn't disappear overnight, but it loses its grip. You no longer need to be perfect because you are already loved. You no longer need to control everything because you trust the One who does. You stop performing for approval because you already have it. And you can finally breathe.

DISCUSSION PROMPTS

1. **Understanding:** What's the difference between trying to *secure yourself* and trusting that God has already secured you?

2. **Personal Response:** What's one area of your life where you're trying to control everything? What would it look like to surrender that to God instead?

3. **Lived Practice:** When anxiety creeps in this week, try praying this simple prayer: "God, You are good. I am Yours. I can trust You with this." How does that feel different than just worrying?

PARENT NOTE

Anxiety in kids, and even in adults, is often a symptom of insecure identity. When we believe our worth depends on performance, we live in constant fear of failure. When we believe our security depends on control, we live in constant stress. Your job as a parent is not to eliminate anxiety, but to help your kids trace it back to the root and replace it with truth.

Be careful not to minimize their feelings with phrases like "Just trust God more!" or feed the performance trap with "You'll do better next time!" Instead, ask curious questions: "What are you afraid will happen if you don't succeed? What do you think that says about your worth?" Then gently point them back to their identity in Christ.

Important distinction: surrendering to God doesn't mean being irresponsible or passive. Your kids still need to study, work hard, and take their commitments seriously. But their worth is not on the line. Their effort flows from security, not anxiety.

ACTION STEP

Before bed tonight, each person names one thing they are trying to control and prays a short prayer of surrender.

It can be as simple as: "God, I can't control [this], but I trust You with it." Let it be a practice of releasing the weight you were never meant to carry.

ONE-SENTENCE ANCHOR

When your identity is anchored in a good God, anxiety loses its power and trust takes root.
"Cast all your anxiety on him because he cares for you." — 1 Peter 5:7

SCRIPTURE READING

Matthew 6:25–34
Philippians 4:6–7
Psalm 55:22
Isaiah 26:3
1 Peter 5:6–7

DAY 5 RELATIONSHIPS—REFLECTING GOD'S PATIENCE AND FAITHFULNESS AT HOME

OPENING SCENARIO

It's been a long day, and your kids are bickering again. Your son snaps at his sister for borrowing his charger without asking. She fires back that he never shares anything. Voices escalate. You step in, exhausted, and hear yourself say, "Why can't you two just get along? I'm so tired of refereeing!"

But later, when the house is quiet, the thought hits you: How often do I snap at them the same way? You think about the impatience in your tone this morning when your daughter couldn't find her shoes. The frustration you felt when your son forgot his homework again. The way you've been short with your spouse all week.

Then you remember yesterday's conversation about God's patience and faithfulness. You wonder, if God is patient with me, endlessly patient, what would it look like to reflect that at home?

CONVERSATION STARTER

Honest moment: Who in this family do you think shows the most patience? Who shows the least? (And yes, parents can answer too.)

SHORT TEACHING

Here's a truth easy to forget: the way God treats us is meant to shape how we treat each other. If God is patient, faithful, and kind toward us even when we fail, forget, and frustrate Him, then our homes should be places where patience, faithfulness, and kindness are the norm, not the exception.

But let's be honest: that's hard. It's easy to be patient with strangers and short-tempered with family. It's easy to show grace to people we barely know, yet we hold grudges against the people we live with. Why? Because home is where we're most tired, most vulnerable, and most ourselves. It's where the gap between who we want to be and who we actually are comes into full color.

Here's the good news: **God doesn't just call us to reflect His character;** He empowers us to do it. When you're tempted to explode at your sibling for the third time today, you can pause and remember how many times God has been patient with you. When you're frustrated that someone in your family keeps making the same mistake, you can remember that God is faithful to you even when you're not faithful to Him.

This doesn't mean pretending everything's fine or letting bad behavior slide. It means responding from a place of security, not scarcity. You don't have to hoard patience like it's running out, because God's patience toward you never does. **You don't have to withhold forgiveness as if it were a limited resource, because God's faithfulness toward you is new every morning** (Lamentations 3:23).

When your family begins to reflect God's patience and faithfulness, the atmosphere changes; conflict doesn't disappear, but it's no longer toxic. Mistakes don't vanish, but they become opportunities for grace. Home becomes a place where people are being formed, not just managed.

DISCUSSION PROMPTS

1. **Understanding:** What does it mean to reflect God's patience and faithfulness in everyday family life? What would that look like?

2. **Personal Response:** Think about a recent time when someone in this family was patient with you (or you with them). How did that feel? What made it possible?

3. **Lived Practice:** This week, when you're tempted to snap or hold a grudge, pause and ask yourself: "How has God been patient with me today?" Then respond to your family member the way God responds to you.

PARENT NOTE

This one might be a little hard to hear, but the truth is your kids will learn more about God's character by watching you than by anything you say. If they see you showing patience when they make mistakes, they'll start to believe that God is patient too. If they see you keeping your promises even when it's hard, they'll start to trust that God is faithful.

But if they see you lose your temper, hold grudges, or give up on them when they struggle, they'll internalize a version of God who acts the same way.

This isn't about being a perfect parent; it's about being honest and willing to make things right. When you lose patience (and you will), admit it. Say you're sorry. Show them what it looks like to receive grace and then pass it on. Your kids don't need perfect parents. They need parents who are being shaped and transformed by the same God they're learning to trust.

Coaching tip: When conflict happens, try not to rush to fix it or shut it down. Sometimes, the most important teaching moment is helping your kids put words to what happened and talk about a better way forward. You might say, "I was impatient. That wasn't okay. Here's what I could have done differently."

ACTION STEP

Tonight, go around the table and have each person name one way someone in the family has shown them patience or faithfulness recently.

Be specific with your examples. You might say, "You helped me when I forgot my lunch," or "You forgave me when I said something mean." Then take a moment to thank God together for His patience and faithfulness toward each of you.

ONE-SENTENCE ANCHOR

The patience and faithfulness God shows us are meant to overflow into how we treat each other.

"Be kind to one another, tenderhearted, forgiving one another, as God in Christ forgave you." — Ephesians 4:32

SCRIPTURE READING

Colossians 3:12–14
1 Corinthians 13:4–7
Lamentations 3:22–23
Ephesians 4:32
Psalm 86:15

DAY 6 CULTURE LENS—CONTROL, SUCCESS, AND SELF-RELIANCE

OPENING SCENARIO

It's a Saturday morning, and you're scrolling through social media while your kids are stuck on their screens in the other room. You see another post from a parent whose kids just won another award, got accepted into another program, or have another achievement to celebrate. You feel that familiar twinge, part comparison, part pressure. Are we doing enough?

Meanwhile, your son is watching videos of influencers talking about "grinding," "hustling," and "making it happen." The message is clear: your destiny is in your hands. If you're not winning, you're not trying hard enough.

Later, at dinner, your daughter casually mentions she's stressed about an upcoming test. You start to encourage her, but she cuts you off: "It's fine. I'll figure it out." She's eleven, and she's already learned that asking for help is a weakness, that she has to have it all together, that success is all on her shoulders.

You realize, this isn't just about school, it's about the world we're all swimming in.

CONVERSATION STARTER

Let's talk: What messages do you hear every day about success, control, and figuring life out on your own? Where do those messages come from?

SHORT TEACHING

We live in a culture that puts three things above all else: **control, success, and self-reliance.** If we're not careful, these values can quietly take the place of our trust in God, often without us even noticing.

Control says: *You feel like you're in charge of every outcome. If something goes wrong, it's easy to think it's because you didn't plan well enough, work hard enough, or stay on top of things. It's exhausting. Every uncertainty feels like a threat, and every mistake feels like a failure of willpower.*

Success says: *Your worth is tied to your achievements. Winning matters, being the best matters. If you're not excelling, it feels like you're falling behind. It's a race that never ends, and the finish line always seems to move farther away.*

Self-reliance says: *You start to believe you don't need anyone. Asking for help feels like weakness. Real strength seems like doing it all on your own. It's lonely. It cuts you off from community, from guidance, and even from God.*

Here's the problem: **these values run counter to everything in God's kingdom. Jesus calls** us to let go of control, not grab for it. He defines success as faithfulness, not achievements. And He invites us into dependence on Him and on each other because that's where real strength is found.

When your family starts to notice these cultural messages, you can push back. You can name the lie, hold up the truth, and choose a different path. You can celebrate effort over outcomes, trust over control, and community over self-reliance. **And you can teach your kids that the pressure to have it all together doesn't come from God; it comes from a world that doesn't know Him.**

DISCUSSION PROMPTS

1. **Understanding:** Where do you see messages about control, success, and self-reliance in your everyday life? (School, social media, friends, sports, etc.)

2. **Personal Response:** Which of these three controls, success, or self-reliance, do you find most challenging? How does it show up in your daily life?

3. **Lived Practice:** This week, when you feel pressure to perform, control, or do it all on your own, pause and ask: "Is this message from God, or from the culture around me?"

PARENT NOTE

This conversation is so important because culture is shaping your kids' worldview, whether you notice it or not. The messages they absorb from school, media, and peers are quietly shaping beliefs about worth, identity, and success. Unless you point out those messages and offer a counter-example, they'll often become the default.

Your job isn't to shield your kids from culture or pretend it doesn't exist. It's to help them develop discernment. Teach them to notice when a message goes against Scripture. Ask questions that make the invisible visible:

- "What does that show say about what makes someone valuable?"
- "What does that influencer believe about success?"

Watch for this: Kids who grow up under pressure to control, succeed, and be self-reliant often become anxious perfectionists or discouraged quitters. Neither reflects the freedom of the gospel. Your home can be a place where they learn a better way, where mistakes aren't the end, asking for help is a strength, and worth isn't something you have to earn.

ACTION STEP

As a family, choose one area where you've been chasing control, success, or self-reliance and try practicing the opposite this week.

Maybe it's asking for help instead of doing it all alone. Maybe it's about celebrating effort rather than just the results. Maybe it's letting go of one thing you can't control and trusting God with it. Do it together, and take time to talk about how it feels to do things differently.

ONE-SENTENCE ANCHOR

The world tells us to control, achieve, and rely on ourselves, but God calls us to trust, be faithful, and depend on Him.

"Trust in the LORD with all your heart, and do not lean on your own understanding." — *Proverbs 3:5*

SCRIPTURE READING

Proverbs 3:5–6
Matthew 11:28–30
2 Corinthians 12:9–10
Jeremiah 17:5–8
James 4:13–15

DAY 7 PRACTICE—FAMILY GRATITUDE AND RELEASING ONE WORRY TO GOD

OPENING SCENARIO

It's Sunday evening, and the week ahead already feels overwhelming. Your son has three tests, a project due, and a game he's nervous about. Your daughter is worried about a rocky friendship. You're staring at a work deadline and a house that won't clean itself. Your spouse is mentally running through the logistics of getting everyone where they need to be.

Everyone's carrying something, and no one is talking about it because what would talking even do? The week is coming whether you're ready or not.

But then you remember the last six days of conversations, the truth your family has been discovering: God is good, present, and powerful. Our identity is secure in Him. We don't have to carry everything alone. And you think: What if we actually practiced that tonight? What if we stopped talking about trust and really lived it?

CONVERSATION STARTER

Before we dive in: What's one thing you're grateful for today? And what's one thing you're worried about this week?

SHORT TEACHING

Here's what we've been learning all week: our view of God shapes everything. It shapes how we face stress, how we treat each other, how we respond to pressure, and how we carry or let go of the weight of life.

But belief without practice is just theory. **Tonight, we're going to turn belief into action through two simple rhythms: gratitude and release.**

Gratitude reorients our hearts. When we name what we're thankful for, we remind ourselves that God is good, He provides, and even in hard seasons, His faithfulness is real. Gratitude isn't pretending everything is fine; it's choosing to notice God's presence in the middle of whatever we're facing.

Release is where surrender becomes tangible. Instead of white-knuckling our worries or trying to control outcomes we can't manage, we practice handing them to God out loud, together, as a family. We name the thing we're anxious about, and then we say: "God, this is Yours. I'm trusting You with it."

These aren't magical formulas. They're spiritual disciplines, small, repeated practices that train our hearts to trust instead of fear, and to rest instead of strive. When your family does them together, you're not just learning theology, you're living it.

DISCUSSION PROMPTS

1. **Understanding:** Why do you think gratitude and releasing worry are both important? What happens if we only do one without the other?
2. **Personal Response:** What's one thing you're genuinely grateful for right now? And what's one worry you've been carrying that you need to release to God?
3. **Lived Practice:** How can we make gratitude and release a regular part of our family rhythm, not just tonight, but ongoing?

PARENT NOTE

Tonight is about building muscle memory. **You're not just having another conversation, you're starting a practice your family can**

return to again and again. The goal is to make gratitude and release feel normal, accessible, and doable in everyday life.

Don't overcomplicate it. You're not performing a ritual or checking a spiritual box. You're simply creating space for your family to notice God's goodness and entrust Him with what you can't control. If your kids are reluctant or distracted, that's okay. Keep it short. Keep it real. Keep showing up.

Important reminder: This isn't about eliminating worry or pretending to have it all together. It's about teaching your kids that faith is something you practice, not just something you believe. When they see you releasing your worries to God, not perfectly, but honestly, they'll learn that trust is a choice they can make too.

ACTION STEP

Tonight, do this together as a family:

1. **Go around the table and each person shares:**
    - One thing they're grateful for today.
    - One worry they're carrying this week.
2. **After everyone shares, pray together—short and simple:**
    - Thank God for the things you named.
    - Release each worry to Him out loud: "God, we trust You with [this]."
3. **End with this simple declaration together:**
   "God is good. We are His. We can trust Him."

ONE-SENTENCE ANCHOR

Gratitude reminds us of God's goodness; release reminds us we don't have to carry what only He can hold.
"Do not be anxious about anything, but in everything by prayer and supplication with thanksgiving let your requests be made known to God." — Philippians 4:6

SCRIPTURE READING

Philippians 4:6–7
Psalm 34:1–8
1 Thessalonians 5:16–18
Matthew 6:25–34
Psalm 55:22

DAY 8 BIG QUESTION—IF GOD IS GOOD, WHY SUFFERING?

OPENING SCENARIO

Your daughter comes home from school quieter than usual. Later, while you're making dinner, she leans against the counter and says, "A kid in my class has cancer. She's only ten." Her voice cracks. "If God is good like we've been talking about, why would He let that happen? Why doesn't He … fix it?"

You pause, searching for words. You want to give her an honest answer that won't shatter her faith. But you also know this question doesn't have an easy answer because you've asked it yourself when the job fell through, when the miscarriage happened, when the diagnosis came.

She's staring at you, waiting. And you realize: this is the question that tests everything we've been learning. If we can't reconcile God's goodness with the reality of suffering, the whole foundation starts to crack.

CONVERSATION STARTER

Let's start with honesty: Have you ever wondered why God allows hard or painful things to happen? What made you ask that question?

SHORT TEACHING

This is one of the oldest and hardest questions in the world. **If God is good and powerful, why is there suffering?** And here is the truth. There is no simple answer that makes pain disappear or confusion go away.

But there are still truths we can hold onto, even when we do not understand everything.

First, suffering exists because the world is broken. When sin entered the world, it not only affected our hearts but also everything. Disease, death, disasters, and relational pain are all part of living in a world that is not the way it was meant to be. God did not create cancer or cruelty. He created a good world. But when humanity chose to go its own way, brokenness followed.

Second, God does not stand outside suffering. He enters into it. Jesus did not stay in heaven, distant and untouched. He came to earth and lived among us. He experienced rejection, betrayal, physical pain, and death. He understands what it is like to suffer. **And because He does, we can trust that God is not indifferent to our pain. He is present with us in it.**

Third, God is using even the broken pieces for a greater purpose. We do not always see it in the moment, but Scripture promises that God is at work redeeming, restoring, and making all things new. Suffering is not the end of the story. Resurrection is.

Does this mean suffering is easy or always makes sense? No. Does it mean we will not still ask "Why?" Absolutely not. But it does mean we do not have to choose between believing that God is good and acknowledging that life is hard. Both can be true. And in the middle of this tension, we trust the God who is with us, not because we have all the answers, but because He has proven Himself faithful.

DISCUSSION PROMPTS

1. **Understanding:** What is the difference between saying that "God causes suffering" and saying that "God allows suffering in a broken world"? Why does this distinction matter?

2. **Personal Response:** Have you ever experienced something hard and wondered where God was? Looking back, can you

see ways He was present, even if it did not feel that way at the time?

3. **Lived Practice:** When you face something painful or confusing this week, how can you hold onto God's goodness while still acknowledging that the pain is real?

PARENT NOTE

This conversation may feel difficult because you cannot fix this question for your children. You cannot explain every instance of suffering or tie everything together with a simple theological answer. And honestly, that is okay. Your job is not to have all the answers. It is to help your children bring their honest questions to God, rather than allowing those questions to push them away from Him.

Some children will wrestle with this intellectually. Others will feel it deeply on an emotional level. Meet them where they are. Do not rush to answer. Sit in the tension with them. Acknowledge their confusion and listen carefully. **And gently point them to the cross, where God's goodness and the reality of suffering meet, and where redemption begins.**

Avoid these pitfalls:

- "Everything happens for a reason." (This can minimize real pain and may imply that God orchestrates tragedy.)
- "God needed another angel." (This is not biblical and can make God sound callous.)
- "Just have more faith, and it'll make sense." (Faith does not erase mystery—it helps us trust God in the middle of it.)

Better approach: "I don't know why this happened. But I know God is good, and I know He's with us. And I trust that He's working even when we can't see it."

ACTION STEP

Tonight, talk about one hard thing your family has faced and one way you saw God's presence or faithfulness in the middle of it.

It does not have to be a happy ending. It can just be a moment of grace, a provision, a sense of peace, or a reminder that you were not alone. Then, thank God together not for the suffering, but for His presence in it.

ONE-SENTENCE ANCHOR

God's goodness doesn't mean life will be easy—it means He is with us, even in the hardest moments.

"Even though I walk through the valley of the shadow of death, I will fear no evil, for you are with me." — Psalm 23:4

SCRIPTURE READING

Psalm 23:4
Romans 8:28
John 16:33
2 Corinthians 1:3–5
Revelation 21:3–5

DAY 9 REFLECTION ANCHOR—WHO GOD IS DETERMINES HOW WE LIVE

OPENING SCENARIO

It's the end of the first week, and honestly, it's been a lot. You've talked about God's character, identity, anxiety, patience, cultural pressure, and suffering. Your children have asked hard questions. You've prayed together. You've practiced gratitude and letting go.

And now, as you're cleaning up after dinner, your son says something that stops you in your tracks: "I think I get it now. Like… if God really is good and He's really with us, then we don't have to freak out about everything, right?"

Your daughter chimes in: "Yeah. And we can be nicer to each other because God's been patient with us."

You smile. They're connecting the dots. **They're starting to see that theology isn't just information, it's transformation.** Who God really is shapes how we live.

CONVERSATION STARTER

Let's look back: What is one thing you learned about God this week that surprised you or changed the way you think?

SHORT TEACHING

Here's what we've been building toward all week: **Who God is determines how we live.**

If God is good, we don't have to live in fear; we can trust Him.

If God is just, we don't have to take revenge; we can leave justice in His hands.

If God is powerful, we don't have to control everything; we can surrender.

If God is present, we don't have to carry life alone; we can depend on Him.

This is why theology matters. Not because it is intellectual or impressive, but **because it is deeply, practically, life-changingly relevant**. When your view of God shifts, everything else shifts with it. Your anxiety decreases because you trust His goodness. Your relationships improve when you reflect on His patience. Your identity stabilizes because it is rooted in His truth, not the world's approval.

But here's the key: this only works if we actually believe it. It is not enough to know about God. We have to know Him, and let that knowledge reshape how we think, speak, and act every single day.

Over the next 81 days, we will keep building on this foundation. We will talk about who we are, why we are broken, how Jesus rescues us, what it means to grow, and how to live with purpose and hope. But everything, everything comes back to this: **Who is God? And how does that change me?**

DISCUSSION PROMPTS

1. **Understanding:** What's one way your view of God has changed this week? How has that affected the way you think or live?

2. **Personal Response:** If you really believed—deep down—that God is good, present, and powerful, what's one thing you'd do differently this week?

3. **Lived Practice:** How can we keep reminding each other of these truths as a family? What rhythms or habits will help us remember who God is?

PARENT NOTE

Take a moment tonight to celebrate. You have just spent a week laying a theological foundation with your family, and that matters more than you know. You have modeled what it looks like to take God seriously, to ask hard questions, and to practice faith together.

Do not underestimate what is happening. **Your children are learning that theology is not boring or irrelevant; it is the lens through which they interpret everything.** And you are teaching them that faith is not just something you inherit or perform, it is something you live out loud, together.

Moving forward, use this reflection rhythm every ninth day. Let it be a chance to pause, look back, and celebrate what God is doing in your family. Do not rush past it. Let your children articulate what they are learning in their own words. Ask them what is sticking. Listen for where the Spirit is working.

And remember, you are not just teaching content. You are forming disciples, and that **happens one conversation, one question, one honest prayer at a time.**

ACTION STEP

Tonight, go around the table one last time and finish this sentence:
"Because God is __________, I can __________."

(Examples: "Because God is good, I can trust Him with my worries." "Because God is patient, I can be patient with my sister.")

Then, pray together, thanking God for who He is and asking Him to continue shaping your family through what you are learning.

ONE-SENTENCE ANCHOR

Who God is determines how we live—and that changes everything.

"And we all, with unveiled face, beholding the glory of the Lord, are being transformed into the same image from one degree of glory to another." — 2 Corinthians 3:18

SCRIPTURE READING

2 Corinthians 3:18
Psalm 34:8
Romans 12:1–2
Colossians 1:9–12
Philippians 1:9–11

UNIT

2

HUMAN IDENTITY

(IMAGO DEI)

DAY 1 WHY IDENTITY QUESTIONS FEEL INTENSE TODAY

OPENING SCENARIO

Your daughter scrolls through her phone before dinner, and you notice her expression change, brows furrowed, shoulders tense. She finally looks up. "Everyone at school is changing their profile bios again," she says. "Like, every week it's something different. Who they're into, what pronouns they use, what labels they identify with. And I just… I don't even know who I am."

Your son overhears and shrugs. "Just pick something. Everyone's making it up anyway." But you hear the defensiveness in his voice. Lately, he's been unusually quiet about his friendships, and you wonder if he's struggling with the same questions in his own way.

Later, as you fold laundry, your thoughts drift to your day: the performance review that left you doubting your abilities, the comparison spiral on social media, the nagging question, **Am I enough? And it hits you, identity confusion isn't just a teenage thing. It's everywhere. And it's exhausting.**

CONVERSATION STARTER

Let's be honest: Where do you feel the most pressure to figure out "who you are"? What makes identity questions feel so heavy right now?

SHORT TEACHING

We live in a moment where identity is treated like a choose-your-own-adventure story. You're told to "find yourself," "be your authentic self," and "define your own truth." The culture says your identity is entirely up to you, fluid, customizable, and always evolving. And if you're not constantly refining it, you're falling behind.

But here's the problem: when identity is something you have to create, it becomes an unbearable burden. Because how do you know if you got it right? What if you change your mind? **What if the identity you chose doesn't fit anymore? What if the approval you built it on disappears?**

The pressure is crushing, and it's not just on teenagers. Adults feel it too. We're all asking the same questions: Am I valuable? Do I matter? What makes me… me? And we're looking for answers in achievement, relationships, appearance, performance, labels, and online validation, none of which are stable enough to hold the weight of a human soul.

Here's the truth the world won't tell you: your identity isn't something you create. It's something you receive. You are made in the image of God. That's not a label you choose or a performance you maintain; it's a reality that's been true since the moment you existed. Your worth, your dignity, your purpose, they're gifts, not achievements.

And that changes everything. When identity is received, not earned, you can finally stop performing, stop comparing, and stop scrambling to prove you're enough. **Because you already are.**

DISCUSSION PROMPTS

1. **Understanding:** What's the difference between *creating* your identity and *receiving* it? Why does that distinction matter?

2. **Personal Response:** Where do you feel the most pressure to prove who you are or figure yourself out? What would it feel like to believe your identity is already secure?

3. **Lived Practice:** This week, whenever you feel the pressure around your identity, whether it's comparison, performance anxiety, or seeking approval, pause and remind yourself: "I am made in God's image, and my worth is already settled."

PARENT NOTE

This may be one of the most important conversations you'll have with your kids because the world is aggressively presenting them with a counterfeit version of identity. They're being told that identity is something they must define for themselves, self-authored and endlessly customizable. And if they don't figure it out quickly enough, label it clearly enough, or perform it confidently enough, they may begin to feel like they are failing.

As a parent, your role is to offer a better story, one rooted in Scripture, not culture. But be careful: don't dismiss their questions or minimize the pressure they feel. This isn't simply "just a phase" or a problem unique to "kids these days." It is a real and persistent cultural pressure, and they need you to recognize that reality while gently pointing them toward something more stable and trustworthy.

Watch for this: Kids who internalize the pressure to construct their own identity often become either anxious performers constantly evaluating themselves and wondering if they measure up or identity-hoppers, repeatedly trying on different versions of themselves without ever feeling settled. Both are signs of deeper insecurity. Your role is to help anchor them in the unchanging truth of who they belong to.

Important clarification: Saying identity is "received" doesn't mean your kids can't have preferences, interests, unique personalities, or seasons of growth and discovery. It means their core worth and dignity are not something they must earn or constantly defend. They can explore who they're becoming without the crushing pressure of having to prove who they are.

ACTION STEP

Tonight, each person shares one label or identity marker they feel pressure to live up to (smart, athletic, popular, successful, etc.). Then, together, say this out loud: *"That's not where my worth comes from. I am made in the image of God, and that's enough."*

ONE-SENTENCE ANCHOR

Your identity isn't something you create—it's a gift you receive from the God who made you.

"So God created man in his own image, in the image of God he created him; male and female he created them." — *Genesis 1:27*

SCRIPTURE READING

Genesis 1:26–27
Psalm 139:13–16
Ephesians 2:10
1 Peter 2:9
Colossians 3:3

DAY
2

MADE IN GOD'S IMAGE—DIGNITY, CREATIVITY, RESPONSIBILITY

OPENING SCENARIO

Your son is working on an art project at the kitchen table, sketching, erasing, and starting over. He's been at it for an hour, completely absorbed. You pause to watch him, noticing the concentration on his face, and the way he tilts his head when something doesn't quite look right. There's something almost sacred about it.

Later, your daughter helps her younger sibling build a blanket fort, narrating an elaborate storyline as they go. She's inventing rules, assigning roles, and creating an entire imaginary world. And you think: Where does that come from, the impulse to make, to build, to imagine?

And then it hits you: **they're reflecting something deeper**. The creativity, the problem-solving, and the care they're putting into these small acts aren't random. They are echoes of the God who made them. They're image-bearers. And you realize that you've been watching theology unfold in everyday life all afternoon.

CONVERSATION STARTER

Let's start here: What's something you've made or created recently—big or small? What did you enjoy about it?

SHORT TEACHING

When the Bible says we're made in God's image, it's not talking about what we look like. It's talking about **who we are and what we're**

designed to do. Being made in God's image means three powerful things:

First, it means we have dignity. Every single person, no matter their age, ability, background, or behavior, has inherent worth. Not because of what they accomplish or contribute, but simply because they bear God's image. You cannot earn it, and you cannot lose it. It's a gift woven into the very fabric of your being.

Second, it means we have creativity. God is the ultimate Creator, and we reflect that in our own way. When you solve a problem, write a story, cook a meal, build something, or come up with a new idea, you are echoing the God who spoke the universe into being. Creativity isn't just for artists; it's for anyone who makes, repairs, imagines, or innovates. It's part of what it means to be human.

Third, it means we have responsibility. God entrusted the world to us not to exploit or hoard, but to steward and care for it. That includes how we treat creation, how we use our time and gifts, and most importantly, how we treat one another. Because if every person is made in God's image, then every person deserves honor, protection, and love.

Here's why this matters in everyday life: when you understand that you're made in God's image, you stop measuring your worth by comparison or performance. You stop seeing yourself as a mistake or an accident. You begin to recognize that you were made on purpose, for a purpose, and that truth changes how you see yourself, how you treat others, and how you move through the world.

DISCUSSION PROMPTS

1. **Understanding:** What does it mean practically to say someone has "dignity because they're made in God's image"? How should that change the way we treat people?

2. **Personal Response:** Where have you seen creativity, problem-solving, or care show up in your own life recently? How is that a reflection of being made in God's image?

3. **Lived Practice:** This week, when you're tempted to compare yourself to others or feel worthless, remind yourself: "I bear God's image. I have dignity, creativity, and purpose."

PARENT NOTE

This is foundational because if your kids don't internalize the truth that they are made in God's image, they'll look for their worth elsewhere. They'll try to earn it through performance, extract it from relationships, or manufacture it through accomplishments. And none of it will ever be enough.

Your job is to help them see image-bearing in action. Point it out when they create something. Celebrate when they solve a problem. Affirm when they show care for someone else. And say it out loud: "You know what that is? That's you reflecting the God who made you."

Important nuance: Being made in God's image doesn't mean we're perfect or always reflect Him well. Sin has distorted the image, but it hasn't erased it. We still bear God's likeness, even in our brokenness. That's why every person deserves dignity, and why transformation is always possible.

Coaching tip: Kids often struggle to connect abstract theological truths to real life. Help them by asking specific questions: "When you helped your friend today, whose kindness were you reflecting?" "When you built that, whose creativity were you echoing?" Make it tangible and practical.

ACTION STEP

Tonight, go around the table, and each person answers this:
"One way I've seen someone in this family reflect God's image this week is..."

Be specific. Name the creativity, the care, the problem-solving, the dignity they showed someone else. Let your family practice seeing the image-bearing in everyday moments.

ONE-SENTENCE ANCHOR

You are made in God's image, which means you have dignity, creativity, and responsibility that can't be taken away.
"You are fearfully and wonderfully made." — Psalm 139:14

SCRIPTURE READING

Genesis 1:26–28
Psalm 139:14
Ephesians 2:10
James 3:9
Colossians 3:10

DAY 3

MISUNDERSTANDINGS—IDENTITY BASED ON PERFORMANCE OR APPROVAL

OPENING SCENARIO

Your daughter comes home from tryouts and goes straight to her room without saying a word. Later, you find her lying on her bed, staring at the ceiling.

"I didn't make the team," she says quietly. Then, after a long pause: "I guess I'm just not good at anything."

You try to encourage her, but she cuts you off. "Please don't say I'm good at other things. That doesn't count. This is what mattered."

And suddenly you realize: she has tied her entire sense of worth to whether she made the middle school volleyball team.

Meanwhile, your son is constantly checking his phone, refreshing his social media posts to see how many likes he's getting. When you ask him about it, he shrugs. "I just want to know if people care."

Translation: I need other people's approval to know that I matter.

Two kids. One problem.

They believe different versions of the same lie: your worth depends on what you achieve and whether others validate you.

CONVERSATION STARTER

Let's be real: When do you feel most valuable or confident? What has to happen for you to feel like you're "enough"?

SHORT TEACHING

Here's one of the most damaging lies our culture teaches: that your identity is based on performance and approval. You're only as valuable as your last achievement. You're only as worthy as the validation you receive. If you succeed, you matter. If you fail, it can feel like you don't.

And here's the exhausting part: the standard never stops moving. You make the team, but now you have to be a starter. You get the grade, but now you have to stay at the top. You get the likes, but now you need more. Performance-based identity is like a treadmill that keeps speeding up the longer you run.

The same goes for approval. When your worth depends on what other people think, you're constantly performing for an audience that's often fickle, distracted, and unable to give you the lasting assurance you need because no amount of human approval can fill the deep need in your soul to know that you are loved, seen, and valued.

Here's the truth: your worth is not performance-based. It is rooted in your existence. You don't have to earn it. You don't have to maintain it. You don't have to prove it. You matter because you were made in God's image, and that was true before you accomplished anything, and it remains true even when you fail.

This doesn't mean effort and growth don't matter. They absolutely do. But they flow from security, not insecurity. You work hard because you're faithfully stewarding the gifts God gave you, not because your worth is on the line. You care about growth because you're becoming who God made you to be, not because you're trying to prove that you are enough.

When you root your identity in God instead of performance or approval, failure stops being devastating, and success stops being the ultimate measure of your value. You're free to try, fail, learn, and grow because your worth was never up for debate in the first place.

DISCUSSION PROMPTS

1. **Understanding:** What's the difference between working hard to prove your worth and working hard to steward the gifts God has given you faithfully?
2. **Personal Response:** Where do you feel the most pressure to perform or seek approval? What would it feel like to know your worth does not depend on that?
3. **Lived Practice:** This week, when you fail at something or do not receive the approval you hoped for, practice saying this out loud: "My worth doesn't come from this. I am loved and valued no matter what."

PARENT NOTE

This is where your kids are most vulnerable because a performance-based identity is reinforced everywhere. School grades, sports teams, social media likes and metrics, and peer approval all send the same message: you are what you achieve and who approves of you.

And here's the hard part: as parents, you might unintentionally reinforce this message too. If your affirmation is primarily tied to accomplishments ("I'm so proud you got an A!" "Great job winning the game!"), Your kids may begin to internalize the idea that their worth is conditional. They'll believe love and approval come only when they succeed and disappear when they don't.

What to do instead: Affirm character and effort, not just outcomes. Celebrate kindness, persistence, integrity, and growth. And most importantly, make sure your kids know they are deeply loved and delighted in, whether they succeed or fail.

Watch for this: Kids caught in a performance-based identity often become either chronic overachievers (terrified of failure) or chronic underachievers (convinced they will fail anyway, so why try?). Both are symptoms of the same wound: the belief that their worth must be earned.

ACTION STEP

Tonight, each person shares one recent failure or disappointment—and then someone else in the family responds with this phrase:
"That doesn't change who you are or how much you're loved."

Let your family practice disconnecting worth from outcomes. Let them hear—and say—the truth that identity is secure, even when performance isn't perfect.

ONE-SENTENCE ANCHOR

Your worth is not based on what you do or who approves of you—it's based on whose you are.
"But God shows his love for us in that while we were still sinners, Christ died for us." — Romans 5:8

SCRIPTURE READING

Romans 5:8
Galatians 1:10
Ephesians 1:4–6
1 John 3:1
Psalm 147:10–11

DAY 4 IDENTITY AND EMOTIONS—SHAME VS. WORTH

OPENING SCENARIO

It's a quiet Tuesday evening when your son walks into the kitchen, his shoulders slumped and eyes downcast. He won't make eye contact. Finally, he mutters, "I messed up today." You ask what happened, and he tells you he lied to a teacher to avoid trouble and now he feels terrible.

But here's what catches you off guard: he doesn't just feel bad about what he did. He feels bad about who he is. "I'm such a liar," he says. "I'm a terrible person." His voice is heavy with something deeper than regret; it's shame.

Later, your daughter overhears the conversation and says, "At least he cares. I mess up all the time, and I feel... nothing. Like, I know I should feel bad, but I don't. Does that mean something's wrong with me?"

Two kids. Two different struggles. One drowning in shame. One numb to conviction. And you realize: **both of them are confused about how their emotions relate to identity and worth.**

CONVERSATION STARTER

Let's talk: When you mess up, what do you usually feel? And do those feelings ever make you question who you are or whether you're a good person?

SHORT TEACHING

Here's something we need to understand: emotions are real, but they aren't always reliable guides to truth.

When you do something wrong, it's good and right to feel conviction that's your conscience saying, "This doesn't align with who you're meant to be." But there's a difference between conviction and shame.

Conviction says, "You did something wrong, and it matters. Now you need to make it right." It's specific, truthful, and ultimately redemptive. It leads to confession, repentance, and change.

Shame says, "You are doing something wrong. You're defective, broken, and unworthy." It's global, condemning, and paralyzing. It doesn't lead to change; it leads people to hide, to believe lies about themselves, and to fall into despair.

Here's the critical difference: conviction addresses your behavior while protecting your worth. Shame attacks your worth because of your behavior. One leads to healing. The other leads to destruction.

But there's another side to this. Feeling nothing when you sin is also a problem. If you've become numb to conviction, it might mean you've stopped believing your actions matter, or worse, that you've stopped believing you matter to God. Numbness isn't freedom. It's a form of spiritual disconnection.

The truth is this: your emotions, whether shame, numbness, guilt, or regret, do not define your worth. Your worth is anchored in the unchanging reality that you are made in God's image, deeply loved, and fully known by Him.

Yes, sin is real, and it matters. **Yes, you need to acknowledge it, confess it, and turn away from it. But your failures do not erase your identity.** They reveal your need for grace.

DISCUSSION PROMPTS

1. **Understanding:** What's the difference between feeling guilty about something you did and feeling ashamed of who you are? Why does that distinction matter?

2. **Personal Response:** Do you tend to struggle more with shame (feeling like you're a bad person) or numbness (not feeling much when you mess up)? What do you think is behind that?

3. **Lived Practice:** This week, when you mess up, practice this: Name what you did wrong. Confess it. Receive forgiveness. Then remind yourself: "This doesn't define me. I am still loved and valuable."

PARENT NOTE

This conversation is important because shame is one of the enemy's most effective weapons. **If the enemy can convince your kids that their sin defines who they are, he can trap them in cycles of hiding, self-hatred, and despair.** Your job is to help them learn the difference between conviction (which comes from the Spirit and leads to life) and shame (which comes from the enemy and leads to death).

But be careful not to swing too far the other way. **Some kids learn to rationalize sin or minimize its impact, which can lead to numbness and moral apathy.** If your child isn't bothered by wrongdoing, don't ignore it or brush it aside. Gently explore: "Do you think what you did mattered? Why or why not?" Help them connect their behavior to its consequences and to the kind of person they are becoming.

Coaching Tip: When your child confesses sin or expresses shame, your response matters more than you may realize. If you react with anger, disappointment, or withdrawal, you may unintentionally reinforce shame. If you minimize or dismiss it, you may end up reinforcing numbness instead. Instead, model something like this: "Thank you for being honest. What you did was wrong, and we need to address it. But you are still loved, and we are going to work through this together."

Watch for this: Kids who are trapped in shame often become perfectionists or people-pleasers, desperately trying to prove they are good enough. **Kids who grow numb often become cynical or reckless, feeling disconnected from moral responsibility.** Both need the gospel:

you are worse than you think (sin is real), and you are more loved than you dare believe (grace is greater).

ACTION STEP

Tonight, practice this as a family:
If someone has been carrying shame about something, invite them to name it briefly and then have someone else speak this truth out loud: "That was wrong, but it does not define you. You are forgiven, and you are loved."

If someone has been feeling numb or disconnected, gently explore it together: "Why do you think you're not feeling much about this? What might help you reconnect to what is true?"

ONE-SENTENCE ANCHOR

Shame says you are what you did; grace says you are who God says you are—and those are not the same.
"There is therefore now no condemnation for those who are in Christ Jesus." — Romans 8:1

SCRIPTURE READING

Romans 8:1
Psalm 103:10–12
1 John 1:9
Hebrews 4:15–16
2 Corinthians 7:10

DAY 5 RELATIONSHIPS—HONORING OTHERS AS IMAGE-BEARERS

OPENING SCENARIO

It's Saturday morning, and your kids are already arguing with each other. Your son keeps making snarky remarks about your daughter's outfit. She fires back with a sharp comment about his video game obsession. Within minutes, they're both shouting, and you're stepping in to break it up again.

Later, you're scrolling through a group text with other parents and cringe at how one mom is being talked about behind her back. Then you overhear your daughter on the phone with a friend, casually mocking a classmate's presentation from yesterday. And your son is in the other room, trash-talking his opponents in an online game with language that makes you pause and wince.

It's everywhere: **casual cruelty, dismissive language, and the habit of treating people like obstacles, annoyances, or objects of ridicule.** And you think: If we truly believed that every person is made in God's image, would we speak to each other this way?

CONVERSATION STARTER

Honest question: How do you talk about people when they're not around? How do you talk to people when you're frustrated with them?

SHORT TEACHING

Here's a truth that should change every conversation, every conflict, and every relationship: every single person you encounter is made in the image of God. That means every person, no matter how annoying, difficult, different, or frustrating, possesses inherent dignity and worth.

When you forget that, it becomes easy to treat people as if they are less than human. You dismiss them. Mock them. Use them. Ignore them. You reduce them to a label, a stereotype, or an inconvenience. **And in doing so, you're not just disrespecting a person, you're also dishonoring the God whose image they bear.**

This applies at home. Your sibling who drives you crazy? An image-bearer. Your parent who doesn't get you? An image-bearer. The classmate you can't stand? An image-bearer. The stranger at the grocery store who's moving too slowly? **An image-bearer. Every. Single. One.**

Honoring people as image-bearers doesn't mean pretending they're perfect or ignoring when they do wrong. It means choosing to treat them with dignity, even when it's difficult. It means speaking about them with respect, even when they are not in the room. It means listening, being patient, and choosing kindness not because they've earned it, but because the image of God in them deserves it.

And here's what's beautiful: **when you start treating others as image-bearers, it begins to change you, too. You become less cynical.** Less quick to criticize. More compassionate. Because you start seeing people more the way God sees them, flawed, yes, but still valuable. Still worthy of love.

DISCUSSION PROMPTS

1. **Understanding:** What does it mean in practical terms to" honor someone as an image-bearer"? How would that change the way we speak to people or speak about them?

2. **Personal Response:** Think about someone you struggle with at school, at home, or online. How might your attitude or actions change if you truly saw them as someone made in God's image?

3. **Lived Practice:** This week, when you're tempted to mock, dismiss, or speak harshly about someone, pause and remind

yourself: "This person bears God's image." Then choose a response that reflects dignity and respect.

PARENT NOTE

This is one of the most countercultural truths you'll teach your kids because our world is built on ranking, labeling, and dismissing people. Social media often rewards mockery. **Entertainment frequently normalizes cruelty**. And casual disrespect toward others is often treated as humor rather than recognized as sin.

Your kids are absorbing this every day. They're learning to treat people like content, competition, or obstacles. And unless you actively intervene, they may begin to accept it as normal without even realizing it.

Your role is to address it directly. When you hear mocking language, dismissive comments, or cruel humor, stop and ask: "Do you think that person is made in God's image? How do you think God feels when we talk about His image-bearers that way?" Don't shame them, guide them, and teach them.

Model this in your own life. Your kids will learn more from watching how you talk about the difficult neighbor, the annoying coworker, the frustrating family member, or even the public figure you strongly disagree with. **Do you honor them as image-bearers, even when you disagree with or critique their actions**? Or do you reduce them to an enemy, an idiot, or a caricature?

Watch for this: Kids who grow up mocking others often struggle with insecurity themselves; they may tear others down to feel superior. Kids who grow up dismissing others often struggle with empathy; they have learned to see people as objects rather than as souls.

ACTION STEP

Tonight, as a family, think of one person you have recently been dismissive, harsh, or unkind toward (even if it was only in your thoughts or in words spoken when they were not present).

Then pray for that person by name and ask God to help you see them the way He sees them. Let this be an intentional practice of repentance and renewed perspective.

> ### ONE-SENTENCE ANCHOR
>
> **Every person is made in God's image, which means they deserve to be treated with dignity and respect.**
> *"Whoever despises his neighbor is a sinner, but blessed is the one who is generous to the poor." — Proverbs 14:21*

SCRIPTURE READING

James 3:9–10
Matthew 5:43–48
Proverbs 14:21
Luke 6:27–31
1 Peter 2:17

DAY 6 CULTURE LENS—COMPARISON AND SOCIAL MEDIA PRESSURE

OPENING SCENARIO

Your daughter is lying on her bed, scrolling. She's been quiet all afternoon, and when you ask if she's okay, she doesn't look up. "I'm fine," she says, but her voice tells a different story.

Later, she shows you a post from a classmate, a perfectly curated photo of a birthday party she wasn't invited to. Everyone looks happy, beautiful, and effortlessly cool. Your daughter stares at it and says, "Why does everyone else's life look so perfect? What's wrong with me?"

Meanwhile, your son is in his room, comparing his gaming stats to streamers with millions of followers. "I'll never be that good," he mutters. "What's even the point?"

Two kids. Same phone. Same poison: the relentless pressure of comparison. And you realize this isn't just about social media. It's about a whole generation being told to measure their worth by how they stack up against everyone else's highlight reel.

CONVERSATION STARTER

Let's be honest: When you're on social media or comparing yourself to others, how do you usually feel afterward—better or worse? Why do you think that is?

SHORT TEACHING

Social media is built on a lie: the idea that you can truly know someone's life just by looking at their feed. You see the polished photos, the witty captions, and the carefully chosen moments. And your brain whispers, Their life must be better. They seem happier. More popular. More talented. More… everything.

But here's the truth: you're comparing your behind-the-scenes life to everyone else's highlight reel. You're seeing their best moments and comparing them to your worst. You're seeing their carefully managed image and comparing it to your real, messy life. And that comparison slowly crushes your joy.

Comparison almost always leads to one of two places: pride or discouragement. Either you feel superior because you found someone you can look down on, or you feel worthless because it seems like everyone else is doing better than you. Both are toxic. Both grow out of the same lie: that your worth is determined by how you measure up to someone else.

But here's what God says: your value isn't measured by comparison. It's measured by the fact that you were created in His image. You're not in competition with anyone. You're not falling behind. You're not "less than" because someone else seems "more than." You are exactly who God made you to be, with the gifts, opportunities, and calling He has entrusted specifically to you.

This doesn't mean social media is evil or that you need to delete everything. But it does mean you should use it wisely rather than letting it shape your identity. You need to recognize when it's fueling comparison, feeding insecurity, or replacing real relationships with carefully curated performances. And sometimes you may need to step back and refocus your heart on what is true. Remember this: the God who created you does not rank you against others. He delights in you.

DISCUSSION PROMPTS

1. **Understanding:** Why do you think comparison feels so strong on social media? What makes it hard to remember that you're only seeing a small part of someone's story?

2. **Personal Response:** When do you feel most tempted to compare your life to someone else's? What usually triggers it, and how do you typically feel afterward?

3. **Lived Practice:** Try this challenge during the coming week: Every time you catch yourself comparing, pause and name one thing you're grateful for in your own life or in the gifts God has given you. Practice gratitude instead of falling into comparison.

PARENT NOTE

This conversation is urgent because comparison is one of the most common and damaging pressures in your kids' lives. And social media has intensified it. Every scroll can become a comparison trap. Every post is a carefully curated moment. And every metric, likes, followers, comments, can start to feel like a measure of personal worth.

Your kids are being trained to believe their value is relative rather than intrinsic. Unless you intentionally challenge that message, it can become the lens through which they see themselves and others.

Your role as a parent or mentor is to teach them healthy media awareness. Help them ask thoughtful questions such as: "What might I not be seeing behind this post?" "What is this making me feel, and is that feeling based on truth?" "Am I using this to connect with people, or to compete with them?"

Model healthy boundaries with technology. If you're constantly comparing yourself to others online, your kids will notice and learn from it. If you talk about people mainly in terms of status, success, or appearance, your kids may begin to believe those things matter more than character. Your relationship with social media and comparison quietly teaches them what is normal.

Watch for this: Kids caught in constant comparison often move in one of two directions. Some become image-obsessed, always performing to gain approval. Others become image-avoidant, withdrawing because they feel they can't compete. Both responses grow out of the same wound: the belief that a person's worth must be earned by being "better than" someone else.

ACTION STEP

Tonight, do a "social media audit" as a family.
Invite each person to share: Is there someone you follow online who tends to make you feel worse about yourself? What accounts tend to trigger feelings of comparison or insecurity for you?

Then, as a family, talk about what might be helpful moving forward. Do you need to unfollow, mute, or take a break from certain accounts? Let this be a simple practice of guarding your heart and mind.

ONE-SENTENCE ANCHOR

Your worth is not measured by comparison to others; it is rooted in the God who created you, made you unique, and loves you completely.
"For we dare not classify or compare ourselves with some who commend themselves. But they, measuring themselves by themselves and comparing themselves among themselves, are not wise." — 2 Corinthians 10:12 (NKJV)

SCRIPTURE READING

2 Corinthians 10:12
Galatians 6:4–5
Psalm 139:13–14
1 Thessalonians 5:11
James 2:1–4

DAY 7 PRACTICE—CHARACTER-BASED AFFIRMATIONS AROUND THE TABLE

OPENING SCENARIO

It's Thursday night, and dinner feels a little flat. Everyone's tired. Conversations are brief and surface-level. Your son barely looks up from his plate. Your daughter seems distracted, her mind clearly somewhere else. And you realize: **When was the last time we intentionally encouraged one another?**

You think about the last week. How many times did you correct behavior but forget to affirm their character? How many moments did you focus on what went wrong instead of noticing what went right? And then you remember the conversations your family has been having about identity, worth, and being made in God's image.

What if tonight, instead of letting exhaustion win, you chose to do something different? What if you intentionally spoke life into each other, not based on achievements or performance, but based on who each person is becoming?

CONVERSATION STARTER

Before we start: When was the last time someone told you something good about your character (not your accomplishments)? How did it feel?

SHORT TEACHING

Here's something we often forget: words shape who we are. The things spoken over us, especially by the people closest to us, become part of how we see ourselves. If the dominant messages we hear are criticism, correction, or conditional approval, we can start to believe that we're never quite enough. But if we hear regular, sincere affirmations of our character, we begin to believe we are genuinely valued.

Notice the keyword: character. Not performance. Not achievements. Not appearance. Character-based affirmations celebrate who someone is becoming, not just what they've done. They say, "I see kindness in you. I see courage in you. I see faithfulness, patience, integrity, humility." And those words do something powerful; they anchor identity in truth.

This is what God does for us. He doesn't just love us in theory. He speaks truth over us. He calls us beloved, chosen, His own. And those words shape us. They influence how we see ourselves and how we move through the world.

When your family makes character-based affirmation a regular practice, something shifts. You stop defining each other by mistakes and start celebrating growth. You stop waiting for perfection and start noticing progress. **And you create a culture where people feel truly seen, not just for what they produce, but for who they are.**

DISCUSSION PROMPTS

1. **Understanding:** What's the difference between praising someone's accomplishments (like "Great job on the test!") and affirming their character (like "I see how hard you worked and didn't give up")? Why does this distinction matter?

2. **Personal Response:** What's one character quality you notice and appreciate in someone at this table? When have you seen it in action recently?

3. **Lived Practice:** How can we make affirmation a regular part of our family life, not just when someone does something impressive, but as a steady reminder of who they are becoming?

PARENT NOTE

This practice is simple, but it's truly transformative because your kids are hungry for words that affirm their worth apart from performance. **They're used to hearing "Good job" when they succeed. They're used to hearing "Do better" when they fail.** But what they desperately need to hear is: "I see who you're becoming, and I'm proud of the person God is shaping you into."

Character-based affirmation isn't flattery or empty praise. It's noticeable. It's paying attention to the small moments when your child shows patience, kindness, courage, humility, or perseverance and naming them out loud. For example: "I saw how you helped your sibling without being asked. That's kindness." "I noticed you kept trying even when it was hard. That's perseverance."

Make this a regular rhythm. Once a week, go around the table and affirm each person's character. Don't skip yourself model receiving affirmation with humility and gratitude. And don't let perfectionism creep in. You're not looking for flawless people. You're celebrating image-bearers who are growing.

Watch for this: Kids who rarely hear character-based affirmation often become either approval-addicts, desperate for validation, or approval-avoiders, convinced they'll never measure up. Regular, sincere affirmation roots them in truth and frees them from the performance trap.

ACTION STEP

Tonight, go around the table and have each person give one character-based affirmation to someone else in the family.
Use this framework: *"[Name], one thing I see in you is [character quality], and I saw it when you [specific example]."*

Examples:

- "Dad, I see patience in you, and I saw it when you helped me with my homework even though I was frustrated."
- "Sis, I see kindness in you, and I saw it when you shared your snack with me without me asking."

Let this be the start of a new rhythm in your home.

ONE-SENTENCE ANCHOR

The words we speak over each other shape identity—so let's speak truth, not just correction.
"Therefore, encourage one another and build one another up, just as you are doing." — 1 Thessalonians 5:11

SCRIPTURE READING

1 Thessalonians 5:11
Ephesians 4:29
Proverbs 16:24
Hebrews 10:24–25
Colossians 3:16

DAY 8 BIG QUESTION—ARE WE WHAT WE FEEL?

OPENING SCENARIO

Your son is sprawled on the couch, staring at the ceiling. When you ask what's wrong, he says, "I just don't feel like a Christian. I know I'm supposed to believe all this stuff, but I don't really feel anything. Does that mean I'm not actually saved?"

Later, your daughter is in tears over something a friend said. "I feel like nobody really likes me. I feel annoying and weird, and like everyone tolerates me." You try to reassure her, but she shakes her head. "You don't get it. This is how I feel. And if I feel it, doesn't that make it true?"

Two kids. Two struggles. One question lies beneath both: **Are we what we feel?** And you realize: this is one of the most confusing and ultimately important questions of our time.

CONVERSATION STARTER

Let's start here: Do you think your feelings are always an accurate picture of reality? Or can you feel something that isn't true?

SHORT TEACHING

Here's a truth that can save you years of confusion and heartache: your feelings are real, but they're not always reliable. You can feel unloved and still be deeply loved. You can feel like a failure and still be growing. **You can feel distant from God and still be secure in Him. Feelings matter, but they don't define truth.**

Our culture has trained us to believe the opposite. We're told, "Your feelings are your truth. If you feel it, it's valid. You have to honor what you feel." And while it's true that feelings shouldn't be dismissed or suppressed, elevating them to the level of ultimate truth is dangerous.

Here's why: feelings are shaped by circumstances, body chemistry, fatigue, fear, lies, and countless other factors. They shift. They fluctuate. They're influenced by what you ate, how much you slept, what you scrolled through, and what someone said to you just a few hours ago. Feelings are real and important, but they aren't the foundation of your identity.

Your identity is anchored in objective truth: You are made in God's image. He loves you. You are called, known, and chosen. These things are true whether you feel them or not. On the days when your feelings scream otherwise, you get to choose which voice you will listen to.

This doesn't mean ignoring your emotions. It means learning to steward them wisely. When you feel something, name it. Explore it. Ask: "Where is this coming from? Is this feeling based on truth, or is it based on fear, lies, or circumstances?" **And then, gently but firmly, bring your feelings to God and let His truth reorient you.**

DISCUSSION PROMPTS

1. **Understanding:** Can you think of a time when you felt something strongly but later realized it wasn't true? What helped you recognize the truth?

2. **Personal Response:** What's a feeling you've been struggling with lately? If you tested that feeling against Scripture, what would God's truth say about it?

3. **Lived Practice:** This week, when a strong feeling arises, especially about your worth, identity, or God's love, pause and ask: "Is this feeling based on truth, or is it coming from something else?" Then speak God's truth out loud to counter the lie.

PARENT NOTE

This conversation is so important because a **feelings-based view of identity is one of the most common and influential ideas of our time**. Your kids are being taught that their subjective feelings are the ultimate authority on who they are. And if feelings = truth, then objective reality can seem optional.

This creates confusion and instability. Feelings change. They contradict themselves. They're unreliable narrators. And if your child's identity is built on feelings, it will be as unstable as their emotions on any given day.

Your role is to teach them to steward their feelings, not worship them. Help them name what they're feeling, explore where it's coming from, and test it against Scripture. Model this yourself. Let them hear you say things like: "I'm feeling anxious right now, but I know God is in control. I'm going to choose to trust Him, even though I don't feel peaceful yet."

Important nuance: Saying "feelings aren't the ultimate truth" doesn't mean dismissing emotions or telling kids to "just get over it." Feelings are signals that tell us something is happening inside us. But they're not the final word on reality. We honor feelings by listening to them. We protect identity by anchoring it in something far more stable.

Watch for this: Kids who confuse feelings with truth often become emotionally reactive (led entirely by whatever they're feeling in the moment) or emotionally avoidant (suppressing feelings because they feel too overwhelming). Both responses are unhealthy. The goal is emotional awareness grounded in theological truth.

ACTION STEP

Tonight, each person shares one strong feeling they've had recently—and then someone else responds with a truth from Scripture that speaks to that feeling.

Examples:

- "I feel like I'm not good enough." → "God says you are fearfully and wonderfully made."
- "I feel like God doesn't hear me." → "God says He is near to the brokenhearted and hears your prayers."

Practice letting truth reorient feelings together.

ONE-SENTENCE ANCHOR

Your feelings are real and important, but your identity is anchored in unchanging truth, not shifting emotions.
"Let us hold fast the confession of our hope without wavering, for he who promised is faithful." — Hebrews 10:23

SCRIPTURE READING

Hebrews 10:23
Jeremiah 17:9
Proverbs 3:5–6
Romans 12:2
2 Corinthians 5:7

DAY
9

REFLECTION ANCHOR—WORTH IS GIVEN, NOT EARNED

OPENING SCENARIO

It's been a full week since you started talking about identity, and honestly, it's been a lot to process. You've wrestled with comparison, shame, performance pressure, and the weight of cultural lies. Your kids have asked hard questions. You've had some honest, uncomfortable conversations.

But tonight, something shifts. Your daughter is setting the table, and out of nowhere, she says, "You know what's amazing? I don't have to be the best at anything to matter." She pauses. "Like… I do. Because God made me."

Your son overhears and nods. "Yeah. And even when I mess up, it doesn't change that."

You stop what you're doing and listen. Because **they're getting it,** they're starting to internalize the truth that's been woven through every conversation this week: worth is given, not earned. And you realize: this is what transformation looks like.

CONVERSATION STARTER

Let's reflect: What's one thing you've learned this week about identity that's starting to change the way you think or feel about yourself?

SHORT TEACHING

Here's the anchor truth of this entire unit: your worth is given, not earned. You don't have to achieve it. You don't have to prove it. You don't have to perform for it or maintain it through sheer willpower. **It's a gift, handed to you the moment God made you in His image.**

This truth changes everything. When worth is given, failure stops being fatal. You can try, fall short, and try again because your value isn't on the line. When worth is given, comparison stops being crushing. You can celebrate others' gifts without feeling diminished, because their success doesn't threaten your identity. When worth is given, approval stops being addictive. You can care what people think without needing it to survive, because your core identity is secure.

But here's the reality: this truth has to be practiced, not just believed. The world will keep telling you the opposite. It will keep whispering that you're only as valuable as your last achievement, your latest validation, or your most recent performance. And unless you actively rehearse the truth out loud, together, regularly, the lies will creep back in.

That's why these nine days mattered. You've been laying a foundation. You've been naming the lies, holding up the truth, and practicing what it looks like to root your identity in something unshakable. And now, as you move forward, this becomes the lens through which you see everything else.

When you understand that worth is given, you're free to grow, serve, love, and become who God made you to be, **not to prove you're enough, but because you already are.**

DISCUSSION PROMPTS

1. **Understanding:** What's the difference between living like worth is *earned* and living like worth is *given*? How would each approach change your daily life?

2. **Personal Response:** What's one lie about identity or worth that you're still tempted to believe? What truth do you need to keep rehearsing to counter it?

3. **Lived Practice:** How can we keep reminding each other of this truth as a family? What rhythms or habits will help us remember that worth is given, not earned?

PARENT NOTE

Take a moment tonight to celebrate what God has been doing in your family this week. You've introduced your kids to a powerful, counter-cultural truth: their worth is not something they have to earn or prove. And even if they don't fully understand it yet, **you have planted seeds that the Holy Spirit will continue to nurture and grow.**

Moving forward, your role is to keep returning to this foundation. When your child feels anxious about a test, remind them: "Your grades do not measure your worth." When they feel hurt by social rejection, remind them: "Your value is not determined by who includes you." When they fail, remind them: "This mistake does not define who you are."

And most importantly, practice these truths in your own life. Your kids will learn far more from watching how you respond to your own failures, insecurities, and identity struggles than from anything you say. Let them see you holding on to God's truth. Let them hear you pray honestly when you feel ashamed or discouraged. Let them watch you turn away from comparison and choose gratitude instead.

This is slow, long-term work. Identity formation does not happen in just a few days. It grows over years of steady, faithful encouragement and reminders. But you have begun well. And God is faithful to finish the work He has started.

ACTION STEP

Tonight, go around the table one last time and finish this sentence: *"One way I want to live differently because I know my worth is given, not earned, is..."*

Then pray together, thanking God for His unchanging love and asking Him to keep anchoring your family in this truth.

ONE-SENTENCE ANCHOR

Your worth is a gift from God, not a grade you earn—and that changes everything about how you live.
"See what kind of love the Father has given to us, that we should be called children of God; and so we are." — *1 John 3:1*

SCRIPTURE READING

1 John 3:1
Ephesians 1:4–6
Romans 8:38–39
Psalm 139:13–18
Zephaniah 3:17

UNIT
3

Brokenness and Sin

DAY 1 WHY GOOD INTENTIONS STILL GO WRONG

OPENING SCENARIO

Your son storms into the house after school, drops his backpack on the floor, and snaps at his sister without any clear reason. You call him out, and he explodes: "I didn't mean to! I was having a bad day! Why does everyone always think I'm trying to be mean?"

Later, when things calm down, he sits at the table with his head down, looking discouraged. "I don't understand," he says quietly. "I don't want to act like this. I don't want to yell at people or lose my temper. But I keep doing it anyway. What's wrong with me?"

Meanwhile, you may find yourself wrestling with the same kind of question. You snapped at your spouse earlier that morning over something trivial. You've been feeling impatient with the kids all week. And every night you tell yourself, "Tomorrow I'll do better." But tomorrow comes, and the same habits reappear, **good intentions… the same failures. And you begin to wonder if something inside you is deeply broken.**

CONVERSATION STARTER

Let's be honest: Have you ever genuinely wanted to do the right thing—but still ended up doing the wrong thing anyway? What was that like?

SHORT TEACHING

Here's one of the most frustrating realities of being human: **good intentions alone are not enough.** You can genuinely want to be kind, patient, honest, and self-controlled and still fail. Sometimes again and again. And it's not because you're uniquely flawed or weak-willed. It's because something deeper is happening inside the human heart.

The Bible has a word for it: sin. And before you tune out, thinking this is just religious language, stay with me because understanding sin is one of the most practical and freeing truths the Bible offers.

Sin isn't just "bad behavior." It's not simply a list of things you're told not to do. Sin is a condition of the heart. It's a brokenness that runs deeper than your choices; it affects your desires, your thoughts, and your will. It's the reason you can know what's right and still choose what's wrong. It's the reason your desires become distorted, your motives become mixed, and your will feels divided. It's the gap between the person you want to be and the person you often find yourself becoming.

This is why simply trying harder cannot fix the problem. You can muster willpower, make promises, set goals, and force yourself to hold it together for a while, but eventually, you'll crack because sin isn't just a behavior problem. It is a heart problem. And heart problems require more than good intentions; they require deep transformation.

Here's the good news: recognizing this truth is not defeating it; it is the beginning of freedom. When you stop pretending you can fix yourself through sheer determination and start admitting your need for God's help, you are finally in a place where God can work because the gospel isn't for people who appear to have everything together. **It's for people who are honest enough to admit that they don't.**

DISCUSSION PROMPTS

1. **Understanding:** What's the difference between *sin as behavior* (doing bad things) and *sin as a condition* (a brokenness inside us)? Why does that distinction matter?

2. **Personal Response:** Can you think of a time when you really wanted to do the right thing but still failed? What do you think was going on beneath the surface?

3. **Lived Practice:** This week, when you fail at something you genuinely wanted to do well, instead of just beating yourself up, pause and ask: "What does this reveal about what's going on in my heart?"

PARENT NOTE

This conversation is very important for your family because **if your kids don't understand sin correctly, they will either minimize it or feel overwhelmed by it.** They may shrug it off and say, "Everyone makes mistakes." Or they may spiral into shame and think, "I'm the worst person ever." Neither of these responses helps them grow.

Your role is to help them see sin as serious but not hopeless. It's real. It affects every person. It runs deeper than behavior. **But it is not the final word. The gospel of Jesus Christ is the final word.**

Avoid these pitfalls:

- Making sin primarily about external behavior ("Don't lie, don't cheat, don't be mean"). This turns faith into moralism and misses the heart.
- Using sin language to shame or control ("God's going to be so disappointed in you"). This distorts God's character and produces fear rather than transformation.
- Pretending sin isn't that big a deal ("We all mess up sometimes!"). This minimizes the cost of the cross and undercuts the need for a Savior.

A better way to explain it might be this: "You're not a bad person just because you struggle. You're a broken person like all of us, who needs God's help. And the amazing news is that God doesn't just forgive our brokenness. He also begins to heal it."

Pay attention to this pattern: Kids who grow up with a shallow understanding of sin often become either self-righteous, believing they are basically good on their own, or discouraged and hopeless, believing they are beyond help. Both responses miss the heart of the gospel. The goal is to help them develop honest self-awareness while also having confident hope in God's power to transform their lives.

ACTION STEP

Tonight, invite each family member to share one area where they continue to struggle, even though they genuinely want to do better.

Don't just name the behavior, try to talk about what might be underneath it.

For example: "I keep snapping at people. I think underneath it, I'm trying to control things because I feel anxious."

Then pray together as a family, asking God to help you understand your hearts more clearly and to begin His work of transformation in each of you.

ONE-SENTENCE ANCHOR

Good intentions aren't enough to overcome the brokenness inside us—we need God's power to transform what we can't fix on our own.
"For I do not do the good I want, but the evil I do not want is what I keep on doing." — Romans 7:19

SCRIPTURE READING

Romans 7:15–20
Jeremiah 17:9
Psalm 51:1–12
Romans 3:23
James 1:14–15

DAY 2 SIN AS DISORDERED LOVE AND MISTRUST, NOT JUST BAD BEHAVIOR

OPENING SCENARIO

Your daughter is scrolling through social media late at night again, even after she promised to put her phone away. When you confront her, she becomes defensive: "I wasn't doing anything bad. I was looking at things. It's not like I was lying or stealing or hurting anyone."

But you've started to notice a pattern. The longer she stays up scrolling, the more anxious she seems to become. The more she compares herself to others, the more insecure she feels. And when you gently point this out, she deflects: "You're making a big deal out of nothing. I'm just… I don't know. It helps me feel less alone." **And suddenly something begins to make sense. This isn't just about breaking a household rule. It's about where she is turning for comfort, identity, and connection.** She's not finding those things in her relationship with God; she's looking for them in likes, comments, and the illusion of belonging online. And you realize: this is often what sin looks like in everyday life. Not just breaking rules, but loving the wrong things in the wrong ways.

CONVERSATION STARTER

Let's think deeper: Is sin just about breaking rules, or is it about something more? What do you think is really going on when we choose the wrong thing?

SHORT TEACHING

Here's a truth that can change the way you think about sin: sin is disordered love and misplaced trust. **It's not primarily about behavior; it's about what you love most and whom you choose to trust.**

Think about it. Why do you lie? Because you care more about protecting your reputation than about telling the truth. Why do you gossip? Because you enjoy the feeling of being "in the know" more than protecting someone's dignity. Why do you lose your temper? Because in that moment, you value control or being right more than showing patience. **Sin happens when we love good things in the wrong way, or when we love lesser things more than we love God.**

And underneath disordered love, there is often mistrust. Sin is saying, "God, I'm not sure I can trust You to provide what I truly need, so I'll try to take it for myself." It's Eve reaching for the fruit because she did not trust that God's provision was enough (Genesis 3:1–6). It's the Israelites building a golden calf because they did not trust that God was still with them (Exodus 32:1–4). It's us scrolling, performing, manipulating, or trying to control situations because deep down, we struggle to trust that God is good, present, and enough for us.

This is why simply changing behavior does not solve the deeper problem. You can stop the external action without addressing the misplaced love beneath it, and it will eventually surface elsewhere. The only real solution is for your loves to be reordered and your trust to be restored. And that is something only God can ultimately do.

When you begin to see sin this way, it becomes less about "Don't do this" and more about "What am I loving right now, and what am I trusting instead of God?" **And that is a deeper and more life-changing question.**

DISCUSSION PROMPTS

1. **Understanding:** What does it mean that sin is "disordered love"? Can you think of an example where you loved something good, but in the wrong way or at the wrong time?

2. **Personal Response:** Think about a sin you often struggle with. What do you think you're loving more than God in that moment? What are you finding difficult to trust God to provide?

3. **Lived Practice:** This week, when you're tempted to sin, pause and ask yourself: "What am I really reaching for right now? What do I think this will give me that God cannot?"

PARENT NOTE

This is where the conversation can become truly transformative because most kids (and adults) tend to think of sin as just a list of behaviors to avoid. And that mindset produces either legalism (obsessive rule-keeping) or license (shrugging off sin as no big deal)—neither of these leads to genuine transformation.

When you help your kids see sin as disordered love and misplaced trust, you're teaching them to trace behavior back to the heart. You're helping them ask deeper, more meaningful questions:

"Why did I do that? What was I hoping to get? What was I afraid of losing? What am I trusting more than God right now?"

This is also where you can begin to teach them the difference between **symptoms and roots.** The symptom is the behavior. The root is the disordered love or mistrust underneath. And until the root is addressed, the symptom will persist.

Coaching tip: When your child sins, don't just address the behavior. Ask curious questions that help them explore the heart:

- "What were you feeling right before you did that?"
- "What were you hoping would happen?"
- "What do you think you were trusting more than God in that moment?"

Watch for this: Kids who only ever hear "Don't do that" without understanding the reason behind it often grow into one of two patterns: compliant rule-followers (externally obedient but unchanged in the heart) or rebellious rule-breakers (who come to believe that faith is only about restrictions).

Teaching them to see sin as a form of disordered love invites them into heart-level transformation, not just mere behavior management.

ACTION STEP

Tonight, pick one recurring struggle or temptation in your life and trace it back to the heart.
Ask yourself (or each other): "What am I loving in the wrong way? What am I struggling to trust God to provide?"

Write your answer down. Then pray together, asking God to reorder your loves and help you trust Him more fully.

> **ONE-SENTENCE ANCHOR**
>
> **Sin is loving the wrong things or loving good things in the wrong ways—and underneath it all is a failure to trust God.**
> *"You desire and do not have, so you murder. You covet and cannot obtain, so you fight and quarrel." —James 4:2*

SCRIPTURE READING

James 4:1–3
1 John 2:15–17
Matthew 6:19–21
Romans 1:25
Psalm 37:4

DAY 3 MISUNDERSTANDINGS—SHAME-ONLY VS. RESPONSIBILITY AND HOPE

OPENING SCENARIO

Your son comes to you late at night, his eyes red. He confesses that for weeks he's been lying about finishing his homework. He's been pretending it's done, hiding assignments and making excuses. Now he's failing two classes.

"I'm such a screw-up," he says, his voice breaking. "I can't do anything right. I'm the worst. God probably hates me."

He's spiraling not just into confession, but into deep shame. And you realize he's confusing what he did with who he is.

Meanwhile, your daughter overhears the conversation. Later, she comes to you privately and says, "I mean… everyone makes mistakes, right? God forgives, so it's not really that big of a deal."

She's minimizing, shrugging it off. And you realize **she's swung in the opposite direction, dismissing sin instead of drowning in it.**

Two kids. Two opposite responses. And neither one lands in the right place: **honest responsibility paired with confident hope.**

CONVERSATION STARTER

Let's talk: When you do something wrong, do you tend to beat yourself up and feel like you're a terrible person? Or do you tend to shrug it off like it's no big deal? Why do you think that is?

SHORT TEACHING

Here's a tension we need to hold: **sin is serious, but it is not hopeless**. Learning to hold these two truths together is one of the most important lessons you can learn.

On one side is shame. Shame says, "You are what you did. You're not just someone who sinned, you're a sinner, and that's all you are. You're ruined, broken, unforgivable."

Shame doesn't lead to repentance. It leads to hiding, self-hatred, and despair. It is the voice of the enemy, not the voice of the Spirit.

On the other side is minimization. Minimization says, "It's not that bad. Everyone does it. God forgives anyway, so why worry about it?"

Minimization doesn't lead to freedom. It leads to apathy, repeated sin, and a dull conscience. It is not grace, it's cheap grace, and it ignores the cost of what Jesus did.

The biblical response is neither of these. It is a responsibility paired with hope.

Responsibility says, "What I did was wrong. It matters. It hurt others, it hurt me, and it grieved God. I need to own it, confess it, and make it right."

Hope says, "But this does not define me. I am forgiven. I am loved. And God is powerful enough to change me."

This is the gospel: You're worse than you think. Sin runs deeper than behavior.

And you're more loved than you dare believe. Grace runs deeper than sin.

Both truths matter. Hold them together, and you will find freedom. Pull them apart, and you will fall into either shame or apathy.

DISCUSSION PROMPTS

1. **Understanding:** What's the difference between *shame* (I am bad) and *conviction* (I did something bad and need to make it right)? Why does that distinction matter?

2. **Personal Response:** Do you tend to be harder on yourself (shame) or easier on yourself (minimization) when you sin? What would it look like to take sin seriously *and* hold onto hope?

3. **Lived Practice:** This week, when you sin, practice this response: "What I did was wrong, and it matters. *And* I am forgiven and loved. Now, how do I make this right and move forward?"

PARENT NOTE

This is one of the most important conversations you'll have because how **your kids process sin will shape their entire spiritual lives.**

If they land in shame, they may become performance-driven perfectionists or give up entirely, convinced they'll never be good enough.

If they land in minimization, **they may become spiritually apathetic,** treating grace as a license to keep sinning without consequence.

Your job is to help them hold the tension: sin is serious, and grace is real. This takes discernment, because different kids need different emphasis.

A shame-prone child needs generous doses of grace and assurance. A child prone to minimizing needs to understand the weight of sin and the cost of the cross.

Model this yourself. Let your kids see you take responsibility for your sin without spiraling into shame. Let them hear you say things like:

"I was wrong. I shouldn't have spoken to you that way. That was sinful, and I'm sorry. And I'm grateful that God forgives me and is changing me."

Avoid these extremes:

- Over-emphasizing sin without grace → produces fear and legalism
- Over-emphasizing grace without responsibility → produces apathy and entitlement

The gospel holds both: You are deeply broken *and* deeply loved. Your sin cost Jesus everything *and* His love covers it completely.

Watch for this: Shame-driven kids often avoid confession because they can't bear the weight of their failure. Minimization-driven kids often confess flippantly without genuine repentance. Teach them what true confession looks like: honest, specific, humble, and hopeful.

ACTION STEP

Tonight, practice confession as a family using this framework:

1. **Name it specifically:** "I did [this], and it was wrong because [why it matters]."
2. **Own it humbly:** "I take responsibility. I'm not making excuses."
3. **Receive grace:** "And I trust that God forgives me and is transforming me."
4. **Make it right:** "Here's what I need to do to repair this."

Let this become a rhythm—honest responsibility paired with confident hope.

ONE-SENTENCE ANCHOR

Sin is serious enough that Jesus died for it—and grace is powerful enough that it covers it completely.
"If we confess our sins, he is faithful and just to forgive us our sins and to cleanse us from all unrighteousness." — 1 John 1:9

SCRIPTURE READING

1 John 1:8–10
Psalm 32:1–5
Romans 8:1
2 Corinthians 7:10
Micah 7:18–19

DAY 4 PERSONAL PATTERNS AND HABITS

OPENING SCENARIO

It's another chaotic morning. Your daughter is frantically searching for her shoes again. Your son forgot his lunch again. And you snap at both of them in frustration again.

As you drive to school in tense silence, the thought hits you: **Why do we keep repeating the same patterns?**

Later, your son admits he's been staying up way too late playing video games, even though he knows it makes him exhausted and irritable the next day.

"I don't know why I keep doing it," he says. "I know it's dumb. I just… can't seem to stop."

Your daughter confesses she's been stress-eating every night, scrolling through her phone while mindlessly snacking.

"It's like I'm not even thinking about it. I do it."

And you realize: **sin isn't just about one-time choices. It's about patterns. Habits. Ruts we fall into without noticing.** Those patterns are shaping who we're becoming.

CONVERSATION STARTER

Let's be honest: What's one habit or pattern in your life that you know isn't good for you, but you keep doing it anyway? Why do you think it's hard to stop?

SHORT TEACHING

Here's something we often miss: **sin isn't just about isolated bad choices. It's about patterns that become habits, and habits that shape character.**

You don't wake up one day and suddenly become an angry, dishonest, or selfish person. You get there through small, repeated choices that carve grooves in your soul.

The Bible talks about this as the power of habit. Every time you give in to temptation, you make it easier to give in next time. Every time you respond in anger, you strengthen that pathway in your heart. Every time you choose comfort over discipline, you train your will to default to ease. And over time, those choices stop feeling like choices; **they feel automatic. You become what you repeatedly do.**

This is why sin is so insidious. It doesn't just damage you in the moment; it forms you over time. If you're not intentional about breaking unhealthy patterns, they shape your character in ways you never intended.

But here's the hope: **the same principle works in reverse.** Just as sinful habits form you toward brokenness, godly habits form you toward Christlikeness. Every time you choose patience over anger, honesty over deception, discipline over comfort, you're retraining your heart. You're carving new grooves.

And over time, those choices stop feeling like sheer willpower and start feeling like a part of who you are.

This doesn't happen overnight. It takes time, repeated practice, and God's power working in your life. **But the patterns you practice today are shaping the person you will become tomorrow.** And that is both a gentle warning and an encouraging invitation.

DISCUSSION PROMPTS

1. **Understanding:** What's the difference between a one-time sin and a sinful pattern or habit? Why are patterns harder to break?

2. **Personal Response:** What's one unhealthy pattern or habit you've noticed in your own life? How do you think it's shaping you over time?

3. **Lived Practice:** What's one small, positive habit you could start practicing this week that would move you toward who you want to become? (Examples: pausing before reacting, putting your phone away during meals, reading Scripture before bed, etc.)

PARENT NOTE

This is where theology meets practical discipleship, because your **children are forming habits right now, whether they realize it or not.** The question is not whether they are being shaped. The real question is how and toward what. Your role is to help them notice their patterns, not to shame them, but to invite them into intentional growth gently. Ask questions like:

- "What do you usually do when you feel stressed?"
- "What is the first thing you reach for when you feel bored?"
- "How do you normally respond when someone corrects you?"

These are not moral failures that need to be condemned. They are patterns to notice and, when necessary, gently redirect.

Model healthy habit formation in your own life. Let your kids see you developing rhythms of prayer, Scripture reading, gratitude, and confession. When you notice unhealthy patterns in yourself, name them honestly and out loud: "I've been reaching for my phone every time I feel anxious. I don't think that's helping. I'm going to try praying instead."

Remember: Breaking a bad habit is only half the battle. You also need to replace it with a good one. Otherwise, it is easy to fall back into the old pattern. That is why accountability, community, and God's power are so important. **Transformation is not only about stopping sin.** It is about forming new pathways toward holiness.

Pay attention to this: Kids with unexamined habits can become reactive and impulsive, driven by patterns they may not even recognize. Teaching them to notice, name, and redirect their habits is one of the most practical and lasting gifts you can give them.

ACTION STEP

Tonight, have each person identify one unhealthy pattern or habit they want to break and one positive habit they want to build in its place.

Write them both down. Then choose one small, concrete step to take this week to begin building the new habit.

Examples:

- "I want to stop scrolling on my phone before bed. I'm going to put my phone in another room and read a book instead."
- "I want to stop snapping at my sibling. I'm going to pause, take three deep breaths, and respond calmly."

ONE-SENTENCE ANCHOR

The patterns you practice today are shaping the person you're becoming tomorrow—choose habits that form you toward Christ.

"Do not be conformed to this world, but be transformed by the renewal of your mind." — Romans 12:2

SCRIPTURE READING

Romans 12:2
Galatians 6:7–9
Hebrews 12:1–2
1 Corinthians 9:24–27
Colossians 3:5–10

DAY 5 RELATIONSHIPS—APOLOGY, FORGIVENESS, AND REPAIR

OPENING SCENARIO

Your kids had a massive fight this afternoon. **Your son said something cruel.** Your daughter fired back with something just as hurtful. Both are now sulking in separate rooms, arms crossed, refusing to talk to each other.

You call them together and ask your son to apologize. He rolls his eyes and mutters, "Sorry." It's flat, insincere, and clearly said to get you off his back.

Your daughter crosses her arms even tighter. **"Whatever. I don't forgive you."**

You take a deep breath and realize: neither of them really knows how to handle this. They don't know how to apologize honestly and humbly. They don't know how to forgive without pretending it didn't hurt. And they definitely don't know how to repair what was broken.

They need more than a script. They need a clear, practical framework.

CONVERSATION STARTER

Let's talk: When was the last time you apologized to someone? Was it genuine, or were you trying to make the situation go away? And when was the last time you truly forgave someone?

SHORT TEACHING

Here's a truth that can transform your relationships: **sin doesn't just need to be confessed, it also needs to be repaired.**

Because when you hurt someone, whether through words, actions, or neglect, you create a break in the relationship. **And unless you repair it, that break can deepen and grow over time.**

Let's break this down into three parts:

1. Apology.
A real apology isn't "I'm sorry you're upset" or "Sorry, but you did it too." A real apology is specific, humble, and takes full responsibility. It sounds like this:

"I was wrong when I [specific action]. That was hurtful and sinful. I'm sorry. Will you forgive me?"

Notice what's not in there: no excuses, no blame-shifting, and no minimizing, just honest ownership.

2. Forgiveness.
Forgiveness doesn't mean pretending it didn't happen or that it didn't hurt. **It means choosing to release the other person from what they owe you.** It's saying,

"You hurt me, and it mattered. But I'm not going to hold this against you or punish you for it. I'm choosing to let it go."

Forgiveness is costly. It requires you to absorb the hurt rather than return it. But it's also freeing because holding a grudge is like drinking poison and expecting the other person to suffer.

3. Repair.
Sometimes an apology and forgiveness are enough. But sometimes you also need to rebuild trust and make things right. If you broke something, you replace it. If you lied, you commit to telling the truth moving forward. **If you betrayed trust, you recognize that it must be rebuilt over time.**

Repair means following through. It's not just words; it's consistent, changed behavior that proves the apology was real.

When families learn to apologize, forgive, and repair well, conflict stops being toxic and starts being a tool for growth. You're not just managing sin, you're learning and growing through it together.

DISCUSSION PROMPTS

1. **Understanding:** What's the difference between a real apology and a fake one? What makes forgiveness hard, and why is it necessary anyway?

2. **Personal Response:** Think about a conflict you've had recently. Did you apologize well? Did you forgive? Was there a repair? What could have made it better?

3. **Lived Practice:** This week, if conflict happens, practice this framework: honest apology, genuine forgiveness, and practical repair. Don't just move on—do the work to make it right.

PARENT NOTE

This is one of the most practical and essential skills you can teach your kids, because they will hurt people and be hurt in turn. The question is whether they'll learn to handle relational conflict with grace, humility, and wisdom, or whether they'll default to avoidance, defensiveness, and resentment.

Your home is the training ground. Every sibling conflict, every parent-child clash, every hurt feeling becomes an opportunity to practice apology, forgiveness, and repair. Don't waste those moments by simply shutting conflict down or forcing a hollow "say you're sorry." Use them to teach and model a better way.

Model it yourself. When you wrong your child, apologize genuinely. Don't minimize it or hide behind your authority. Say,

"I was wrong when I spoke to you that way. That was unkind. I'm sorry. Will you forgive me?"

Let them see you practice what you're teaching.

Teach your kids the difference between cheap forgiveness and costly grace. Cheap forgiveness says, "It's fine, no big deal. Let's move on." Costly grace says, "You hurt me, and it matters. But I'm choosing to forgive you because that's what God has done for me."

Watch for this:

- Kids who are forced to apologize without understanding often become resentful or learn to give insincere apologies.
- Kids who are told to "just forgive and forget" without processing the hurt often end up suppressing their anger, which surfaces later.
- Kids who never see repair modeled often begin to believe relationships are disposable when things get hard; you move on.

Teach them to stay, to own it, to forgive, and to rebuild. That's the gospel lived out in everyday relationships.

ACTION STEP

Tonight, if there's any unresolved conflict in the family, walk through the framework together:

1. **Apology:** The person who caused harm takes full responsibility. No excuses.
2. **Forgiveness:** The person who was hurt chooses to release the offense.
3. **Repair:** Together, name one concrete step toward rebuilding trust or making things right.

If there's no current conflict, role-play it. Practice the language so it's familiar when the moment comes.

ONE-SENTENCE ANCHOR

Sin breaks relationships, but apology, forgiveness, and repair can restore and strengthen them.

"Be kind to one another, tenderhearted, forgiving one another, as God in Christ forgave you." — Ephesians 4:32

SCRIPTURE READING

Ephesians 4:32
Matthew 5:23–24
Colossians 3:12–13
Matthew 18:21–22
Luke 17:3–4

DAY 6 CULTURE LENS—BLAME-SHIFTING AND MORAL RELATIVISM

OPENING SCENARIO

You're watching the news with your kids, and a story breaks about a public figure caught in a scandal. Instead of taking responsibility, the person blames their upbringing, their circumstances, their accusers, anyone but themselves.

Your son shrugs. "I mean, they're probably right. If you grew up like that, you'd do the same thing. You can't really hold them responsible."

Later, your daughter is telling you about a conflict at school. When you gently suggest her friend might have been in the wrong, she pushes back: "But who are we to judge? Everyone has their own truth. What's wrong for you might not be wrong for her."

And you realize: your kids are absorbing a cultural narrative that says personal responsibility is optional and that moral truth is subjective. And if you don't address it, it will slowly undermine everything you've been teaching about sin, repentance, and transformation.

CONVERSATION STARTER

Let's talk: When someone does something wrong, do you think it's fair to hold them responsible? Or does it depend on their circumstances, background, or personal perspective?

SHORT TEACHING

Our culture has two major narratives about sin, and both of them are destructive.

The first is blame-shifting. Blame-shifting says, "I'm not responsible for my actions because of my past, my circumstances, my upbringing, or what someone else did to me." It's the oldest trick in the book, literally. Adam blamed Eve. Eve blamed the serpent. And we've been doing it ever since.

Here's the problem: while circumstances and past pain absolutely shape us, they don't remove responsibility. You can acknowledge that someone was hurt or faced injustice and still hold them accountable for their choices. Compassion and responsibility aren't opposites; they belong together.

The second narrative is moral relativism. Moral relativism says, "There's no such thing as objective right and wrong. Everyone gets to decide their own truth. What's wrong for you might be fine for me." It sounds tolerant and open-minded, but it's actually deeply destructive because **if there's no such thing as real sin, there's no need for real repentance, real forgiveness, or a real Savior.**

Here's the truth Scripture teaches: sin is real. It's objective. It's not just a matter of opinion or perspective. And while we extend grace and compassion to those who struggle, we don't erase accountability. You are responsible for your choices, even when hard circumstances shape them.

This doesn't mean you ignore context or show no mercy. It means you hold two truths together: "Yes, life has been hard for you, and you are still responsible for how you respond. And there is grace, power, and hope available to help you choose differently."

When you lose personal responsibility or objective morality, **you lose the gospel. Because the gospel requires both: you are guilty of real sin, and Jesus offers real forgiveness.**

DISCUSSION PROMPTS

1. **Understanding:** What's the difference between explaining why someone did something wrong and excusing their behavior?

Can you have compassion for someone's circumstances and still hold them accountable?

2. **Personal Response:** Have you ever blamed your circumstances or someone else for your own sin? What would it look like to take full responsibility instead?

3. **Lived Practice:** This week, when you're tempted to shift blame or think "everyone has their own truth," pause and ask: "Am I avoiding responsibility? Is there actually a real right and wrong here?"

PARENT NOTE

This is one of the most important cultural conversations you'll have because blame-shifting and moral relativism are everywhere. Your kids are absorbing these narratives from school, media, peers, and even well-meaning adults who want to be compassionate but end up removing accountability in the process.

Your job is to help them see the difference between explanation and excuse. You can acknowledge someone's pain, trauma, or difficult circumstances without removing their responsibility for how they respond. **Compassion and accountability aren't opposites; they work together.**

Teach them discernment. When someone says "you can't judge," ask: "Is that true, or are they avoiding responsibility?" When someone says "everyone has their own truth," ask: "Does that actually make sense? Can two contradictory things both be true?"

Model personal responsibility yourself. When you mess up, don't blame your stress, your upbringing, or someone else's behavior. Say, "I was wrong. That was my choice. I'm responsible, and I'm going to make it right." Let your kids see that taking ownership isn't a weakness, it's a sign of maturity.

Watch for this: Kids who grow up in a blame-shifting, relativistic culture often struggle to develop a strong moral compass. They either become paralyzed, unable to make clear moral judgments, or self-righteous, judging others while excusing themselves.

The gospel offers a third way: honest self-awareness, humble repentance, and confident hope in transformation.

ACTION STEP

Tonight, talk about one area where our culture promotes blame-shifting or moral relativism.
It could be something you've seen in the news, on social media, or even in everyday conversations.

Then ask: "What does Scripture say about this? What's true, and what's a cultural lie we need to reject?"

> ### ONE-SENTENCE ANCHOR
>
> **You are responsible for your choices—and there is grace, power, and hope available to help you choose well.**
> *"Each of us will give an account of himself to God." — Romans 14:12*

SCRIPTURE READING

Romans 14:12
Ezekiel 18:20
Galatians 6:4–5
Proverbs 28:13
James 1:13–15

DAY 7 PRACTICE—SIMPLE CONFESSION AND REPAIR FRAMEWORK

OPENING SCENARIO

It's Sunday evening, and the week ahead feels heavy. You know there are unresolved tensions in the house. Your son still hasn't apologized for the way he spoke to his sister on Friday. Your daughter is holding a grudge against you for something you said in frustration on Wednesday. And honestly, you haven't been great either; you snapped at your spouse this weekend and haven't gone back to make it right.

Everyone's just… carrying it, pretending everything is fine, moving on without truly resolving anything. And you know from experience that unaddressed sin doesn't just disappear; it builds up, hardens over time, and eventually erupts.

But what if tonight, instead of just letting it sit, you chose to respond differently? **What if you made a confession and repaired a regular rhythm, not just a crisis response?**

CONVERSATION STARTER

Before we dive in, take a moment to reflect: Is there anything from this past week something you said, did, or didn't do that's still sitting heavy on your heart? Is there something you need to make right?

SHORT TEACHING

Here's a truth that will change your family culture: confession and repair aren't just for big, dramatic sins; they're for everyday life. Every sharp word. Every broken promise. Every moment of impatience, selfishness, or neglect. Sin doesn't wait for a crisis to do damage, and neither should confession.

The problem is, most of us don't know how to confess to a regular practice. We either avoid it entirely, hoping it will just blow over, or we do it poorly, offering a quick "sorry" without real ownership or meaningful change. **What we need is a simple, repeatable framework that makes confession and repair feel normal rather than intimidating.**

Here's the framework:

1. Name it specifically. Don't be vague. Don't say, "If I hurt you" or "for whatever I did." Say exactly what you did wrong: "I spoke to you harshly when you asked me a question. That was unkind and impatient."

2. Own it humbly. No excuses. No "but you did this first." Just take full responsibility: "I was wrong. That's on me."

3. Ask for forgiveness. Don't assume it asks, "Will you forgive me?" clearly and directly.

4. Make it right. If there's a way to repair what was broken, name it and follow through: "I'm going to work on pausing before I respond, and I want you to know you can tell me when I'm being harsh."

This isn't complicated, but it is countercultural. Because the world teaches us to defend, deflect, and minimize, **while the gospel teaches us to confess, repent, and repair. And when families practice this regularly, it can truly change everything.**

DISCUSSION PROMPTS

1. **Understanding**: Why do you think it's important to make confession and repair a regular practice, rather than something we only do in a crisis?

2. **Personal Response:** What makes confession hard for you? Is it pride, fear, or simply not knowing what to say?
3. **Lived Practice:** What would it look like to make confession and repair a weekly rhythm in our family? How could we intentionally build this into our routine?

PARENT NOTE

Tonight is about establishing a sustainable, **grace-filled rhythm** that becomes part of your family's DNA. Confession isn't meant to be rare or dramatic; it's meant to be normal. And the more consistently you practice it, the less intimidating it becomes.

Your role as a parent is to lead by example. Don't wait for your kids to confess first; model it by going first. Let them see you own your sin, ask for forgiveness, and follow through on repair. When they see that you're not afraid to be vulnerable and honest, they'll learn that **confession is a safe and natural part of family life.**

Make it a rhythm. Some families do this weekly with Sunday night check-ins, where everyone shares if there's anything that needs to be confessed or repaired. Others do it as needed, but with a clear framework that everyone understands. **The key is consistency and grace.**

Here's an important reminder: This isn't about creating a culture of constant guilt or hypervigilance about sin. It's about creating a culture where sin is addressed quickly and grace flows freely. You're not looking for perfection; you're practicing humility, honesty, and repair.

Watch for this: Kids who grow up in homes where confession is normal become adults who can own their mistakes, repair relationships, and extend grace. **On the other hand, kids who grow up in homes where sin is ignored or minimized often struggle** with accountability and relational health.

ACTION STEP

Tonight, practice the confession-and-repair framework as a family.

If there's unresolved sin from the past week, work through it together using the four steps:

1. Name it specifically.
2. Own it humbly.
3. Ask for forgiveness.
4. Make it right.

If there's nothing current, practice it anyway by role-playing or talking through past situations so the language becomes familiar when you need it.

Then commit: "We're going to make this a regular practice in our home." Decide together how often and when, **whether through a weekly check-in, as needed, or another rhythm that works for your family.**

ONE-SENTENCE ANCHOR

Confession and repair aren't just for crises—they're for everyday life, keeping relationships healthy and hearts humble.
"Therefore, confess your sins to one another and pray for one another, that you may be healed." —James 5:16

SCRIPTURE READING

James 5:16
1 John 1:8–9
Proverbs 28:13
Matthew 5:23–24
Psalm 32:1–5

DAY 8 BIG QUESTION—ARE PEOPLE BASICALLY GOOD?

OPENING SCENARIO

You're watching a movie with your kids, and the villain gets a redemption arc. By the end, the character who started cruel and selfish has become kind, even heroic. Your daughter sighs happily. "See? Deep down, everyone's basically good. They need the right circumstances to bring it out."

Your son nods. "Yeah, I think most people would do the right thing if they weren't, like, desperate or hurt or whatever."

Later, you're scrolling through the news and see yet another story of corruption, violence, or betrayal. And you think about your own heart, the jealousy you felt today, the harsh thought you had, or the moment you chose comfort over doing what was right. And you begin to wonder: **Are people basically good, or is something deeper at work?**

CONVERSATION STARTER

Let's wrestle with this: Do you think people are basically good, just making mistakes? Or is there something broken inside all of us that runs deeper than circumstances?

SHORT TEACHING

This is one of the most important questions you'll ever answer because how you answer it shapes everything. If you believe people are basically good, then sin is just a mistake, a misstep, or something caused by external circumstances. **Fix the circumstances, and you fix the person.**

But if you believe people are fundamentally broken, then sin isn't just situational, it's internal. It's woven into the fabric of who we are. And no amount of better circumstances, education, or good intentions will fix it. We need transformation, not just improvement.

Here's what Scripture says: We are not basically good. We are made in God's image, which gives us dignity and worth. But we are also deeply broken by sin, which means our desires, motives, and wills are compromised. Left to ourselves, we don't naturally choose what's right. We choose what serves us, what feels good, what protects us.

This isn't pessimism, it's honesty about the human condition. And actually, it's the only worldview that makes sense of human history. If people were basically good, why is there so much evil? Why do well-intentioned people still hurt each other? Why do you know what's right and still choose what's wrong?

Because sin isn't just what we do, it's who we are apart from grace. And that's why we need a Savior. Not someone to give us tips on how to be better. Not someone to improve our circumstances. **But someone to rescue, redeem, and transform us from the inside out.**

Here's the hope: While we're not basically good, we're not beyond hope. God's grace is more powerful than our sin. His Spirit can do what we can't. He can change our hearts, reorder our desires, and make us new. But it starts with being honest about the problem.

DISCUSSION PROMPTS

1. **Understanding:** What's the difference between believing people are "basically good" and believing people are "made in God's image but broken by sin"? Why does that distinction matter?

2. **Personal Response:** Have you ever thought you were basically a good person, only to be surprised by your own sinful thoughts or actions? What did that reveal about your heart?

3. **Lived Practice:** This week, when you're tempted to minimize sin (in yourself or others) by saying, "they're basically good," pause and ask: "Is that really true, or is there a deeper brokenness that needs God's transforming power?"

PARENT NOTE

This question is foundational because it determines whether your **kids think they need the gospel.** If they believe they're basically good, then Jesus becomes optional, just a nice teacher or moral example, but not a necessity. But if they understand they're broken and in need of rescue, then **Jesus becomes everything.**

Your job is to help them see the reality of sin without crushing them with despair. Yes, we're broken. Yes, our sin runs deep. And yet, we are deeply loved and fully redeemable. **Both truths matter.**

Avoid these extremes:

- **Over-optimism:** "You're a good kid. Just try harder." This underestimates sin and overestimates human ability.
- **Over-pessimism:** "You're completely wicked and hopeless." This crushes the soul and fails to recognize the image of God and the power of grace.
- **The gospel holds both:** You are worse than you think (sin is serious), and you are more loved than you dare believe (grace is powerful).

Watch for this: Kids who believe they're basically good often become either self-righteous (looking down on "bad people") or self-deluded (blind to their own sin). Kids who understand their brokenness, paired with grace, often become humble, compassionate, and grateful because they know they're no better than anyone else and that they've been rescued.

ACTION STEP

Tonight, talk honestly as a family:
"What's one area where we've seen that people (including ourselves) are not basically good? Where have we seen sin show up even with the best intentions or circumstances?"

Then ask: "How does understanding our brokenness make the gospel more beautiful and necessary?"

ONE-SENTENCE ANCHOR

We are not basically good; we are deeply broken by sin and in desperate need of a Savior who alone can make us new.
"None is righteous, no, not one; no one understands; no one seeks for God." — Romans 3:10-11

SCRIPTURE READING

Romans 3:10–12, 23
Jeremiah 17:9
Genesis 6:5
Psalm 51:5
Ephesians 2:1–5

DAY 9 REFLECTION ANCHOR—NAMING BROKENNESS OPENS THE PATH TO HEALING

OPENING SCENARIO

It's been nine days of hard conversations. You've talked about why good intentions fail, what sin really is, the difference between shame and responsibility, patterns and habits, blame-shifting, and whether people are basically good. It's been… a lot to take in.

But tonight, something unexpected happens. Your son, who's usually defensive when confronted, says quietly at dinner, "I think I've been blaming everyone else for my bad attitude. Yes, things have been hard, but I've been choosing to be angry. And I don't want to keep living that way."

Your daughter nods. "Me too. I've been pretending I'm fine, but I've been really unkind to people when I'm stressed. And I don't think I can change that on my own."

You sit back, stunned. **Because they're not just acknowledging sin, they're owning it.** And in that honesty, you see something beautiful: the beginning of real, heart-level transformation.

CONVERSATION STARTER

Let's reflect: What's one thing you've learned about sin, brokenness, or yourself over the past nine days that's been hard to admit but also freeing?

SHORT TEACHING

Here's the paradox of the gospel: the path to healing starts with naming the wound. **You can't fix what you won't acknowledge. You**

can't be healed from something you're pretending doesn't exist. And that's why naming brokenness honestly, humbly, and specifically is one of the most important things you'll ever do.

Our instinct is to hide, excuse, or minimize. We don't want to admit how broken we really are. It's humbling. It's uncomfortable. **And we're afraid that if we're fully honest, we'll be rejected, shamed, or left hopeless.**

But here's the truth: God already knows. He sees it all: every sinful thought, every selfish motive, every broken pattern. And he doesn't recoil. He doesn't reject you. He moves toward you in grace. And when you finally stop hiding and start owning the truth about your brokenness, you position yourself to receive what He's been offering all along: forgiveness, healing, and transformation.

This is what these nine days have been about. **Not to crush you under the weight of your sin, but to free you from the exhausting work of pretending you're fine.** Because when you stop performing and start being honest, you can finally receive the power and grace you need to change.

Naming brokenness isn't the end of the story; it's the beginning. It's the first step toward repentance, which leads to forgiveness, which leads to transformation. And all of it flows from the simple, courageous act of telling the truth about yourself.

DISCUSSION PROMPTS

1. **Understanding:** Why do you think naming your brokenness is so hard? And why is it also necessary for healing and growth?

2. **Personal Response:** What's one area of brokenness or sin you've been avoiding, minimizing, or hiding? What would it take to name it and bring it honestly before God finally?

3. **Lived Practice:** How can we make honesty about sin a regular part of our family culture, not just something we do in crisis, but a normal, ongoing rhythm of confession, grace, and growth?

PARENT NOTE

Tonight is about celebrating honest self-awareness. If your kids are starting to own their sin without drowning in shame, that's evidence of the Spirit's work. Don't minimize it, affirm it. Let them know that their honesty is a sign of maturity and faith, not weakness.

But also remind them: **this is just the beginning. Naming brokenness** is the first step, but it's not the whole journey. The next unit will focus on Jesus, the One who doesn't just diagnose the problem but also provides the solution; the One who meets us in our brokenness and makes us new.

Your job as a parent: keep modeling honest confession. Keep creating a safe space where sin can be named without fear of rejection. And keep pointing your kids to the gospel, the good news that our brokenness is not the final word.

Watch for this: Kids who learn to name their sin honestly often become spiritually healthy adults quick to repent, humble in relationships, and deeply grateful for grace. Kids who learn to hide, excuse, or minimize their sin often struggle with pride, defensiveness, and shallow faith.

ACTION STEP

Tonight, go around the table one last time and finish this sentence:
"One area of brokenness I'm ready to stop hiding and start addressing is..."

Then pray together, thanking God that He already knows and loves you, and that He is already at work to heal and transform you.

ONE-SENTENCE ANCHOR

Naming your brokenness isn't defeat—it's the first step toward the healing and transformation only God can give.

"If we say we have no sin, we deceive ourselves, and the truth is not in us. If we confess our sins, he is faithful and just to forgive us our sins and to cleanse us from all unrighteousness." — 1 John 1:8-9

SCRIPTURE READING

1 John 1:8–9
Psalm 32:1–5
Psalm 51:1–12
Luke 18:9–14
James 4:6–10

UNIT

4

Jesus and Redemption

(Christology)

DAY 1 WHY JESUS MATTERS BEYOND RELIGION

OPENING SCENARIO

Your daughter is working on a school project on world religions and has been reading about Buddha, Muhammad, and various spiritual teachers. At dinner, she says casually, "They all basically teach the same thing, right? Be a good person, don't hurt others, try to be enlightened or something. Jesus was just another good teacher."

Your son shrugs. "Yeah, I mean, He had some good ideas, the Golden Rule and all that. But I don't really get why Christianity is supposed to be so different from everything else."

Later, you overhear a conversation between them where your daughter says, "Honestly, I think religion is just about making you a better person. If you're kind and try hard, then you're good." And you realize: they've reduced Jesus to a moral philosopher. They don't understand why He's actually necessary.

CONVERSATION STARTER

Let's start here: If someone asked you why Jesus matters—why He's different from other religious teachers—what would you say?

SHORT TEACHING

Here's a question that changes everything: **What problem is Jesus solving?** Because if you think the human problem is just ignorance that we don't know how to be good, then sure, Jesus is just another teacher—a wise one, maybe the best one, but fundamentally the same category as other moral philosophers.

But that's not the **problem the Bible diagnoses.** The problem isn't that we don't know what's right. **The problem is that we're broken, enslaved to sin, and incapable of saving ourselves.** We know what's right and still choose what's wrong. We try to be good and still fail. We make resolutions and still fall back into the same patterns.

This is why Jesus isn't primarily a teacher. He's a Savior. He didn't come just to give us information or moral examples. He came to do what we couldn't do: to live the perfect life we should have lived, to die the death our sin deserved, and to rise again, breaking the power of sin and death. **Jesus doesn't just show us the way; He is the way.**

Here's what makes Christianity different from every other religion: every other system teaches what you must do to reach God, **but Christianity proclaims what God has already done to reach you. It's not "try harder, and maybe you'll make it."** It's "you can't make it on your own, so God came down, took your place, and made a way."

This isn't just a nicer version of religion; it's **fundamentally different**. Religion says, "earn it." Jesus says, "receive it." Religion says, "perform." Jesus says, "rest." Religion says, "Climb up." Jesus says He came down.

When you understand this, Jesus stops being optional and starts being everything. **Because if you're broken beyond self-repair, and you are, then you don't need tips;** you need rescue. And that's exactly what Jesus offers.

DISCUSSION PROMPTS

1. **Understanding:** What's the difference between Jesus as a *good teacher* and Jesus as a *Savior*? Why does that distinction matter?

2. **Personal Response:** Have you ever thought of Christianity as just "being a good person and following Jesus' example"? How does understanding Jesus as Savior change that?

3. **Lived Practice:** This week, when you think about your faith, ask yourself: "Am I treating Jesus like a helpful teacher, or like the Savior I desperately need?"

PARENT NOTE

This conversation is critical because if your kids don't grasp why Jesus is necessary, they'll drift into moralism or apathy. **They'll either try to earn God's approval through good behavior (and burn out) or conclude that faith is just one option among many (and walk away).**

Your job is to help them see that the gospel isn't moralism with Jesus's name attached. It's not, "try to be like Jesus and maybe God will accept you." **It's "you can't be like Jesus, so Jesus became like you, took your sin, and gave you His righteousness."**

Watch for this: Many kids (and adults) unconsciously believe they're saved by grace but grow by effort. **They know Jesus died for them, but they think transformation is up to them. This leads to exhausting religion**. The gospel is better: Jesus both saves you and transforms you; it's grace all the way down.

Coaching tip: When your kids mess up, resist the urge to say, "What would Jesus do?" That makes Jesus a moral example they can't live up to. Instead, say, "You can't do this on your own, but Jesus can change you. **Let's ask Him for help." Point them to dependence, not performance.**

ACTION STEP

Tonight, talk about the difference between these two statements:

1. "Christianity is about being a good person by following Jesus' teachings."
2. "Christianity is about being rescued by Jesus because we can't save ourselves."

Which one have you believed? Which one is actually true? How does that change everything?

ONE-SENTENCE ANCHOR

Jesus didn't come to teach us how to live—He came to rescue us from what we couldn't escape on our own.

"For the Son of Man came to seek and to save the lost." — Luke 19:10

SCRIPTURE READING

Luke 19:10
John 14:6
Acts 4:12
1 Timothy 1:15
Titus 3:4–7

DAY
2
WHO JESUS IS—FULLY GOD AND FULLY HUMAN

OPENING SCENARIO

Your son is reading a graphic novel about superheroes, and he casually says, "Jesus was kind of like a superhero, right? Like, He had powers and did miracles."

Your daughter overhears and rolls her eyes. "He wasn't a superhero. He was just a really good man who inspired people. The miracle stories are probably exaggerated."

You pause, realizing that **one thinks Jesus was divine but not really human. The other thinks He was human but not really divine.** And neither one truly grasps who He is. And if they get this wrong, everything else begins to fall apart.

CONVERSATION STARTER

Let's wrestle with this: Do you think Jesus was God? A good man? Both? And why does it matter?

SHORT TEACHING

Here's one of the most important truths in all of Christianity: **Jesus is fully God and fully human. Not half-and-half. Not God pretending to be a man.** Not just a really spiritual human. **Fully both at the same time.**

This is called the Incarnation, and it's mind-bending. But it's also essential. Here's why:

If Jesus wasn't fully God, He couldn't save us. Only God has the power to defeat sin and death. Only God can offer forgiveness that truly lasts. Only God's life is valuable enough to pay for the sins of the whole world. **A good man, no matter how impressive, can't do that. We needed God Himself to step in.**

But if Jesus wasn't fully human, He couldn't represent us. He had to live the life we were supposed to live, perfectly obedient, fully trusting, without sin. He had to face real temptation, real pain, and real death. If He were just God pretending to be human, **then His life and death wouldn't truly count for us. We needed someone who was genuinely one of us.**

So Jesus is both fully God, with the power to save, and fully human, able to stand in our place. And because He's both, His death on the cross accomplishes what nothing else could: **the perfect God-man takes the penalty for sin, satisfies God's justice, and offers us His righteousness.**

This isn't just theological trivia; it's the very heartbeat of the gospel. When you grasp who Jesus is, fully God and fully human, you start to understand the magnitude of what He did. God didn't stay distant and demand that you climb up to Him. **He came down. He became one of us. And He did for us what we couldn't do for ourselves.**

DISCUSSION PROMPTS

1. **Understanding:** Why does it matter that Jesus is both fully God and fully human? What would be missing if He were only one or the other?

2. **Personal Response:** Have you ever thought of Jesus as just a great teacher or just a distant God? How does understanding Him as both fully God and fully human change the way you relate to Him?

3. **Lived Practice:** This week, when you pray or think about Jesus, remind yourself: "He is powerful enough to save me (fully God) and close enough to understand me (fully human)."

PARENT NOTE

This is foundational theology, and your kids need to understand it clearly because every heresy and distortion of Christianity gets Jesus wrong. **Some make Him less than God (just a prophet or teacher). Some make Him less than human** (a spiritual being who only appeared human). Both of these views undermine the gospel.

Your job is to help them hold the tension: Jesus is 100% God and 100% human. Not 50/50. Not switching between the two. Fully both mysteriously and perfectly.

Use everyday language. Don't get lost in technical terms like "hypostatic union" or "two natures." Just say, "**Jesus is God, the same God who created the universe**. And He is human. He got tired, hungry, sad, and tempted, just like us. He is both. And that is what makes salvation possible."

Point to Scripture. Show them passages where Jesus displays divine power (calming storms, forgiving sins, rising from the dead) and human limitations (weeping, praying, suffering). Let the Bible shape their understanding.

Watch for this: Kids who see Jesus as only divine often struggle to relate to Him. He feels distant and untouchable. Kids who see Jesus as only human often reduce Him to a moral example, impressive but ultimately unable to save. The full truth frees them to trust Him and know Him.

ACTION STEP

Tonight, read one passage in which Jesus shows His divinity and one in which He shows His humanity.

Examples:

- **Divinity:** Mark 4:35–41 (calming the storm)
- **Humanity:** Luke 22:39–44 (praying in anguish before the cross)

Talk about what each passage reveals about who Jesus is—and why both matter.

ONE-SENTENCE ANCHOR

Jesus is fully God and fully human—which means He has the power to save us and the compassion to understand us.
"The Word became flesh and dwelt among us, and we have seen his glory, glory as of the only Son from the Father, full of grace and truth." —John 1:14

SCRIPTURE READING

John 1:1, 14
Philippians 2:5–11
Hebrews 4:14–16
Colossians 1:15–20
Matthew 1:23

DAY 3 MISUNDERSTANDINGS—MORAL TEACHER ONLY VS. DETACHED SAVIOR

OPENING SCENARIO

You're at a family gathering, and your uncle, who doesn't go to church but considers himself spiritual, says, "I think Jesus had some great teachings: love your neighbor, don't judge people, and forgive. That's all good. But I don't think you need all the religious baggage. Just follow His example, and you'll be fine."

Later, your grandmother, who's been a churchgoer her whole life, responds, "Well, what matters is that Jesus died for our sins. The teachings are nice, but salvation is what really counts. As long as you believe that, you're saved."

Your kids are listening to both, and on the way home, your daughter asks, "So… which one is right?" And you realize: **they're both missing something. One reduces Jesus to morality. The other reduces Him to a transaction. And neither one captures the full, beautiful reality of who He truly is.**

CONVERSATION STARTER

Let's talk: Do you think Jesus is more like a wise teacher who shows us how to live, or more like a distant Savior who saves us but doesn't really relate to our everyday lives? Or is He something else entirely?

SHORT TEACHING

There are two common distortions of Jesus, and both are dangerous because they leave out half the story.

The first distortion: The Moral Teacher Only.

This view says, "Jesus was a great man with good ideas. If we follow His teachings and try to be like Him, we'll be fine." It's appealing because it feels empowering to do the work and get the credit. But here's the problem: **Jesus didn't come primarily to give you a moral example. He came to save you.** If all you needed was better teaching, God could have sent a philosopher. But teaching doesn't fix a broken heart. **You need transformation, not just information.**

The second distortion: The Detached Savior.

This view says, "Jesus died for my sins, so I'm saved. That's what matters. The rest of His teachings, His life, His example, that's secondary." It reduces salvation to a transaction: Jesus did His part (the cross), and I do my part (believe), and now everything is settled. But here's the problem: **Jesus didn't just die to get you into heaven. He died and rose again to bring you into a restored relationship with God and to transform you into His likeness.** Salvation isn't just forgiveness; it's restoration and transformation.

The truth holds both together. Jesus is your Savior and your Lord. He rescues you from sin and teaches you how to live. He died for you and calls you to follow Him. **He's not just a moral example you can never live up to, and He's not a distant transaction that doesn't touch your daily life. He's the living, present, powerful God who saves you, knows you, and is actively transforming you.**

When you reduce Jesus to only one of these, you lose the fullness of the gospel. But when you hold them together, **you discover a Savior who is both powerful enough to rescue you and personal enough to walk with you every day.**

DISCUSSION PROMPTS

1. **Understanding:** What's wrong with seeing Jesus as only a moral teacher? What's wrong with seeing Him as only a distant Savior? What are we missing in each of these views?

2. **Personal Response:** Which distortion are you more tempted toward: treating Jesus like a good example you're trying to copy, or treating Him like a distant transaction that doesn't affect your daily life?

3. **Lived Practice:** This week, practice seeing Jesus as both the One who saved you from sin and the One who is with you in everyday moments, teaching, guiding, and transforming you.

PARENT NOTE

This conversation is crucial because both distortions are rampant in Christian culture. Some churches emphasize Jesus the Teacher and barely mention the cross. Others emphasize Jesus the Savior and barely mention discipleship. Your kids need to see that the gospel includes both.

The Moral Teacher only leads to exhausting religion, trying to be good enough, and never succeeding. Kids who grow up with this version often burn out or walk away, convinced Christianity is just a set of impossible standards.

The Detached Savior leads to shallow faith without transformation. Kids who grow up with this version often live indistinguishably from the world, **treating Jesus like "fire insurance" rather than Lord.**

Your job: Help your kids see that Jesus is both/and, not either/or. He's the Savior who rescues and the Lord who leads. He forgives your past and transforms your future. He died for you and calls you to live for Him.

Model this yourself. Let your kids see you depending on Jesus for both salvation and daily guidance. Let them hear you pray for forgiveness and for wisdom. Let them watch you trust Jesus to save you and follow Jesus in how you live.

Watch for this: Kids who only see Jesus as a moral teacher often become performance-driven and anxious. Kids who only see Jesus as a distant Savior often become complacent and apathetic. The full gospel produces grateful, transformed, mission-oriented disciples.

ACTION STEP

Tonight, talk about one area of life where you need Jesus as Savior (rescue, forgiveness, power) and one area where you need Jesus as Lord (guidance, example, wisdom).

Then pray together, thanking Him for being *both*—the One who saves you *and* the One who walks with you.

ONE-SENTENCE ANCHOR

Jesus is not just a moral teacher or a distant Savior—He's the living Lord who rescues, knows, and transforms us.

"I am the way, and the truth, and the life. No one comes to the Father except through me." —John 14:6

SCRIPTURE READING

John 14:6
Matthew 11:28–30
1 Peter 2:21–24
Hebrews 12:1–2
Colossians 2:6–7

DAY 4 IDENTITY THROUGH CHRIST—ACCEPTANCE AND BELONGING

OPENING SCENARIO

Your daughter comes home from youth group unusually quiet. Later, she tells you that the speaker talked about being "in Christ" and having a new identity. "But I don't really get it," she says. "I know Jesus saved me, but what does that have to do with who I am now? I still feel like the same person, insecure, anxious, always trying to figure out if I'm good enough."

Your son overhears and adds, "Yeah, I've been a Christian my whole life, but I still feel like I have to earn God's approval. Like, if I mess up too much, maybe He's disappointed in me or frustrated with me."

And you realize: **they know Jesus died for their sins, but they haven't grasped what that means for their identity.** They're still living like orphans, trying to earn a sense of belonging, instead of as children who already have it.

CONVERSATION STARTER

Let's talk honestly: Do you feel like you have to earn God's love and acceptance? Or do you believe you already have it because of Jesus?

SHORT TEACHING

Here's one of the most revolutionary truths of the gospel: **when you trust in Jesus, your identity fundamentally changes.** You're not just forgiven and sent on your way; you're brought into Christ Himself. **The Bible uses the phrase "in Christ" repeatedly, and it means that your entire identity is now securely rooted in Him.**

Think about what that means:

You are fully accepted. Not because of what you've done, but because of what Jesus did. God doesn't look at you and see your failures, your insecurities, your mess-ups. **He sees you in Christ, covered in Jesus' perfect life and righteousness.** You are as accepted as Jesus is. Let that truth sink in.

You fully belong. You're not a hired servant hoping to earn your keep. **You're not a distant acquaintance God tolerates. You are a child of God, adopted, loved, and called by name.** You belong in His family, and nothing you do can take that away.

This is why performance-based identity is such a lie. You're not trying to become accepted; you already are. You're not striving to earn belonging; it's already yours. **Your worth is secure because it's anchored in Christ, not in you.**

Does this mean you can do whatever you want and it doesn't matter? No. But it does mean you obey out of gratitude and security, not fear and insecurity. You grow because you're loved, not to be loved. You serve because you belong, not to belong.

When you really grasp this, everything changes. Anxiety decreases because your worth isn't on the line. Comparison fades because you're not competing for approval. Shame loses its grip because your identity is secure. **You're free to grow, fail, try again, and become who God made you to be, not to earn His love, but because you already have it.**

DISCUSSION PROMPTS

1. **Understanding:** What does it mean to be "in Christ"? How is that different from just being forgiven?

2. **Personal Response:** Do you live as if your acceptance and belonging are already settled, or as if you're still trying to earn them? What would change if you really believed they are completely secure?

3. **Lived Practice:** This week, when you feel insecure or anxious about your worth, remind yourself: "I am in Christ. I am fully accepted, and I fully belong. Nothing I do can change that."

PARENT NOTE

This is gospel identity 101, and it's life-changing, but it's also easily misunderstood or forgotten. Your kids might intellectually know they're saved, but still emotionally live like they're on probation. Your job is to help them connect the dots between salvation and identity.

Key phrase to reinforce: "You are in Christ." Use it often. When they mess up: "You're still in Christ." When they succeed: "That's who you are in Christ." When they're anxious: "Remember who you are in Christ." Let that language become a normal rhythm in your home.

Model this yourself. Let your kids hear you preach the gospel to your own heart. When you're anxious or insecure, say out loud, "I'm already accepted in Christ, I don't have to earn this." Let them see that gospel identity **isn't just for new believers, it's a daily reminder for a lifetime.**

Watch for this: Kids who don't grasp their identity in Christ often become either legalistic (trying to earn God's favor) or apathetic (assuming grace covers everything, so effort doesn't matter). **The gospel produces a third way: joyful, grateful obedience that flows from security, not insecurity.**

Important clarification: Being secure in Christ doesn't mean there are no consequences for sin or that growth doesn't matter. It means your worth and belonging aren't contingent on your performance. You're loved whether you succeed or fail. **And that security empowers growth, it doesn't undermine it.**

ACTION STEP

Tonight, each person finishes this sentence:
"Because I am in Christ, I am..."

Use Scripture to fill in the blank. Examples:

- "Because I am in Christ, I am forgiven." (Ephesians 1:7)
- "Because I am in Christ, I am a new creation." (2 Corinthians 5:17)
- "Because I am in Christ, I am loved and chosen." (Ephesians 1:4–5)

Write them down. Post them somewhere visible. Let these truths shape how you see yourself this week.

ONE-SENTENCE ANCHOR

In Christ, you are fully accepted and fully belong—not because of what you've done, but because of what He's done.
"But to all who did receive him, who believed in his name, he gave the right to become children of God." —John 1:12

SCRIPTURE READING

John 1:12
Romans 8:14–17
Ephesians 1:3–6
2 Corinthians 5:17
Galatians 3:26–27

DAY 5 RELATIONSHIPS SHAPED BY SACRIFICIAL LOVE

OPENING SCENARIO

It's a typical weeknight, and your daughter is complaining again about having to help clean up after dinner.

"Why do I always have to do this? It's not fair. No one else does as much as I."

Your son fires back, "That's not true! I do tons of stuff, and you never notice!"

The bickering escalates, and you step in, exhausted. Later, when things calm down, you sit with both of them and ask,

"What do you think love actually looks like? Is it just a feeling? Is it fairness keeping score of who does what?"

They both pause, unsure. And you realize: **they don't have a clear picture of what real love is. They think it's about fairness, reciprocity, and getting what they deserve.**

They haven't yet grasped the kind of love Jesus modeled: sacrificial, costly, and other-centered.

CONVERSATION STARTER

Let's think about this: What does love actually mean? Is it just a feeling? Is it about fairness, only doing for others if they do the same for you? Or is it something more?

SHORT TEACHING

Here's what Jesus does to our understanding of love: He redefines it entirely.

The world's version of love is conditional: "I'll love you if you love me back. I'll serve you if you serve me. I'll forgive you if you deserve it." It's transactional. It keeps score. It's rooted in fairness and reciprocity.

But Jesus' love is different; it is sacrificial. He didn't die for us because we earned it or deserved it. He died for us while we were still sinners, broken, hostile, and indifferent to Him. **He gave everything, expecting nothing in return.**

This is the standard. This is what love truly looks like.

And here's the shocking part: Jesus doesn't just call us to admire His love; He calls us to live it out in our families, friendships, and everyday interactions. He says, "Love one another as I have loved you." Not "as much as they deserve" or "as long as it's fair," but as I have loved you.

What does that look like practically? It means serving without keeping score. It means forgiving when you've been wronged. It means choosing patience when you're frustrated. It means giving up your preferences, your comfort, your rights for the sake of someone else. Not because they earned it, but because that's what Jesus did for you.

This kind of love is not something you can produce on your own. You can't manufacture it through willpower or good intentions. **It only flows from being loved by Jesus first.** When you truly grasp how much He sacrificed for you, how undeserved, how costly, how complete His love is, it begins to overflow into the way you love others.

And that changes everything. **Relationships stop being about fairness and start being about grace.** You stop keeping score and begin serving freely. You stop demanding your rights and start laying them down. Because that's what Jesus did, and He is the model.

DISCUSSION PROMPTS

1. **Understanding:** What's the difference between conditional love ("I'll love you if…") and sacrificial love ("I'll love you no matter what")? Why is one so much harder?

2. **Personal Response:** Think about your relationships at home. Are you loving sacrificially like Jesus, or are you keeping score and expecting fairness?

3. **Lived Practice:** This week, look for one opportunity to love someone sacrificially, whether by serving them, forgiving them, or giving something up for them without expecting anything in return.

PARENT NOTE

This is where theology becomes intensely practical because **your kids' relationships are the testing ground for whether they really understand Jesus' love.** If they've truly grasped how sacrificially Jesus loved them, it should start to show in how they treat each other, you, and the people around them.

But be patient. Sacrificial love is learned, not automatic. Your kids won't wake up one day and suddenly serve joyfully without being asked. It's a slow, repeated process of being reminded of Jesus' love, practicing small acts of sacrifice, and depending on the Spirit's power.

Your job: Model it. Let your kids see you serving sacrificially, doing things you don't have to do, forgiving when it's hard, and giving without expecting thanks. And when they're keeping score or demanding fairness, gently point them back to Jesus: "Did Jesus keep score with us, or did He give freely?"

Don't weaponize this truth. Sacrificial love isn't about guilting your kids into compliance. It's not, "Jesus died for you, so you better clean your room without complaining." That's manipulation, not discipleship.

Instead, invite them into the beauty of it: "Jesus loved us freely. What would it look like for us to love each other the same way?"

Watch for this: Kids who grow up with transactional love, fairness, and scorekeeping often become resentful adults who struggle with generosity and grace. Kids who grow up experiencing and practicing sacrificial love become adults who reflect Christ and build healthy, life-giving relationships.

ACTION STEP

Tonight, each person shares one way someone in the family has loved them sacrificially recently—serving, forgiving, or giving without keeping score.

Then challenge each other: "This week, let's each look for one opportunity to love someone else that way—without expecting anything in return."

> ### ONE-SENTENCE ANCHOR
>
> **Jesus' love is sacrificial and costly—and He calls us to love others the same way He loved us.**
> *"By this we know love, that he laid down his life for us, and we ought to lay down our lives for the brothers."* — *1 John 3:16*

SCRIPTURE READING

1 John 3:16
John 15:12–13
Philippians 2:3–8
Ephesians 5:1–2
Romans 5:6–8

DAY 6 CULTURE LENS—HUMILITY VERSUS SELF-PROMOTION

OPENING SCENARIO

Your son is scrolling through social media, watching influencers talk about "building your brand," "manifesting success," and "believing in yourself." The message is clear and consistent: you are your own greatest advocate. **Promote yourself. Make sure people see your value. If you don't put yourself first, no one else will.**

Later, your daughter is stressed about a group project because she's worried she won't get enough credit. "What if everyone thinks it was all her idea? What if I don't get noticed?" She's not being selfish; she's responding to what she's been taught by the culture around her: visibility equals value. **If you're not seen, it can feel like you don't matter.**

And you realize something deeper is happening: **they're being trained to self-promote constantly. The culture tells them that humility is weakness**, that obscurity is failure, and that their worth depends on being recognized, praised, and celebrated. But this stands in direct contrast to the life Jesus modeled.

CONVERSATION STARTER

Let's be honest for a moment: do you feel pressure to promote yourself to make sure people see you, notice you, and give you credit? Where do you think that pressure comes from?

SHORT TEACHING

Here's one of the most countercultural truths of Christianity: **Jesus calls us to humility, not self-promotion.** And in a world obsessed with personal branding, visibility, and recognition, that can sound completely upside down.

The culture says: "Advocate for yourself. No one else will. Make sure you're seen, celebrated, and acknowledged. Your value depends on your visibility."

But Jesus turns that idea on its head. He was God in the flesh, the most important person who ever lived, and yet He chose a life of quiet humility. He spent most of His life in obscurity. He washed feet. He served the marginalized. He often stepped away from the spotlight. And when He was finally lifted, it was on a cross, the ultimate picture of humility and self-sacrifice.

And then He says to us: **"If you want to be great, become a servant. If you want to be first, put yourself last. Whoever exalts himself will be humbled, and whoever humbles himself will be exalted."**

This doesn't mean you should hide your gifts or refuse to use them. It doesn't mean you should have low self-worth or pretend you don't matter. Instead, it means your worth isn't tied to being seen. **You can serve faithfully in obscurity because God sees you. You can give without recognition because God notices.** You can even defer credit to others because your identity is secure in Christ, not in applause.

Here's where the freedom comes in: **when you stop needing to be seen, you're free to serve truly.** When you stop performing for validation, you're free to love without strings attached. When you stop promoting yourself, you're free to celebrate others without jealousy or insecurity.

Humility isn't weakness. **It's a quiet strength rooted in security.** And it's the way of Jesus.

DISCUSSION PROMPTS

1. **Understanding:** What's the difference between *using your gifts faithfully* and *self-promoting for validation*? How can you tell which one you're doing?

2. **Personal Response:** Where do you feel the most pressure to be seen, recognized, or celebrated? What would it look like to serve faithfully even if no one noticed?

3. **Lived Practice:** This week, look for one opportunity to serve, give, or help someone without telling anyone else about it. Practice humility in the hidden places.

PARENT NOTE

This conversation matters deeply because the pressure to self-promote is already shaping your kids' hearts. **Social media rewards visibility. School culture rewards self-advocacy.** Even well-meaning adults say, "Make sure you stand out. Get noticed." And all of it can train them to believe their worth depends on being seen.

Your role is to teach them a radically different way: **faithful service in the hidden places, the work no one sees,** the kindness no one applauds, the obedience that doesn't come with recognition. This is where true character is formed.

Model this in your own life. Let your kids see you serving without seeking credit. Let them watch you celebrate others' successes without jealousy. Let them hear you say, "I don't need recognition for this. God sees, and that's enough."

But also affirm them in a healthy and meaningful way. Humility doesn't mean acknowledging someone's gifts or efforts. It means doing so in a way that doesn't tie their worth to visibility. **Say things like: "You did that really well. Even if no one else noticed, I'm proud of you, and God is too."**

Pay attention to this pattern: kids who grow up in a culture of self-promotion often become either anxious performers, exhausted by the constant need to be seen, or cynical non-participants, convinced that nothing matters unless it's recognized. **The gospel offers a better way: quiet, faithful service rooted in security, not visibility.**

ACTION STEP

Tonight, invite each person to share one thing they've done recently that no one else noticed or acknowledged.

Then, as a family, celebrate it together, not to replace the recognition they didn't receive, but to gently remind them: God sees, and that's enough.

ONE-SENTENCE ANCHOR

Jesus calls us to humility and service, not self-promotion—because our worth is secure in Him, not in being seen.
"Whoever exalts himself will be humbled, and whoever humbles himself will be exalted." — Matthew 23:12

SCRIPTURE READING

Matthew 23:11–12
Philippians 2:3–8
John 13:12–17
Mark 10:43–45
Colossians 3:23–24

DAY 7 PRACTICE—INTENTIONAL UNSEEN SERVICE

OPENING SCENARIO

It's Saturday morning, and you notice something unusual: the kitchen is clean. You didn't ask anyone to do it. No one mentioned it. But the dishes are done, the counters are wiped, and everything is put away.

Later, you find out it was your son. He woke up early, saw the mess from last night, and just cleaned it up. When you thank him, he shrugs. "It's fine. I just thought it needed to be done."

And you realize: **this is what unseen service looks like, no announcement, no expectation of credit, just quiet faithfulness.** And you think, what if this became a regular practice? What if you intentionally looked for ways to serve without needing to be noticed?

CONVERSATION STARTER

Let's think about this: When was the last time you did something helpful without telling anyone or expecting credit? How did it feel?

SHORT TEACHING

Here's a spiritual discipline that's rare in our culture but powerful in its impact: **intentional, unseen service.** It's the practice of doing something good, helpful, or kind without telling anyone, without expecting thanks, and without seeking recognition.

This goes against much of what our world teaches. We're trained to share, announce, and broadcast every good deed: "Look what I did!" "See how generous I am!" "Aren't you proud of me?" We've turned service into a performance, and performance requires an audience.

But Jesus calls us to something very different. He says, "When you give to the needy, don't let your left hand know what your right hand is doing, so that your giving may be in secret. And your Father who sees in secret will reward you."

Notice the pattern: **you serve, no one knows, God sees, and that's enough.**

Why does this matter? Because unseen service shapes your heart. It reveals whether you're serving to love others or to be loved. **It shows whether you're generous for God's glory or for your own.** It helps form you into someone who finds joy in simply being faithful, not in the applause that might follow.

And here's the beautiful irony: **when you stop needing to be seen, you become more like Jesus.** He spent most of His life in obscurity, serving quietly and loving without recognition. And He calls us to the same pattern: faithful, humble, unseen service, trusting that God sees, and that's all that matters.

DISCUSSION PROMPTS

1. **Understanding:** Why is it often harder to serve when no one will know about it? What does that reveal about our hearts?
2. **Personal Response:** What's one area where you've been serving (or not serving) because you wanted recognition? What would change if you did it simply for God?
3. **Lived Practice:** What's one act of unseen service you could do this week, something helpful, kind, or generous that no one else will know about?

PARENT NOTE

This practice is transformative because it exposes and reshapes motives. When your kids (and you) practice serving without recognition, you quickly discover how much of your "goodness" may actually be performance. And that's not condemnation, it is an invitation. It is a chance to realign your heart and serve out of love, not out of neediness.

Make it a challenge, not a guilt trip. Frame this as an adventure: "Let's see if we can each do one act of unseen service this week, and not tell anyone about it." Create a culture where serving quietly is celebrated privately within the family, but never broadcast.

Model it yourself. Let your kids catch you serving in hidden ways. Do not announce it. Just do it. And if they ask, say, "I saw that it needed to be done." Let them learn by watching.

Here is an important reminder: this is not about never acknowledging service or never expressing gratitude. It is about training the heart to find joy in service itself, not in the recognition that might follow. **Gratitude is good. But if you cannot serve without** it, your heart needs to be reoriented.

Watch for this. Kids who only serve when they are seen often become transactional adults, keeping score, resentful when they are not thanked, and unable to give freely. Kids who learn to serve unseen often become generous, humble, joyful servants who reflect Christ.

ACTION STEP

Tonight, each person commits to one act of intentional unseen service this week.

It could be:

- Cleaning something without being asked
- Helping a sibling without telling anyone
- Doing a chore that is not yours
- Leaving an encouraging note anonymously
- Praying for someone without mentioning it

The rule: *Don't tell anyone.* Let God be your only audience. At the end of the week, you can share with the family—but let the joy be in the doing, not the telling.

ONE-SENTENCE ANCHOR

Unseen service trains your heart to find joy in faithfulness itself—not in recognition, but in knowing God sees.

"But when you give to the needy, do not let your left hand know what your right hand is doing, so that your giving may be in secret."
— Matthew 6:3-4

SCRIPTURE READING

Matthew 6:1–4
Colossians 3:23–24
Mark 9:35
1 Peter 4:10–11
Galatians 5:13

DAY 8 BIG QUESTION—WHY DID JESUS HAVE TO DIE?

OPENING SCENARIO

Your daughter is reading a book for school where a character sacrifices himself to save others, and it sparks a question at dinner: "Why did Jesus have to die? I mean, if God is all-powerful, couldn't He have just forgiven everyone without the crucifixion? It seems… harsh."

Your son nods. "Yes, I have wondered that too. Why could God not just say, 'I forgive you,' and be done with it? Why did someone have to die?"

You pause, **realizing that they do not understand the cross.** They see it as a religious ritual or even divine cruelty, rather than the necessary, beautiful, and costly act of love and justice that it truly is. And if they do not grasp why Jesus had to die, they will not grasp the depth of the gospel.

CONVERSATION STARTER

Let's wrestle with this honestly: If God is loving and powerful, why did Jesus have to die? Why couldn't God forgive sin without the cross?

SHORT TEACHING

This is one of the most important questions you will ever ask, and the answer is at the very heart of the gospel. Here is why Jesus had to die:

Because God is both just and merciful.

God cannot just overlook sin. He is not a lenient grandpa who shrugs and says, "It is fine, no big deal." **Sin is serious. It is rebellion against a holy God.** It is broken trust, shattered relationship, and even cosmic treason. And justice demands that sin be dealt with. If God ignored it, He would not be just, He would be unjust, and the moral fabric of the universe would begin to collapse.

But God is also merciful. He does not want to punish you. He loves you. He desires a relationship with you. So here is the incredible, costly solution: God Himself absorbs the punishment. Jesus, fully God and fully human, takes the penalty you deserve. He stands in your place. He bears the weight of sin, satisfies justice, and makes mercy possible.

The cross is where justice and mercy meet. God does not ignore sin; that would be unjust. And He does not condemn you, that would deny mercy. Instead, He takes the punishment himself. Jesus died the death you deserved so that you can receive the life He deserved.

Here is why it had to be Jesus specifically: Only a perfect sacrifice could pay for sin. A flawed human could not do it, because our own sin disqualifies us. Only someone sinless could bear the weight of others' sin. And only God's life has infinite value, value great enough to cover the sins of the whole world.

So Jesus, fully God, fully human, perfectly sinless, offers Himself. He lives the life you should have lived. He dies the death you should have died. And He rises again, proving that sin and death are defeated.

The cross is not cruel. It is costly love. It is God saying, "I will not ignore your sin. But I will not abandon you to it. I will take it on Myself." And that is the gospel.

DISCUSSION PROMPTS

1. **Understanding:** Why couldn't God forgive sin without the cross? What would be missing if He did?

2. **Personal Response:** When you think about Jesus dying in your place, how does that make you feel? Does it change the way you see your sin or God's love?

3. **Lived Practice:** This week, when you're tempted to minimize sin or take God's forgiveness for granted, pause and remember: *This cost Jesus everything. It's not cheap. It's costly grace.*

PARENT NOTE

This is the gospel in one question, and your kids need to understand it deeply. If they don't grasp why Jesus had to die, they'll either minimize sin ("It's not that bad. God should just forgive.") or despair of grace ("My sin is too big to be forgiven.").

The cross holds both truths together. Sin is worse than you think because it required Jesus' death. Grace is bigger than you imagine because Jesus willingly died to give it to you.

Use everyday analogies. Imagine someone breaks a valuable vase in your home. Justice says they need to pay for it. Mercy says you absorb the cost yourself. The cross is God absorbing the cost of your sin, not ignoring it, but taking the hit Himself.

Point to the substitution. Jesus didn't just die for our benefit like a hero saving the day. He died in our place, like a substitute taking the penalty we deserved. That's the scandal and beauty of the cross.

Watch for this. Kids who don't understand substitutionary atonement often grow up with shallow views of both sin and grace. They either minimize sin, thinking it's no big deal, or live in fear, thinking their sin is too big for grace. **The cross corrects both. Your sin is serious enough to require Jesus' death, and God's love is powerful enough to cover it completely.**

ACTION STEP

Tonight, read the crucifixion account together from one of the Gospels (Matthew 27:32–56, Mark 15:21–41, Luke 23:26–49, or John 19:16–37).

Afterward, talk about what stands out to you. Then ask: "Why did Jesus go through this? What does it tell us about sin? What does it tell us about God's love?"

ONE-SENTENCE ANCHOR

Jesus had to die because sin required justice, and we needed mercy, and the cross is where both were fully satisfied.
"He himself bore our sins in his body on the tree, that we might die to sin and live to righteousness. By his wounds you have been healed."
— 1 Peter 2:24

SCRIPTURE READING

1 Peter 2:24
Isaiah 53:4–6
Romans 3:21–26
2 Corinthians 5:21
Hebrews 9:22

REFLECTION ANCHOR—JESUS REVEALS BOTH GOD'S LOVE AND OUR PATH FORWARD

OPENING SCENARIO

It's the end of the week, and you're tidying up after dinner when your daughter says something that stops you in your tracks: "I used to think Jesus was just… nice. Like, a good person who taught good things. But now I'm starting to see. He's everything. Without Him, none of this makes sense."

Your son nods thoughtfully. "Yeah. It's not just that He died for us. He also shows us what God is really like and how we're meant to live."

You set down the dish towel and listen, because in this moment, **they're connecting the dots.** They're seeing that Jesus isn't optional in faith. He's the center, the heartbeat, the lens through which everything else comes together."

CONVERSATION STARTER

Let's reflect on the past nine days: What's one thing you've learned about Jesus that's changed the way you see God, yourself, or how you're supposed to live?

SHORT TEACHING

Here's the anchor truth of this unit: **Jesus shows us both God's love and the way forward.** He's not just the answer to sin, He's the answer for everything in life.

Jesus shows God's love. Want to know what God is really like? Look at Jesus. He is compassionate toward the broken, patient with those who are struggling, fierce against injustice, and gentle with the weary. Jesus is the perfect representation of God's nature. **When you see Him, you see the Father,** and what you see is relentless, sacrificial, pursuing love.

Jesus shows us the way forward. Want to know how to live? Follow Jesus, not just His teachings, but His example. The way He loved sacrificially, served humbly, and trusted the Father completely. Jesus doesn't just tell us what to do, He shows us how to do it and empowers us through His Spirit.

This is why Jesus is the center of everything. He's not just a part of the Christian faith; He is the faith. He's not one option among many. He is the only way to the Father. He's not just a moral teacher. **He is Savior, Lord, and our model for all of life.**

And here's what that means practically: **When you don't know what God is like, look at Jesus. When you don't know how to live, look at Jesus.** When you feel confused, hurting, or lost, look at Jesus. He is the answer. Always."

DISCUSSION PROMPTS

1. **Understanding:** How does Jesus reveal what God is like? How does He show us the path forward?

2. **Personal Response:** What's one area of your life where you need to look at Jesus more—either to understand God's heart or to know how to live?

3. **Lived Practice:** How can we make "looking to Jesus" a regular practice in our family—not just a theological idea, but a daily rhythm?

PARENT NOTE

This is the culmination of everything you've been building: **Jesus is the lens.** He's the interpretive key to understanding God, yourself, sin, grace, identity, and purpose. If your kids walk away from this unit with one truth, let it be this: *Jesus is central. Everything else flows from Him.*

Keep pointing them to Jesus. When they're anxious: "What would it mean to trust Jesus with this?" When they're confused about God: "What does Jesus show us about who God is?" When they don't know how to respond: "How did Jesus respond in situations like this?"

Model dependence on Jesus yourself. Let your kids see you looking to Him daily—in prayer, in Scripture, in decision-making. Let them hear you say, "I don't know what to do here, but I'm going to ask Jesus for wisdom."

Celebrate growth. If your kids are starting to see Jesus more clearly, name it and thank God for it. Transformation is happening. The Spirit is at work. And the foundation is being laid for a lifetime of following Jesus.

ACTION STEP

Tonight, go around the table and finish this sentence:
"One way Jesus has become more real to me this week is..."

Then pray together, thanking Jesus for who He is—Savior, Lord, revealer of God's love, and the One who shows us how to live.

ONE-SENTENCE ANCHOR

Jesus reveals God's love and shows us the path forward—He is the center of everything.
"No one has ever seen God; the only God, who is at the Father's side, he has made him known." —John 1:18

SCRIPTURE READING

John 1:18
Hebrews 1:1–3
John 14:8–9
Colossians 1:15–20
2 Corinthians 4:6

UNIT
5

GRACE AND SALVATION
(SOTERIOLOGY)

DAY 1 PERFORMANCE FATIGUE AND FEELING NEVER ENOUGH

OPENING SCENARIO

It's Sunday night, and your daughter sits at the kitchen table, staring blankly at her planner. You ask if she's okay, and she shakes her head. "I have three tests this week, a project due, tryouts for the musical, and I promised I'd help with the fundraiser. And I still haven't finished my homework from Friday."

Her voice cracks. "I'm so tired. I feel like I'm always behind, always trying to catch up. And even when I do well, it feels like… It's never enough. There's always something else I should be doing better."

Your son overhears from the couch and mutters, "Welcome to life." But you notice the edge in his voice, he's feeling it too. The relentless pressure to perform, to achieve, to measure up. **The exhaustion of feeling like you're never enough.**

And you realize: this isn't just about school or activities. It's about how they see themselves, how they believe they earn their worth, and how they relate to God. **They're living under the crushing weight of performance, and they don't yet know there's another way.**

CONVERSATION STARTER

Let's be honest: Do you ever feel like no matter how hard you try, it's never quite enough? Where does that pressure come from?

SHORT TEACHING

Here's a reality many of us live with but rarely name: performance fatigue. It's the bone-deep exhaustion that comes from constantly trying to prove you're good enough, valuable enough, worthy enough. It's the treadmill that never stops, the bar that keeps rising, the pressure that never lets up.

And here's the trap: performance fatigue doesn't just affect school or work, it touches your faith too. You start thinking, "If I read my Bible more, pray more, serve more, sin less, maybe then God will be pleased with me. Maybe then I'll be enough."

But here's the problem: you're trying to earn what has already been freely given. You're striving for acceptance that you already have in Christ. **You're performing for approval** that was secured the moment you trusted Jesus. And the exhausting irony is this: the gospel says you're already enough, not because of what you've done, but because of what Jesus has done.

This is what grace means. **Grace is God saying,** "You don't have to earn this. You can't earn this. **It's a gift. Receive it, rest in it, and live from it, not for it."**

When you grasp this, something shifts. You don't stop working hard or caring about growth, but your motivation changes. You're no longer striving out of fear or insecurity. You're responding out of love and gratitude. You're not trying to become acceptable; you are already accepted. And that changes everything.

Performance fatigue is real. And the gospel is the only cure. Not more effort. Not a better discipline. Grace. Rest. **The finished work of Jesus.** You are enough because He is enough."

DISCUSSION PROMPTS

1. **Understanding:** What's the difference between working hard out of gratitude (because you're already loved) and working hard out of fear (trying to earn love)?

2. **Personal Response:** Where do you feel the most performance pressure right now? How would it feel to know you're already fully accepted, no matter what?

3. **Lived Practice:** This week, when you feel performance fatigue creeping in, pause and remind yourself: "I don't have to earn God's love. I already have it. I can rest."

PARENT NOTE

This conversation is urgent because performance fatigue is everywhere, and our kids are feeling it deeply. School, sports, social life, even church, all send the same message: You are what you achieve. You're only as valuable as your last success.

And unless we actively interrupt that message with the gospel, our children will internalize it as truth. They may grow up believing they have to earn love from us, from others, and even from God. And that path leads to burnout, anxiety, and deep discouragement.

Our job: Help them understand the difference between law and grace. Law says, "Do this, and you'll be accepted." Grace says, "You're already accepted, now live from that security." **Both require effort, but the motivation and foundation are completely different**."

"**Model rest for yourself.** If your kids only ever see you hustling, striving, and constantly performing, they'll assume that's what faith requires. Let them see you resting in God's grace. Let them hear you say things like: **"I didn't get everything done today, and that's okay**. My worth isn't tied to my productivity."

Watch for this: Kids who grow up under performance pressure often become either workaholics (constantly striving, never resting) or quitters (giving up because they feel they'll never measure up). The gospel offers a third way: **joyful, sustainable effort rooted in secure identity.**

Important clarification: Resting in grace doesn't mean laziness or apathy. **It means your effort flows from security, not insecurity.** You work hard, grow, and pursue excellence not to earn love, but because you're already loved.

ACTION STEP

Tonight, each person names one area where they feel performance pressure—where they're trying to prove they're "enough."
Then say this out loud together: *"I don't have to earn my worth. I'm already fully loved and accepted in Christ."*

Let this be the beginning of learning to rest in grace instead of striving for approval.

ONE-SENTENCE ANCHOR

You don't have to earn God's love—you already have it, and that frees you to rest and respond in gratitude.
"Come to me, all who labor and are heavy laden, and I will give you rest." — Matthew 11:28

SCRIPTURE READING

Matthew 11:28–30
Ephesians 2:8–9
Romans 5:1–2
Galatians 2:16
Colossians 2:13–14

DAY 2 GRACE EXPLAINED—GIFT, TRUST, AND TRANSFORMATIONS

OPENING SCENARIO

Your son comes to you frustrated after the youth group. "The leader kept talking about grace, and I just don't get it. Like, I know it means God forgives us, but then he said we can't earn salvation, but we also have to obey and grow and all that. So… which is it? Do we have to do stuff or not?"

Your daughter jumps in. "Yeah, and if grace means God forgives everything, then why does it matter if we sin? Can't we do whatever and say 'grace covers it'?"

You pause, realizing: **they've heard the word "grace" a hundred times, but they don't actually understand what it means.** And without clarity, grace becomes either a license to do nothing or a confusing contradiction. **They need the full picture.**

CONVERSATION STARTER

Let's start here: When you hear the word "grace," what do you think it means? And do you think grace changes you, or does it just forgive you?

SHORT TEACHING

Grace is one of the most beautiful, misunderstood words in Christianity. So let's break it down. **Grace has three essential parts: gift, trust, and transformation.**

1. Grace is a gift.
You cannot earn it, deserve it, or work for it. Salvation is a gift from God, given freely to those who trust in Jesus. **Not because you're good enough, but because Jesus is. Not because of what you've done, but because of what He did perfectly.** This is the heart of the gospel: God gives what we could never earn.

2. Grace requires trust.
Receiving a gift means open hands, not clenched fists. **Faith is simply trusting that what Jesus did is enough.** It's not faith plus good works that saves you, it's faith alone, trusting Jesus, not yourself. But here's the key: **real trust changes you.** If you genuinely trust Jesus as your Savior and Lord, it will show in how you live.

3. Grace brings transformation. This is where people often get confused. Grace doesn't just forgive you and leave you the same. It changes you from the inside out. **When you receive God's grace, the Holy Spirit begins working in you, shaping your desires, forming your character, and making you more like Jesus.** You don't obey to earn grace. You obey because of grace. It's the overflow of a transformed heart, not a payment for acceptance.

So here's the summary: **Grace is God's gift of salvation through Jesus. You receive it by trusting Him, not by earning it.** And when you truly receive it, it begins to transform you from the inside out.

Grace isn't cheap; it costs Jesus everything. **And it isn't passive; it actively changes your heart and life.** It's the most powerful force in the universe, and it's yours in Christ."

Discussion Prompts

1. **Understanding:** What's the difference between *earning* salvation and *receiving* it as a gift? Why does that matter?

2. **Personal Response:** Do you tend to think of grace as something you have to earn, or something you receive and then rest in? How does that affect the way you live?

3. **Lived Practice:** This week, when you're tempted to earn God's approval through performance, pause and remind yourself: "Grace is a gift. I received it. And it's transforming me."

PARENT NOTE

This is core gospel teaching, and your kids need to understand it clearly because confusion about grace can lead to either legalism (trying to earn salvation) or license (assuming grace means sin doesn't matter). Both are distortions.

Your job: Help them see that **grace is both/and, not either/or**. It's a gift that transforms you. You're saved by grace alone, and grace produces obedience. You can't earn it, and it changes everything about how you live.

Use the analogy of a gift: Imagine someone gives you a life-saving medication. You don't earn it; it's free. But if you truly believe it will save you, you'll take it. And when you take it, it will change your condition. That's grace. Gift. Requires trust. Produces transformation.

Model grace in your own life. Let your kids see you living in the freedom of grace, not performing for God's approval, but responding to His love. And when they fail, extend grace: "You're forgiven. Let's learn from this and move forward." Don't minimize sin, but don't crush them with condemnation either

Watch for this:

- Kids who think grace is earned often become anxious perfectionists.
- Kids who think grace has no moral implications often become apathetic or reckless.
- Kids who understand grace as a gift, trust, and transformation become grateful, humble, growing disciples.

Important clarification: Saying "you can't earn salvation" doesn't mean effort doesn't matter. It means **effort flows from grace, not toward it.** You don't obey to be saved. You obey because you're saved.

ACTION STEP

Tonight, talk through this framework together:

1. **Gift:** What does it mean that salvation is a gift?
2. **Trust:** What does it look like to truly trust Jesus instead of yourself?
3. **Transformation:** How should grace be changing the way you live?

Then pray together, thanking God for His grace and asking Him to help you receive it fully and live from it daily.

ONE-SENTENCE ANCHOR

Grace is God's free gift of salvation—received by trust, not earned by works—and it transforms us from the inside out.
"For by grace you have been saved through faith. And this is not your own doing; it is the gift of God, not a result of works, so that no one may boast." — Ephesians 2:8-9

SCRIPTURE READING

Ephesians 2:8–10
Titus 3:4–7
Romans 3:23–24
2 Corinthians 5:17
Romans 6:1–2

DAY 3 MISUNDERSTANDINGS—LEGALISM AND CHEAP GRACE

OPENING SCENARIO

You're at a church event, and two conversations are happening at once.

In one corner, a parent is scolding their child: "If you don't read your Bible every day and stop making those mistakes, God's going to be so disappointed in you. You need to try harder." The child looks defeated, shoulders slumped, spirit heavy.

In another corner, a teenager is laughing about something they did over the weekend, something clearly wrong, and when a friend gently questions it, they shrug: "It's fine. God forgives everything. That's what grace is for, right?"

On the drive home, your kids ask, "Which one is right?" And you realize: **both are wrong.** One is crushing legalism. **The other is reckless, cheap grace. Neither one reflects the true gospel.**

CONVERSATION STARTER

Let's talk: Have you ever felt like you had to earn God's approval by being good enough? Or have you ever thought, "It doesn't matter what I do because God forgives everything anyway"?

SHORT TEACHING

Grace is one of the most misunderstood concepts in Christianity, and the two most common distortions are **legalism** and **cheap grace.**

Legalism says: "You're saved by grace, but you stay saved (or prove you're saved) by your performance. You have to obey, work harder, do more, and be better. And if you slip up too much, maybe you were never really saved at all." Legalism turns grace into a starting point, only to burden you with endless religious performance. **It's grace to get in, but it takes work to stay in.** And it's exhausting, joyless, and ultimately hopeless—because you can never do enough.

Cheap grace says: "God forgives everything, so sin doesn't really matter. You can live however you want because grace covers it. There's no need for repentance, growth, or obedience. Just believes **Cheap grace turns grace** into a license to keep sinning without consequence. It's grace without cost, forgiveness without transformation, and faith without fruit. This is not the gospel; it's a distortion.

Here's the truth: grace is free, but it is not cheap. It cost Jesus everything. When you truly receive grace, it does more than forgive you; it transforms you. You don't earn grace by obeying (that's legalism). And you don't ignore obedience because of grace (that's cheap grace). You obey because grace has changed your heart.

Real grace is both costly and transformative. It is a gift that cost Jesus His life. When you receive it, it produces gratitude, humility, and a deep desire to live for the One who saved you. Not perfectly. Not to earn anything. But because love compels you.

So reject both extremes. **Don't try to earn what is already yours. And don't cheapen what cost Jesus everything. Live in the freedom of costly grace.**

DISCUSSION PROMPTS

1. **Understanding:** What's the difference between legalism, cheap grace, and true grace? How can you tell which one you're living in?

2. **Personal Response:** Which distortion are you more tempted toward—trying to earn God's approval (legalism) or assuming grace means sin doesn't matter (cheap grace)?

3. **Lived Practice:** This week, when you're tempted toward either extreme, pause and ask: "Am I trying to earn grace? Or am I treating it as cheap? What does *true* grace look like here?"

PARENT NOTE

This conversation is important because both legalism and cheap grace are common, and both can harm faith. **Legalism produces exhausted, anxious, joyless Christians. Cheap grace produces apathetic, unchanged, fruitless Christians.** Neither reflects the true gospel.

Your job: help your kids navigate this tension. Grace is free and costly. It is a gift that transforms. You cannot earn it, yet it should change you. It's both/and, not either/or.

Watch for signs of legalism in your home:

- Constant emphasis on performance and rule-keeping
- Fear-based motivation ("God will be disappointed")
- Tying acceptance to obedience
- Little joy or freedom in faith

Watch for signs of cheap grace:

- Flippant attitude toward sin
- No evidence of growth or transformation
- Using grace as an excuse to avoid responsibility
- Faith that doesn't affect daily life

Model true grace for yourself. Let your kids see you depending on grace (not performance) while also taking sin seriously and pursuing holiness. Show them what it looks like to live in the freedom of costly grace.

Important clarification: True grace doesn't eliminate conviction or repentance. The Spirit still convicts. You still confess and turn from sin. But **you do it from a place of security, not fear.** You're not trying to earn God's favor—you already have it. You're responding to His love, not performing for His approval.

ACTION STEP

Tonight, talk honestly as a family:

- "Where have we seen legalism (performance-based faith) in our own hearts or church culture?"
- "Where have we seen cheap grace (assuming sin doesn't matter because God forgives)?"
- "What does *true* grace—free but costly, forgiving but transforming—actually look like in our lives?"

ONE-SENTENCE ANCHOR

True grace is free but not cheap—it costs Jesus everything, and it transforms everything about how we live.
"For the grace of God has appeared, bringing salvation for all people, training us to renounce ungodliness and worldly passions, and to live self-controlled, upright, and godly lives." — Titus 2:11-12

SCRIPTURE READING

Titus 2:11–14
Galatians 5:13
Romans 6:1–2, 15
Jude 1:4
1 Peter 2:16

DAY
4

IDENTITY SECURED BY GRACE

OPENING SCENARIO

Your daughter comes home from school looking defeated. She bombed a test she studied hard for, got cut from the team she hoped to make, and discovered that her friends had a get-together without inviting her. She collapses on the couch and says quietly, "I'm such a failure. I'm not good at anything. No one even wants me around."

Your son overhears and says, "At least you try. I've just given up. **What's the point? I'm never going to be good enough anyway.**"

You sit down with both of them, and your heart breaks because they are defining themselves by their failures. They've forgotten that their identity isn't tied to their performance, popularity, or success. **They've forgotten grace.**

CONVERSATION STARTER

Let's be honest: When you fail at something or get rejected, how do you talk to yourself? Do you remember that your worth is secure, or do you spiral into "I'm a failure"?

SHORT TEACHING

Here's a truth that will anchor your soul: your identity is secured by grace, not by performance. That means failure does not define you. **Success does not complete you. Rejection does not diminish you. And approval does not validate you.**

When your identity is rooted in what you do or in what others think of you, it is constantly shifting. **You are only as valuable as your last**

success. You are only as worthy as your latest affirmation. And when those things fail, and they will, your sense of self crumbles.

But when your identity is rooted in grace, everything changes. You are who God says you are: loved. Chosen. Accepted. His child. His workmanship. Redeemed. Forgiven. Secure. And none of this depends on your performance.

Does this mean failure doesn't hurt? No. It still stings. Does it mean rejection doesn't matter? No. It's still painful. But it does not have the power to crush you. Your core identity is settled. You know who you are in Christ, and that does not change based on circumstances.

Here's the freedom in this: when you know your identity is secure, you can take risks. You can try new things without fear of failure. **You can be honest about your struggles without fear of rejection.** You can grow, learn, and even fail because your worth is not on the line.

And here's the humility in this: when you know your identity is secure, you don't need to prove yourself. You don't have to be the best, the smartest, or the most popular. You can celebrate others without jealousy. You can serve without needing credit. You can rest in who God says you are.

Your identity is secured by grace. **Not by what you achieve. Not by who validates you. By Jesus. And that is enough.**

DISCUSSION PROMPTS

1. **Understanding:** What's the difference between identity based on performance (what you do) and identity based on grace (who God says you are)?

2. **Personal Response:** When was the last time failure or rejection made you question your worth? How would it feel to know your identity is secure no matter what?

3. **Lived Practice:** This week, when you fail or get rejected, practice saying this out loud: "This doesn't define me. I am loved, chosen, and secure in Christ."

PARENT NOTE

This is where grace becomes deeply personal because your kids are constantly being told that their worth is conditional. Conditional on grades, performance, appearance, popularity, and achievements. And unless you actively counter that message, they will internalize it.

Your job: reinforce their identity in Christ relentlessly. When they fail, remind them: "You're still loved. You're still valuable. This does not change who you are in Christ." When they succeed, affirm them, but don't let their identity rest on it: "I'm proud of you. And your worth is not tied to this."

Model this yourself. Let your kids see how you handle failure and rejection. Do you spiral into self-condemnation? Or do you remind yourself of your identity in Christ? Let them hear you preach the gospel to your own heart.

Watch for this: kids whose identity is rooted in performance often become either perfectionists (terrified of failure) or quitters (convinced they'll never measure up). Kids whose identity is secured by grace often become resilient, humble, and free because they know who they are and do not depend on outcomes.

Important reminder: securing identity in grace does not mean effort doesn't matter or that failure is meaningless. It means your worth is not contingent on success. You still care about growth, excellence, and responsibility, but from a place of security, not desperation.

ACTION STEP

Tonight, each person shares one recent failure, rejection, or disappointment.

Then, as a family, respond to each one with this truth: *"That was hard. But it doesn't define you. You are loved, chosen, and secure in Christ—and that doesn't change."*

Let this be a practice of anchoring identity in grace, not performance.

ONE-SENTENCE ANCHOR

Your identity is secured by grace—not by success, approval, or performance—and that frees you to live without fear.
"But now in Christ Jesus you who once were far off have been brought near by the blood of Christ." — Ephesians 2:13

SCRIPTURE READING

Ephesians 2:13
Romans 8:38–39
1 John 3:1
Colossians 3:3
2 Corinthians 5:17

DAY 5 GRACE-FILLED RESPONSES IN FAMILY CONFLICT

OPENING SCENARIO

It has been one of those mornings. Your son snapped at his sister over something trivial. She retaliated with a cutting remark. He slammed a door. She stormed off. And now they are both sulking in separate rooms, arms crossed, refusing to apologize.

You call them back to the table, but the conversation goes nowhere. Your son says, "She started it." Your daughter fires back, "He's always mean to me." Neither is willing to take ownership of their part. Neither is willing to extend grace.

And then you realize: **they know about grace theologically, but they have no idea how to practice it relationally.** They can recite that God forgives them, but they cannot forgive each other. **Grace has not yet moved from their heads to their hearts or into their everyday interactions.**

CONVERSATION STARTER

Let's be real: Is it easier to receive grace from God or to extend grace to each other? Why do you think that is?

SHORT TEACHING

Here is one of the most convicting truths in Scripture: the grace you have received from God is meant to overflow into how you treat others. **You are not just saved by grace, you are called to live by grace. And that includes how you respond in conflict.**

Think about it. God has forgiven you of an infinite debt. Every lie, every selfish act, every moment of rebellion covered by Jesus' blood. You did not earn it. You did not deserve it. And yet, God freely forgave you. That is grace.

And then Jesus says, **"Freely you have received; freely give."** In other words, the grace you've been given should shape the grace you extend. If God can forgive you for that much, can't you forgive your sibling for a harsh word? If God can show you patience when you mess up for the hundredth time, can't you show patience to the people you live with?

Here's what grace-filled responses look like in conflict:

1. **Quick to own your part.**
   Don't wait for the other person to apologize first. Don't deflect or blame-shift. Just own it. "I was wrong. I'm sorry."

2. **Quick to forgive.**
   When someone apologizes, don't hold it over them. Don't make them grovel. Just forgive. "I forgive you. Let's move forward."

3. **Quick to extend patience.**
   Remember how many times God has been patient with you. Then extend that same patience to others—even when they're struggling, slow to change, or repeating the same mistakes.

This doesn't mean pretending conflict doesn't hurt. It doesn't mean ignoring sin or enabling bad behavior. **It means responding to others the way God responds to you with grace, truth, and redemptive love.**

When grace fills your home, **conflict becomes an opportunity for growth, not just damage control.** You're not just managing relationships, you're reflecting the gospel in real time.

DISCUSSION PROMPTS

1. **Understanding:** What does it mean to extend grace in conflict? How is that different from just "letting it go" or pretending nothing happened?

2. **Personal Response:** Are you quick to own your part in conflict, or do you tend to wait for the other person to apologize first? Why?

3. **Lived Practice:** This week, when conflict happens at home, practice grace-filled responses: own your part quickly, forgive freely, and extend patience generously.

PARENT NOTE

This is where the rubber meets the road—because **your kids will learn more about grace from how you handle conflict than from anything you teach.** If they see you extending grace in real-time, they'll learn to do the same. If they see you keeping score, demanding fairness, and holding grudges, they'll internalize that too.

Your job: Model grace-filled conflict. When you mess up, own it quickly—without excuses or defensiveness. When your kids apologize, forgive freely—without lectures or shame. When someone is struggling, extend patience—remembering how patient God has been with you.

Don't let conflict fester. Address it, own it, forgive it, and move on. Don't let bitterness or resentment take root. And teach your kids to do the same: **quick to apologize, quick to forgive, quick to repair.**

Watch for this: Kids who grow up in grace-filled homes become adults who can navigate conflict with humility and maturity. Kids who grow up in scorekeeping, grudge-holding homes often become defensive, resentful adults who struggle with forgiveness.

Important clarification: Grace-filled responses don't mean there are no consequences or boundaries. You can forgive someone *and* establish a boundary. You can extend grace *and* require accountability. Grace and truth go together.

ACTION STEP

Tonight, if there's any unresolved conflict in the family, work through it using grace-filled responses:

1. Each person owns their part (no "but you did this first").
2. Each person forgives freely (no holding it over the other).
3. Each person commits to patience going forward (remembering how much grace you've received).

If there's no current conflict, role-play it. Practice the language so it's familiar when the moment comes.

ONE-SENTENCE ANCHOR

The grace we've received from God should overflow into how we respond to others—quick to own, quick to forgive, quick to extend patience.
"Be kind to one another, tenderhearted, forgiving one another, as God in Christ forgave you." — Ephesians 4:32

SCRIPTURE READING

Ephesians 4:32
Colossians 3:12–13
Matthew 18:21–35
Luke 6:37
1 Peter 4:8

CULTURE LENS—EARNING APPROVAL VERSUS RECEIVING GRACE

OPENING SCENARIO

Your daughter is scrolling through Instagram, and you notice her expression shift with every post. She pauses on one photo—a classmate who looks perfect, is doing something impressive, and has hundreds of likes. Your daughter sighs and mutters, "I wish I were like that."

Later, your son is obsessing over a group project, anxious that he'll be judged for not contributing enough. "What if everyone thinks I'm lazy? What if they don't like me?" He's not worried about the actual work—he's worried about **earning approval.**

And you realize: **the culture has trained them to believe their worth depends on other people's validation.** They're performing constantly—on social media, at school, with friends—hoping to earn the approval that will finally make them feel like they're enough. **And it's exhausting.**

CONVERSATION STARTER

Let's talk: Do you ever feel like you're constantly trying to earn people's approval or validation? Where does that pressure come from?

SHORT TEACHING

Here's one of the most insidious lies of our culture: **your worth depends on earning others' approval.** You have to look right, perform well, say the right things, and get the right responses. And if you don't—if people ignore you, criticize you, or forget about you—then you must not matter.

This shows up everywhere. Social media metrics (likes, comments, followers) become a scoreboard for worth. School culture rewards visibility and popularity. Even well-meaning adults ask, "What do you want to be when you grow up?"—tying identity to achievement and recognition.

And so you perform. You curate. You present the best version of yourself and hope people approve. **But it's never enough** because human approval is fickle, conditional, and ultimately incapable of filling the soul-deep need to be fully known and fully loved.

Here's the gospel truth that cuts through all of it: **You don't have to earn approval. You already have it—from the One whose opinion actually matters.**

God doesn't look at your curated highlight reel and decide if you're valuable. **He knows you fully—the good, the bad, the hidden—and He loves you completely.** Not because you performed well. Not because you earned it. But because of Jesus. **You are fully known and fully loved. That's grace.**

And when you truly grasp that, **you stop performing for validation.** You don't need a thousand likes to know you matter. You don't need constant affirmation to know you're valuable. You don't need to prove yourself because your approval is already settled in Christ.

This doesn't mean you stop caring what people think. It means **you stop needing it.** You can receive affirmation with gratitude without being controlled by it. You can face criticism without being crushed by it because **your worth isn't up for a vote.**

DISCUSSION PROMPTS

1. **Understanding:** What's the difference between *wanting* people's approval and *needing* it? How can you tell which one is driving you?

2. **Personal Response:** Where do you feel the most pressure to earn approval—school, social media, friends, family? How would it feel to know you're already fully approved by God?

3. **Lived Practice:** This week, when you're tempted to perform for approval, pause and remind yourself: "I don't have to earn this. I'm already fully known and fully loved by God."

PARENT NOTE

This is one of the most urgent cultural conversations you'll have—because **the pressure to earn approval is crushing your kids.** Every scroll, every interaction, every social dynamic is reinforcing the lie that their worth is conditional on validation.

Your job: Help them see the difference between healthy affirmation (which is good) and needy approval-seeking (which is slavery). They don't have to reject all feedback or become indifferent to what people think. But **they do need to stop building their identity on it.**

Model this yourself. If your kids see you constantly seeking validation—checking social media obsessively, fishing for compliments, spiraling when criticized—they'll learn that approval-seeking is normal. But if they see you resting in God's approval, they'll learn a better way.

Watch for this: Kids who grow up dependent on earning approval often become either people-pleasers (exhausted by trying to keep everyone happy) or approval-avoiders (cynical and withdrawn because they're convinced they'll never measure up). The gospel offers a third way: **secure in God's approval, free to receive human affirmation without being controlled by it.**

Important clarification: Saying "you don't need human approval" doesn't mean you ignore feedback or become arrogant. It means **your core worth isn't contingent on it.** You can listen to input, grow from correction, and appreciate affirmation—without needing it to survive.

ACTION STEP

Tonight, talk about one area where you've been performing for approval—trying to earn validation from others.
Then ask: "What would change if I really believed I'm already fully approved by God?"

Challenge each other: "This week, let's practice living from God's approval instead of performing for human validation."

ONE-SENTENCE ANCHOR

You don't have to earn approval—you're already fully known and fully loved by the One whose opinion actually matters.
"Am I now seeking the approval of man, or of God? Or am I trying to please man? If I were still trying to please man, I would not be a servant of Christ." — Galatians 1:10

SCRIPTURE READING

Galatians 1:10
Proverbs 29:25
1 Thessalonians 2:4
John 12:43
Psalm 118:6

DAY 7 PRACTICE—PAUSE-BEFORE-REACT CHALLENGE

OPENING SCENARIO

Your son is having a rough afternoon. His friend canceled plans at the last minute, his homework is taking forever, and he just spilled juice all over the table. When you gently ask him to clean it up, he snaps: "Why is everything always my fault? I can't do anything right!"

You feel your own frustration rising. You want to fire back with, "Seriously? I just asked you to wipe up the juice!" But something stops you. You take a breath. Pause. And instead say calmly, "I know you're having a hard day. Let's clean this up together."

His shoulders drop. He exhales. "Sorry. I didn't mean to yell." And you realize **that pause changed everything.** Instead of escalating the conflict, you created space for grace. And you wonder: *What if we practiced this intentionally?*

CONVERSATION STARTER

Let's be honest: How often do you react immediately when you're frustrated, hurt, or angry—and then regret it? What would change if we paused first?

SHORT TEACHING

Here's a simple but transformative spiritual practice: **the pause-before-react challenge.** It's exactly what it sounds like: when you're triggered—frustrated, hurt, angry, defensive—you pause before responding. Just a few seconds. A breath. A silent prayer. Enough space to let grace interrupt your impulse.

Why does this matter? Because **most relational damage happens in reactive moments.** Someone says something that bothers you, and you fire back. Someone hurts you, and you retaliate. Someone frustrates you, and you lash out. And before you know it, you've said something you can't take back.

But **the pause gives grace a chance to work.** In that brief moment, you can:

- Ask, "Is this how I want to respond?"
- Pray, "God, help me respond with grace."
- Remember, "I've been shown so much patience—I can extend it here."

The pause doesn't mean you never address the issue. It doesn't mean you suppress your emotions or pretend everything's fine. **It just means you choose your response instead of being controlled by your impulse.**

This is what James means when he says, **"Be quick to listen, slow to speak, slow to anger."** The pause is the practice of being *slow.* Slow enough to listen. Slow enough to think. Slow enough to let the Spirit guide you instead of your flesh.

And here's what's amazing: **when you practice the pause, everything changes.** Conflict de-escalates. Conversations stay productive. Relationships stay healthy because **grace gets the first word, not reaction.**

DISCUSSION PROMPTS

1. **Understanding:** Why is it so hard to pause before reacting? What usually makes you react immediately instead?

2. **Personal Response:** Think about a recent time you reacted in anger or frustration and regretted it. What would have changed if you'd paused first?

3. **Lived Practice:** This week, commit to the pause-before-react challenge. When you're triggered, take three deep breaths and pray silently before responding.

PARENT NOTE

This is one of the most practical, high-impact disciplines you can teach your kids—because **most sin in relationships happens in reactive moments.** Harsh words. Defensive outbursts. Retaliation. All of it flows from impulse, not intention.

Your job: Teach them the pause and model it yourself. When your kids see you pause before responding in conflict, they'll learn that self-control is possible. When they see you react impulsively and then apologize, they'll learn that growth is a process.

Make it a family practice. When conflict happens, call a pause. Literally say, "Let's pause for a second." Take a breath. Pray silently. Then re-engage with grace. Over time, this becomes muscle memory.

Don't shame them when they fail. Reacting impulsively is normal—it's the default. The goal isn't perfection. It's progress. Celebrate when they successfully pause. Extend grace when they don't.

Watch for this: Kids who learn to pause before reacting become adults who can navigate conflict, manage emotions, and respond with wisdom instead of impulse. Kids who never learn to pause often become reactive, defensive, or emotionally volatile adults.

Important reminder: The pause isn't about suppressing emotions or stuffing feelings. It's about **creating space for grace to interrupt the impulse.** You still name what you're feeling. You still address the issue. But you do it with intention, not reaction.

ACTION STEP

Tonight, commit to the 'pause before react' challenge as a family. Every time someone is triggered this week, frustrated, hurt, or angry, they commit to:

1. Take three deep breaths.
2. Praying a silent prayer: "God, help me respond with grace."
3. Choosing a response instead of reacting impulsively.

At the end of the week, share: "How did the pause change the way conflict went?"

ONE-SENTENCE ANCHOR

The pause-before-react creates space for grace to interrupt impulse—and it changes everything.
"Know this, my beloved brothers: let every person be quick to hear, slow to speak, slow to anger."—James 1:19

SCRIPTURE READING

James 1:19–20
Proverbs 15:1
Proverbs 29:11
Ephesians 4:26–27
Colossians 4:6

DAY 8 BIG QUESTION—CAN FAITH FAIL OR FADE?

OPENING SCENARIO

Your daughter comes to you late one night, unable to sleep. "I'm scared," she says quietly. "What if I stop believing? What if I mess up so bad that God gives up on me? What if my faith… fades?"

Your son overhears from his room and calls out, "That happened to a kid at school. He used to be really into church stuff, and now he says he doesn't believe anymore. What if that happens to me?"

You sit on the edge of the bed, and your heart aches because **they're asking one of the deepest, most important questions: Is my faith secure? Or can I lose it?** And the answer matters more than almost anything else.

CONVERSATION STARTER

Let's wrestle with this honestly: Do you ever worry that your faith might fade or fail? What makes you wonder about that?

SHORT TEACHING

This is one of the hardest questions in theology, and Christians have debated it for centuries. But here's what Scripture teaches clearly: **True saving faith is secured by God, not by you.** Let's unpack that.

First, **salvation is not something you maintain by your own effort.** You didn't save yourself—Jesus saved you. And **the same power that saved you is the power that keeps you.** Your faith doesn't depend on your ability to hold on to God. It depends on *God's* ability to hold on to you. And He's stronger than your doubts, your failures, and your struggles.

Jesus says it clearly: **"I give them eternal life, and they will never perish, and no one will snatch them out of my hand."** Not "they might perish if they're not careful." Not "they'll be fine as long as they don't mess up too much." **Never perish. Secure in His hand.**

But here's the tension: **real faith produces real fruit.** The Bible also warns against false faith—people who claim to believe but show no evidence of transformation. If someone walks away from faith entirely and never looks back, the question isn't "Did they lose their salvation?" It's "Did they ever truly have it?"

True faith perseveres. Not perfectly. Not without struggle. But genuinely. You might doubt. You might wrestle. You might go through seasons of dryness or confusion. But **if your faith is real, God will sustain it.** He's faithful even when you're not.

So here's the comfort: **If you're worried about losing your faith, that's actually evidence that your faith is real.** Because people who don't care about faith don't worry about losing it. The very fact that you're wrestling with this question shows that God is at work in you.

Your salvation is secure—not because you're strong, but because God is faithful.

DISCUSSION PROMPTS

1. **Understanding:** What's the difference between struggling with doubt and completely walking away from faith? Can you struggle and still be secure?

2. **Personal Response:** Have you ever worried that your faith might fade or that God might give up on you? How does it feel to hear that God holds you securely?

3. **Lived Practice:** This week, when doubt or fear creeps in, remind yourself: "My faith is secure—not because I'm strong, but because God is faithful."

PARENT NOTE

This question is deeply personal and often anxiety-inducing—especially for kids who tend toward perfectionism or insecurity. Your job is to provide **both assurance and honesty.**

Assurance: True saving faith is secured by God's power, not human effort. If your child has genuinely trusted in Jesus, they are held securely in His hand.

Honesty: The Bible does warn against false profession—people who claim faith but show no fruit. But the warning is meant to provoke self-examination, not paralyze believers with fear.

Don't weaponize this. Never use the "you might not really be saved" threat to manipulate behavior. That's spiritual abuse, not biblical warning. Instead, help your kids look for *fruit*—evidence of the Spirit's work: love, repentance, desire for God, growing obedience. Imperfect fruit is still fruit.

Model faith that perseveres. Let your kids see you wrestle with doubt, ask hard questions, and keep trusting God anyway. Faith isn't the absence of struggle—it's trust that perseveres *through* struggle.

Watch for this: Kids who are constantly worried about losing their salvation often struggle with assurance and live in fear-based faith. Kids who assume faith can never be tested often become complacent. The gospel offers a third way: **confident security that produces humble perseverance.**

Important clarification: Perseverance doesn't mean sinless perfection. It means **directional faithfulness** an overall trajectory toward God, even amid setbacks.

ACTION STEP

Tonight, if anyone is struggling with fear about their faith, talk through these questions together:

1. Have you trusted in Jesus as your Savior?
2. Do you see any evidence of the Spirit's work in your life (love, repentance, desire for God)?
3. When you doubt or struggle, do you turn *toward* God or completely away from Him?

Then remind each other: "God is faithful. He who began a good work in you will complete it."

ONE-SENTENCE ANCHOR

Your faith is secure—not because you hold tightly to God, but because He holds you and will never let go.
"And I am sure of this, that he who began a good work in you will bring it to completion at the day of Jesus Christ." — Philippians 1:6

SCRIPTURE READING

Philippians 1:6
John 10:27–29
Romans 8:38–39
1 Peter 1:3–5
Jude 1:24–25

DAY 9 REFLECTION ANCHOR—GRACE FREES US TO GROW

OPENING SCENARIO

It's the end of another week, and you're sitting around the table reflecting on the past nine days. Your son says, "I think I finally get it. Like, I don't have to be perfect for God to love me. But that doesn't mean I sit around and do nothing. It actually makes me *want* to grow."

Your daughter nods. "Yeah. It's like... because I'm already accepted, I don't have to be afraid of messing up. I can actually try new things and work on stuff without freaking out."

You smile, because **they're getting it.** They're seeing that grace isn't permission to stay the same—it's the power to change. **Grace doesn't make growth optional. It makes growth possible.**

CONVERSATION STARTER

Let's reflect: What's one thing you've learned about grace this week that's changed the way you see yourself, your faith, or how you're growing?

SHORT TEACHING

Here's the anchor truth of this entire unit: **Grace frees us to grow.** And that statement holds together two truths that seem contradictory but are actually inseparable.

First: You are fully accepted as you are. Right now. Not after you improve. Not after you get it together. Not after you stop struggling. **Right now.** You are loved, forgiven, and secure in Christ. Nothing you do—or fail to do—changes that. **That's grace.**

Second: Grace doesn't leave you as you are. It transforms you. When you truly receive grace, **it doesn't just forgive your past—it empowers your future.** The Spirit begins changing your desires, reshaping your character, and forming you into the likeness of Jesus. **That's also grace.**

So here's the paradox: **You don't grow to be accepted. You grow because you're accepted.** You don't obey to earn love. You obey because you're loved. You don't work hard to prove your worth. You work hard because your worth is secure.

And that changes *everything*. When grace frees you, **failure stops being fatal.** You can try, fall short, learn, and try again—because your identity isn't on the line. **Struggle stops being shameful.** You can be honest about where you're weak and ask for help—because you're not pretending to have it all together. **Growth stops being exhausting.** You're not performing out of fear—you're responding out of gratitude.

This is what it means to live by grace. **Not passivity. Not perfectionism. But grateful, humble, Spirit-empowered growth.** Secure in who you are. Free to become who God is making you.

Grace frees us to grow. And that's the gospel.

DISCUSSION PROMPTS

1. **Understanding:** How does grace free you to grow? What's the difference between growing out of fear and growing out of gratitude?

2. **Personal Response:** What's one area where you've been afraid to grow or try because you're scared of failing? How does grace free you to take that risk?

3. **Lived Practice:** How can we keep living in the freedom of grace as a family, remembering that we're accepted *and* being transformed?

PARENT NOTE

This is the culmination of everything you've been teaching about grace. If your kids walk away with one truth, let it be this: **Grace is not opposed to growth. Grace is what makes growth possible.**

Keep reinforcing this. When your kids fail, remind them: "You're still loved. Let's learn from this and keep growing." When they succeed, celebrate it, but anchor it in grace: "This is evidence of God's work in you. Keep leaning into His grace."

Model it yourself. Let your kids see you growing—not perfectly, but intentionally. Let them hear you say, "I messed up here. I'm asking God to help me grow." Show them what it looks like to live in the freedom of grace.

Watch for this: Kids who grasp this truth become resilient, humble, grateful disciples. Kids who miss it become either perfectionists (trying to earn approval) or apathetic (assuming grace means effort doesn't matter). The gospel holds both: **You're fully accepted *and* being transformed.**

Celebrate the journey. Your family has spent nine days wrestling with grace, identity, legalism, approval, and growth. That's significant. Don't rush past it. Thank God for what He's teaching you. And commit to living in the freedom of grace—together.

ACTION STEP

Tonight, go around the table and finish this sentence:
"One way grace has freed me to grow this week is..."

Then pray together, thanking God for His grace—grace that accepts you fully *and* transforms you completely.

ONE-SENTENCE ANCHOR

Grace doesn't just forgive you—it frees you to grow, because you're secure in God's love and empowered by His Spirit.
"For the grace of God has appeared, bringing salvation for all people, training us to renounce ungodliness and worldly passions, and to live self-controlled, upright, and godly lives." — Titus 2:11-12

SCRIPTURE READING

Titus 2:11–14
2 Corinthians 3:17–18
Philippians 2:12–13
2 Peter 3:18
Ephesians 2:8–10

UNIT

6

The Holy Spirit and Everyday Change

DAY 1 WHY CHANGE FEELS DIFFICULT

OPENING SCENARIO

Your son slumps into a chair after school, looking defeated. "I did it again," he says. "I told myself I wasn't going to lose my temper with my friends, and then someone said something stupid and I just... exploded. Why can't I change? I try so hard, and nothing sticks."

Later, your daughter is venting about a habit she's been trying to break. "I keep staying up too late scrolling my phone, even though I know it makes me exhausted the next day. I *want* to stop. I set alarms. I make rules. But I keep doing it anyway. What's wrong with me?"

You recognize the frustration in their voices—because **you've felt it too.** You've tried to be more patient, more disciplined, more consistent. And yet the same patterns keep showing up. The same struggles keep repeating. And you all wonder: **If the Holy Spirit is real and God promises transformation, why does change feel so impossibly hard?**

CONVERSATION STARTER

Let's be honest: What's one thing you've been trying to change about yourself for a while now, but it keeps not sticking? Why do you think it's so hard?

SHORT TEACHING

Here's a truth that's both comforting and sobering: **real, lasting change is difficult because sin runs deeper than behavior.** You're not just fighting bad habits—you're fighting deeply ingrained patterns, disordered desires, and a broken nature that's been shaped over years.

Think about it. You've been training yourself—often unconsciously—to respond to stress, boredom, frustration, or insecurity in certain ways. Maybe you've trained yourself to escape into screens. Or to lash out in anger. Or to retreat into isolation. **These patterns are grooves carved into your soul, and they don't disappear overnight.**

Add to that the reality of spiritual warfare. **The enemy wants you to stay stuck.** He whispers lies: "You'll never change. You've tried before and failed. This is just who you are." And if you believe those lies, you stop trying, or you try in your own strength and burn out.

But here's the hope: **change is difficult, but it's not impossible.** God doesn't expect you to transform yourself through sheer willpower. That's not how sanctification works. **Transformation is a work of the Holy Spirit.** Your job is to cooperate with what God is already doing—through prayer, Scripture, community, and habits that align with His truth.

Change feels difficult because **it *is* difficult.** You're not crazy. You're not uniquely broken. You're human. And humans don't change quickly or easily. But **slow, Spirit-empowered change is still real change.** And over time, with God's help, those grooves can be filled in, and new pathways can be formed.

Don't despair when progress feels slow. **God is patient with your process.** He's not frustrated by how long it's taking. He's committed to completing the work He started in you. And He'll be faithful to do it.

DISCUSSION PROMPTS

1. **Understanding:** Why is real change so difficult? What makes it more than just "trying harder"?

2. **Personal Response:** What's one area where you've been frustrated by slow progress? How does it feel to hear that change is meant to be gradual, not instant?

3. **Lived Practice:** This week, instead of expecting overnight transformation, ask God to help you take *one small step* toward change. What would that look like?

PARENT NOTE

This conversation is essential because **your kids are likely discouraged by how hard change feels.** They've been told (or assumed) that becoming a Christian means everything should get easier. But real discipleship involves struggle, setbacks, and slow growth—and they need to know that's *normal.*

Your job: Normalize the difficulty without excusing sin. Yes, change is hard. Yes, you'll fail sometimes. *And* God is still at work, and growth is still happening—even when it doesn't feel like it.

Don't add to their discouragement. If your kids are genuinely trying to change and struggling, resist the urge to say, "Well, just try harder" or "You're not praying enough." That produces shame, not growth. Instead, say: "Change is hard. I'm proud of you for trying. Let's keep depending on God together."

Model honesty about your own struggles. Let your kids see that *you're* still growing, too. Let them hear you say, "I've been working on this area for years, and I still mess up. But God is patient, and I'm trusting Him to keep changing me."

Watch for this: Kids who expect instant transformation often become discouraged and give up when change is slow. Kids who understand that sanctification is a lifelong process develop patience, humility, and endurance.

Important reminder: Difficulty doesn't mean impossibility. Change is hard, but it's also **possible, promised, and empowered by the Spirit.** Don't let the struggle make you forget the hope.

ACTION STEP

Tonight, each person shares one area where they've been trying to change but struggling.

Then, instead of making grand promises or resolutions, ask together: *"God, what's one small step we can take this week? And will You give us the power to do it?"*

Pray for each other. Commit to checking in at the end of the week—not to judge, but to encourage.

ONE-SENTENCE ANCHOR

Change is difficult because sin runs deep—but it's not impossible, because the Spirit is at work and God is patient with your process.

"And I am sure of this, that he who began a good work in you will bring it to completion at the day of Jesus Christ." — Philippians 1:6

SCRIPTURE READING

Philippians 1:6
Romans 7:15–20
2 Corinthians 3:18
Philippians 2:12–13
Hebrews 12:1–2

DAY 2 WHO THE HOLY SPIRIT IS—PRESENCE AND EMPOWERMENT

OPENING SCENARIO

Your daughter asks a question during dinner that catches you off guard: "So... who exactly is the Holy Spirit? Like, I know God is God, and Jesus is Jesus. But the Holy Spirit feels kind of... vague. Is it just a force? A feeling? What does it actually *do*?"

Your son jumps in. "Yeah, people talk about 'being filled with the Spirit' or 'the Spirit leading them,' but I don't really get what that means. How do you know if it's the Spirit or just your own thoughts?"

You pause, realizing: **they've heard about the Holy Spirit their whole lives, but they don't actually know who He is or how He works.** He's the most mysterious person of the Trinity—and the least understood. **And yet, without the Spirit, transformation is impossible.**

CONVERSATION STARTER

Let's talk: When you think about the Holy Spirit, what comes to mind? Do you think of Him as a person, a force, or something else?

SHORT TEACHING

Here's a truth that will transform how you understand the Christian life: **the Holy Spirit is not a vague force or a mystical feeling. He is a person—the third person of the Trinity—fully God, fully present, and fully active in the life of every believer.**

Let's break that down.

The Holy Spirit is God's presence with you. When Jesus ascended to heaven, He didn't leave His followers alone. He sent the Spirit—God Himself—to dwell *in* them. **The same power that raised Jesus from the dead now lives inside you.** That's not metaphorical. It's real. The Spirit is God's way of being personally, intimately, constantly present with you.

The Holy Spirit is God's power in you. You've probably noticed that you can't transform yourself through willpower alone. You can't overcome sin, grow in holiness, or love sacrificially in your own strength. **You need supernatural power.** And that's exactly what the Spirit provides. He convicts you of sin, guides you into truth, empowers you to obey, produces fruit in your life, and intercedes for you when you don't even know how to pray.

Here's what this means practically: **You are not on your own.** Every moment of every day, God is with you and in you, working to transform you from the inside out. When you're tempted, **the Spirit gives you strength to resist.** When you're confused, **the Spirit gives you wisdom to discern.** When you're struggling, **the Spirit gives you power to persevere.**

And here's the beautiful mystery: **the Spirit doesn't control you like a puppet.** He works *with* you. He leads, and you follow. He empowers, and you act. He transforms, and you cooperate. It's a partnership—God's power and your willing participation.

Without the Spirit, Christianity is just moralism—trying really hard to be good. With the Spirit, Christianity is transformation—being made new from the inside out by God Himself.

DISCUSSION PROMPTS

1. **Understanding:** What does it mean that the Holy Spirit is a person, not just a force? How does that change the way you relate to Him?

2. **Personal Response:** Have you ever experienced a moment where you felt the Spirit's presence or power—giving you strength, wisdom, or conviction? What was it like?

3. **Lived Practice:** This week, try praying *to* the Holy Spirit—not just about Him. Ask Him for help, guidance, and power. Practice recognizing His presence.

PARENT NOTE

This is foundational theology that's often neglected—and **your kids need to understand who the Holy Spirit is and what He does.** Without the Spirit, the Christian life is impossible. With the Spirit, it's empowered.

Your job: Help them see that the Spirit is *personal.* He's not an "it." He's not a vague energy. **He's God—present, active, and intimately involved in their lives.** Use personal language when you talk about Him: "The Spirit is with you." "The Spirit will help you." "The Spirit is at work."

Model dependence on the Spirit yourself. Let your kids hear you pray: "Holy Spirit, I need Your help with this." "Spirit, give me wisdom." "Spirit, show me what to do." Let them see that **you're depending on the same power they have access to.**

Don't create false expectations. Some kids grow up thinking the Spirit's work is always dramatic—visions, feelings, overwhelming experiences. While the Spirit *can* work that way, **most often His work is quiet, steady, and gradual.** He transforms you over time through Scripture, conviction, community, and small faithful choices.

Watch for this: Kids who don't understand the Spirit often try to live the Christian life in their own strength—and burn out. Kids who grasp the Spirit's presence and power learn to depend on Him daily, and they experience sustainable, Spirit-empowered growth.

Important clarification: Saying the Spirit empowers you doesn't mean you're passive. **You still choose. You still act. You still obey.** But you do it in His strength, not yours.

ACTION STEP

Tonight, talk about one area where you need the Holy Spirit's help—strength to resist temptation, wisdom for a decision, power to love someone difficult, etc.

Then pray together—specifically to the Holy Spirit—asking Him for what you need. Practice depending on Him out loud.

ONE-SENTENCE ANCHOR

The Holy Spirit is God's presence with you and God's power in you—transforming you from the inside out.

"But the Helper, the Holy Spirit, whom the Father will send in my name, he will teach you all things and bring to your remembrance all that I have said to you." —John 14:26

SCRIPTURE READING

John 14:26
Acts 1:8
Romans 8:11
Galatians 5:22–25
Ephesians 3:16–17

DAY 3

MISUNDERSTANDINGS—EMOTIONAL EXTREMES VS. STEADY GROWTH

OPENING SCENARIO

Your family is talking about a guest speaker who came to church last week. The speaker was passionate and emotional, and spoke a lot about "being on fire for God" and "feeling the Spirit move." Your daughter seems uncertain. "I didn't really *feel* anything during the service. Does that mean I'm not spiritual enough?"

Meanwhile, your son seems skeptical. "That whole thing felt kind of over-the-top. Do we really need to be that emotional about faith? I thought it was about truth, not feelings."

And you realize: **they're both reacting to extremes.** One equates the Spirit's work with emotional intensity. The other dismisses emotions entirely and reduces faith to intellectual assent. **And neither extreme reflects the full biblical picture.**

CONVERSATION STARTER

Let's talk: Do you think the Holy Spirit's work is mostly about feelings and emotions? Or is it more about truth and obedience, regardless of how you feel?

SHORT TEACHING

When it comes to the Holy Spirit, **there are two common extremes—and both are misunderstandings.**

The first extreme: Emotional intensity equals spiritual maturity. This view says the Spirit's work is always dramatic, emotional, and overwhelming. If you're not crying during worship, feeling goosebumps during prayer, or having powerful spiritual experiences, then something's wrong. **You're not "on fire" enough. You're not "Spirit-filled."**

Here's the problem: **the Spirit's work is not primarily about feelings.** Yes, emotions can be part of it—God made us emotional beings. But equating the Spirit's presence with emotional intensity is dangerous. It produces two results: pride (if you *do* feel something) or despair (if you don't). And it makes faith dependent on subjective experience rather than on objective truth.

The second extreme: Emotions don't matter; only truth does. This view says the Spirit's work is purely intellectual and behavioral. You study Scripture, you obey, and you don't need to feel anything. Emotions are suspect, potentially misleading, and best ignored. **Faith is about facts, not feelings.**

Here's the problem: **God made you with emotions, and He speaks to your whole person—mind, will, and heart.** Dismissing emotions entirely creates cold, detached faith. It can lead to pride ("I don't need emotional experiences—I have the truth") and it misses the beauty of experiencing God's presence in real, affective ways.

The biblical balance is this: The Spirit works primarily through **steady, gradual transformation**—not emotional highs or intellectual knowledge alone. He renews your mind through Scripture. He convicts your conscience. He produces fruit in your character. He guides your decisions. And yes, sometimes He stirs your emotions. **But his work is deeper than feelings and broader than facts.**

Real spiritual maturity isn't measured by how intensely you feel or how much you know. **It's measured by fruit—love, patience, faithfulness, obedience, and Christlikeness over time.**

DISCUSSION PROMPTS

1. **Understanding:** What's wrong with equating the Spirit's work with emotional intensity? What's wrong with dismissing emotions entirely?

2. **Personal Response:** Which extreme are you more tempted toward—relying too much on feelings or ignoring them completely?

3. **Lived Practice:** This week, pay attention to the Spirit's *steady* work—not just dramatic moments. Where do you see Him producing patience, conviction, wisdom, or love in quiet, gradual ways?

PARENT NOTE

This conversation is critical because **your kids are being pulled toward both extremes**—either by hyper-emotional church cultures or by cold, rationalistic faith. Your job is to help them find the biblical balance.

Affirm emotions without making them ultimate. When your child has a meaningful emotional experience in worship or prayer, celebrate it: "That's a gift from God. He meets us in those moments." *And* remind them: "The Spirit is also at work when you don't feel anything. His presence isn't dependent on your emotions."

Affirm truth without dismissing the heart. Teach your kids to love theology, study Scripture, and ground their faith in truth. *And* remind them: "God made you with emotions. He doesn't want cold, detached obedience. He wants your whole heart."

Model the balance yourself. Let your kids see you express emotions in worship—and also depend on truth when feelings are absent. Let them hear you say, "I didn't feel much during church today, but I know God was there. His presence doesn't depend on my feelings."

Watch for this: Kids raised in emotionally intense environments often become either addicted to spiritual highs (and crash when feelings fade) or burned out and cynical. Kids raised in emotionally sterile environments often develop dry, intellectual faith. The goal is **both/and: truth *and* affection, knowledge *and* experience, steady growth *and* occasional mountaintop moments.**

ACTION STEP

Tonight, talk about both extremes:

1. "Have we ever made the Spirit's work too dependent on feelings?"
2. "Have we ever dismissed emotions or experiences as unimportant?"

Then ask: "What does balanced, Spirit-led faith look like in our family—embracing both truth and affection, both steady growth and occasional emotional moments?"

ONE-SENTENCE ANCHOR

The Spirit's work is deeper than emotional intensity and broader than intellectual knowledge—it's steady, transformative, and produces lasting fruit.
"But the fruit of the Spirit is love, joy, peace, patience, kindness, goodness, faithfulness, gentleness, self-control." — Galatians 5:22-23

SCRIPTURE READING

Galatians 5:22–25
1 Corinthians 2:10–13
Romans 8:5–6
Ephesians 5:18–21
1 Thessalonians 5:19–22

DAY 4 INNER LIFE—CONVICTION WITHOUT CONDEMNATION

OPENING SCENARIO

Your son comes to you looking troubled. "I did something I shouldn't have, and I can't stop thinking about it. I feel terrible. Like, I know God forgives me, but I feel... guilty. Is that the Holy Spirit? Or am I just being hard on myself?"

Meanwhile, your daughter overhears and says, "I never really feel guilty about stuff. Like, I know when I mess up, but I don't feel bad about it. Does that mean the Spirit isn't working in me?"

You pause, realizing: **they're both confused about the Spirit's role in conviction.** One feels crushed by guilt. The other feels nothing. And **neither one understands the difference between the Spirit's conviction and the enemy's condemnation.**

CONVERSATION STARTER

Let's talk: When you do something wrong, what do you usually feel? And how do you know if that feeling is from God or from somewhere else?

SHORT TEACHING

Here's one of the most important distinctions you'll ever learn: **the Holy Spirit brings conviction. The enemy brings condemnation. And they feel very different.**

Conviction is specific, truthful, and redemptive. The Spirit says: **"You did this specific thing, and it was wrong. It hurt someone. It dishonored God. You need to confess it, repent, and make it right."** Conviction leads you *toward* God, not away from Him. It produces godly sorrow that leads to repentance. It's uncomfortable, yes—but it's also hopeful. Because **conviction always includes the path forward.**

Condemnation is vague, accusatory, and hopeless. The enemy says, "**You're a terrible person. You always mess up. You'll never change. God is disappointed in you. You're beyond help.**"Condemnation crushes you. It doesn't lead to repentance—it leads to shame, despair, and hiding. **Condemnation doesn't offer a way forward. It just tells you you're worthless.**

Here's how you tell the difference: **Conviction is specific and hopeful. Condemnation is global and hopeless.**

But there's another issue: **what if you *don't* feel anything when you sin?** That could mean a few things. Maybe your conscience has been dulled by repeated sin. Maybe you've rationalized the behavior. Or maybe you're just emotionally numb in that moment. **A lack of feeling doesn't mean the Spirit isn't at work—but it does mean you need to pay attention.**

The Spirit's conviction isn't always a feeling. Sometimes it's just **a quiet awareness: "That wasn't right."** And your job is to respond—whether you feel emotional about it or not. Confess it. Turn from it. Make it right.

Here's the key: **the Spirit convicts to restore, not destroy.** He doesn't beat you down. He doesn't crush you with shame. He lovingly, firmly points out sin—and then empowers you to turn from it and walk in freedom.

DISCUSSION PROMPTS

1. **Understanding:** What's the difference between conviction (from the Spirit) and condemnation (from the enemy)? How can you tell which one you're experiencing?

2. **Personal Response:** When you sin, do you tend to spiral into shame and condemnation, or do you respond to conviction with repentance? What makes the difference?

3. **Lived Practice:** This week, when you feel guilty about something, pause and ask: "Is this conviction or condemnation? Is this leading me toward God or away from Him?" Then respond accordingly.

PARENT NOTE

This is a **life-changing distinction**—and your kids desperately need to understand it. Many Christian kids grow up unable to tell the difference between the Spirit's conviction and the enemy's condemnation, and it cripples their faith.

Your job: Teach them to recognize the Spirit's voice. Conviction is specific, redemptive, and leads to repentance. Condemnation is vague, crushing, and leads to hiding. Help them test what they're feeling against Scripture and the character of God.

When your child confesses sin, affirm conviction without reinforcing condemnation. Say: "Thank you for being honest. That took courage. What you did was wrong, and it matters. *And* you are still loved, still forgiven, and still able to move forward. Let's make this right together."

Watch for this: Kids who can't distinguish conviction from condemnation often become either paralyzed by guilt (afraid to come to God) or numb to sin (ignoring the Spirit's voice entirely). Teach them the difference, and you'll free them to walk in healthy repentance.

Model healthy responses to convince yourself. Let your kids hear you say: "The Spirit convicted me about how I spoke to you earlier. I was wrong. I'm sorry. Will you forgive me?" Show them what it looks like to respond to conviction with humility and hope, not shame.

Important reminder: A tender conscience is a gift. If your child feels convicted when they sin, that's evidence the Spirit is at work. Don't minimize it ("Oh, you're fine, don't worry about it"). But don't let them spiral into condemnation either. **Guide them toward repentance, forgiveness, and restoration.**

ACTION STEP

Tonight, talk about a recent time when someone felt guilty about something.
Ask together: "Was that conviction (specific, redemptive, leading toward God) or condemnation (vague, crushing, leading to shame)?"
Then practice responding: "If it's conviction, what's the next step—confession, repentance, making it right?"

ONE-SENTENCE ANCHOR

The Spirit brings conviction that leads to repentance and restoration—never condemnation that crushes and destroys.
"For godly grief produces a repentance that leads to salvation without regret, whereas worldly grief produces death." — 2 Corinthians 7:10

SCRIPTURE READING

2 Corinthians 7:10
John 16:8
Romans 8:1
Psalm 32:3–5
Hebrews 12:5–11

DAY 5 FAMILY GUIDANCE AND DISCERNMENT

OPENING SCENARIO

Your daughter is facing a decision about which elective to take next semester, and she's genuinely torn. "I don't know what to do. I've prayed about it, but I don't feel like God is giving me a clear answer. How do I know what He wants me to choose?"

Your son is dealing with an unhealthy friendship, and he's unsure whether to address it or step back. "Everyone says, 'Let the Spirit guide you,' but I don't know what that actually means. How do I know if it's the Spirit or just my own thoughts?"

And you realize: **your kids want to follow the Spirit's leading, but they don't know how.** They've been told to "listen to God," but they don't have a framework for discernment. **They need practical guidance, not just spiritual platitudes.**

CONVERSATION STARTER

Let's talk: When you're trying to make a decision, how do you know if the Spirit is leading you? What does "being led by the Spirit" actually look like?

SHORT TEACHING

Here's a truth that will help you navigate decisions with wisdom: **the Holy Spirit leads you, but not always in the dramatic ways you might expect.** He doesn't usually write answers in the sky or give you an audible voice. **Most often, He leads through Scripture, wisdom, conviction, circumstances, and godly counsel.**

Let's break that down practically.

1. **The Spirit leads through Scripture.**
   God has already revealed His will for much of life in the Bible. You don't need to pray about whether lying is okay—Scripture is clear. You don't need special revelation about loving your neighbor—the Bible already says to do it. **Start with what God has already said.** If Scripture addresses your situation, that's your answer.

2. **The Spirit leads through wisdom.**
   God gave you a mind, and He expects you to use it. Pray for wisdom, gather information, consider consequences, and make a thoughtful decision. **The Spirit often guides through sanctified common sense.** You're not just waiting passively for a mystical sign—you're actively seeking wisdom and trusting God to direct your steps.

3. **The Spirit leads through conviction.**
   Sometimes, as you pray and seek God, you'll sense a growing conviction—a settled sense of rightness or wrongness about a decision. It's not just emotion. It's a Spirit-led awareness that aligns with Scripture and wisdom. **Pay attention to that inner witness.** It's one way the Spirit guides.

4. **The Spirit leads through circumstances.**
   Sometimes doors open or close in ways you didn't expect. That doesn't mean every closed door is from God (you still use wisdom), but **the Spirit can guide through the practical realities of your situation.**

5. **The Spirit leads through godly counsel.**
   God often speaks through mature, wise believers. **Don't make big decisions in isolation.** Seek input from parents, mentors, and trusted Christians who know you and love Jesus.

Here's the summary: **The Spirit's leading is rarely dramatic. It's usually steady, multi-faceted, and confirmed through multiple sources.** You pray, you study Scripture, you seek wisdom, you listen to counsel, you pay attention to circumstances—and over time, clarity emerges.

DISCUSSION PROMPTS

1. **Understanding:** What are the five ways the Spirit leads us? Why is it important to look for multiple confirmations instead of waiting for one dramatic sign?
2. **Personal Response:** Think about a decision you're facing right now. How could you apply these five ways of discerning the Spirit's leading?
3. **Lived Practice:** This week, when you're trying to make a decision, walk through this process: What does Scripture say? What does wisdom suggest? What do godly people advise? What are the circumstances? What is the Spirit convicting you toward?

PARENT NOTE

This is **profoundly practical theology**—and your kids need it. They're facing decisions daily: friendships, academics, activities, relationships, technology use, and more. And they need to know **how to discern the Spirit's leading in real, everyday situations.**

Your job: Teach them a process, not just a feeling. Help them see that Spirit-led decision-making involves **prayer, Scripture, wisdom, counsel, and circumstances**—not just waiting for a mystical sign.

Model discernment yourself. When you're facing a decision, let your kids hear you walk through the process out loud: "I'm praying about this. Let me see what Scripture says. I'm going to ask a few wise people for input. I'm looking at the circumstances. Here's what I'm sensing the Spirit might be leading me toward."

Don't overcomplicate it. For most decisions, the Spirit's leading is simple: **What does Scripture say? What does wisdom suggest?** If both points are in the same direction, that's usually your answer. You don't need a fleece or a sign from heaven.

Watch for this: Kids who expect dramatic signs often become paralyzed by indecision (waiting for clarity that never comes). Kids who dismiss the Spirit's leading entirely often become self-reliant (trusting only their own judgment). The biblical balance is **both/and: trust God's guidance *and* use the wisdom He›s given you.**

Important clarification: Sometimes the Spirit *does* lead in dramatic ways—visions, impressions, clear promptings. But that's the exception, not the rule. Don't create unrealistic expectations. **Most often, the Spirit leads through ordinary means.**

ACTION STEP

Tonight, choose one decision your family is currently facing—big or small.

Walk through the five-step discernment process together:

1. What does Scripture say about this?
2. What does wisdom suggest?
3. What do godly people advise?
4. What are the circumstances?
5. What is the Spirit convicting us toward?

Practice discerning the Spirit's leading as a family.

ONE-SENTENCE ANCHOR

The Spirit leads us through Scripture, wisdom, conviction, circumstances, and godly counsel—not usually through dramatic signs.

"Trust in the LORD with all your heart, and do not lean on your own understanding. In all your ways acknowledge him, and he will make straight your paths." — Proverbs 3:5-6

SCRIPTURE READING

Proverbs 3:5–6
James 1:5
Psalm 32:8
Romans 12:2
Acts 16:6–10

DAY 6 CULTURE LENS—DISTRACTION, NOISE, AND ATTENTION

OPENING SCENARIO

It's a quiet Saturday morning—or it should be. But your son has his headphones in, watching videos. Your daughter is scrolling through social media. The TV is on in the background. Notifications are pinging from multiple devices. And you realize: **there hasn't been actual silence in this house in days.**

Later, you try to have a family devotional, but everyone's distracted. Eyes wander. Minds drift. Someone checks their phone mid-prayer. And you think: **How are we supposed to hear the Spirit's voice when we can't even sit still for five minutes?**

The culture has trained you—and your kids—to be constantly stimulated, perpetually distracted, and terrified of silence. **And it's making it nearly impossible to pay attention to God.**

CONVERSATION STARTER

Let's be honest: When was the last time you sat in complete silence for more than a few minutes? How did it feel? Peaceful or uncomfortable?

SHORT TEACHING

Here's a cultural reality we need to name: **we live in a world of relentless distraction.** Notifications, algorithms, entertainment, noise—it's all designed to capture and hold your attention. And the result is that **we've lost the ability to be still, to listen, and to pay attention to what matters most.**

Think about it. How often do you reach for your phone out of habit, not need? How often do you fill silence with noise—music, podcasts, videos—because quiet feels uncomfortable? How often do you multitask through prayer or Scripture reading because focused attention feels impossible?

This isn't just a time management issue. It's a spiritual issue. Because the Holy Spirit often speaks in the quiet, in the stillness, in the moments when you're not distracted by a hundred other voices. And if you're never quiet, **you'll miss Him.**

The Bible is full of commands to **be still. To wait. To listen.** "Be still, and know that I am God." "In quietness and trust shall be your strength." "The LORD is in his holy temple; let all the earth keep silence before him." Over and over, Scripture calls us to *stop, be quiet, and pay attention.*

But our culture conditions us for the opposite. We're trained to stay busy, stay stimulated, stay distracted. And the cost is enormous: **we lose the ability to hear God, to know ourselves, to think deeply, and to rest truly.**

Here's the invitation: **reclaim your attention.** Fight for silence. Create margins. Turn off the noise. Put down the phone. Sit in stillness and invite the Spirit to speak. It will feel uncomfortable at first—because you've been conditioned to fill every moment. But **in the discomfort, you'll find God.**

The Spirit is speaking. The question is: **Are you quiet enough to hear Him?**

DISCUSSION PROMPTS

1. **Understanding:** How does constant distraction and noise affect our ability to hear the Spirit? Why is silence and stillness so important?

2. **Personal Response:** When was the last time you practiced real stillness—no phone, no noise, just you and God? What made it hard or easy?

3. **Lived Practice:** This week, practice five minutes of silence each day. No phone. No music. No distractions. Just sit, breathe, and invite the Spirit to speak. What do you notice?

PARENT NOTE

This is one of the most urgent cultural battles you'll face—because **distraction is stealing your family's spiritual life.** If your kids (and you) are constantly stimulated, they'll never develop the capacity to hear God, think deeply, or rest truly.

Your job: Model stillness. Create space for silence in your home. Turn off the background noise. Put away devices during meals and devotions. And practice listening to prayer as a family.

Don't expect instant success. Stillness is a learned skill that takes time. Your kids will fidget. They'll complain. They'll struggle to sit still. **That's normal.** But over time, with practice, they'll develop the capacity to be quiet and attentive.

Watch for this: Kids who grow up in constant noise and distraction often become anxious, restless adults who can't tolerate silence or solitude. They struggle with prayer, meditation, and intimacy with God because they've never learned to be still.

Important reminder: Technology isn't evil. But **unexamined, constant use is destructive.** Teach your kids to use technology intentionally, not compulsively. And model it yourself.

ACTION STEP

Tonight, practice five minutes of complete silence as a family.
Turn off all devices. Sit together. Invite the Spirit to speak. Don't force conversation—just be still.

Afterward, talk about what it was like. Was it uncomfortable? Peaceful? Hard? What did you notice?

Commit to doing this regularly—daily or weekly—to create space to hear the Spirit.

ONE-SENTENCE ANCHOR

The Spirit often speaks in stillness and silence—but we'll never hear Him if we're constantly distracted by noise.
"Be still, and know that I am God." — Psalm 46:10

SCRIPTURE READING

Psalm 46:10
1 Kings 19:11–13
Isaiah 30:15
Habakkuk 2:20
Psalm 62:5

DAY 7 PRACTICE—SHORT DAILY LISTENING PRAYER

OPENING SCENARIO

Your daughter comes home from school, dumps her backpack on the floor, and immediately starts talking about everything that happened—drama with friends, a hard test, something funny in class. You listen, but you notice something: **she doesn't pause. She doesn't process. She keeps moving.**

Later, you ask her, "Did you talk to God about any of that today?" She shrugs. "I prayed this morning, but it was rushed. I didn't really have time to, like, *listen* or anything."

And you realize: **prayer has become one-way communication in your home.** You talk *to* God, but you rarely talk *with* Him. You ask, request, and confess—but you don't pause to listen. **And you're missing out on one of the most important aspects of a relationship with God.**

CONVERSATION STARTER

Let's talk: When you pray, how much of it is you talking and how much is you listening? Do you ever pause to hear what God might be saying?

SHORT TEACHING

Here's a practice that will transform your relationship with God: **listening prayer.** It's not complicated. It's not mystical. It's simply **creating space in your prayer time to be quiet and attentive to the Holy Spirit's voice.**

Most of us pray like this: "God, here's what I need. Here's what I'm worried about. Here's what I want you to do. Amen." And then we move on. **Prayer becomes a monologue, not a conversation.**

But a real relationship involves both talking *and* listening. And God wants to speak to you—through His Word, through His Spirit, through conviction, comfort, and guidance. But **you have to be quiet enough to hear Him.**

Here's how to practice listening prayer:

1. **Set aside just 5–10 minutes.**
   You don't need an hour. Start small. Just a few minutes of intentional, focused time.

2. **Begin with Scripture.**
   Read a short passage slowly. Let it settle in your heart. Ask, "What is God saying to me through this?" and "What does this passage say about who God is?"

3. **Bring your heart to God.**
   Tell Him what you're feeling, what you're struggling with, what you need. Be honest.

4. **Then be quiet.**
   This is the hardest part. Sit in silence. Don't fill it with more words. Just wait. Pay attention. **Listen for the Spirit's gentle voice, not audible, but an inner witness, a quiet conviction, a sense of peace or direction.**

5. **Write down what comes to mind.**
   Sometimes the Spirit brings Scripture to mind. Sometimes, he convicts you of something. Sometimes, He gives you peace or clarity. Write it down so you don't forget.

6. **Respond.**
   If the Spirit prompts you to action, confess something, forgive someone, make a change, do it. Listening prayer isn't passive. It leads to obedience.

This doesn't require special skill or spiritual maturity. **It just requires the willingness to be quiet and attentive.** And over time, you'll learn to recognize the Spirit's voice and respond to His leading.

DISCUSSION PROMPTS

1. **Understanding:** What's the difference between prayer as a monologue (just talking to God) and prayer as a conversation (talking *and* listening)?

2. **Personal Response:** Have you ever practiced listening prayer? If so, what was it like? If not, what makes it feel hard or intimidating?

3. **Lived Practice:** This week, commit to 5 minutes of listening prayer each day. What do you notice? What does the Spirit bring to mind?

PARENT NOTE

This is a **foundational spiritual discipline** and one that's seldom taught. Most kids grow up thinking prayer is just asking God for stuff. They don't know that **prayer is meant to be a relationship, and a relationship involves listening.**

Your job: Teach them how to listen. Model it yourself. Let your kids see you sitting quietly with your Bible open, waiting on God. Let them hear you say, "I asked God about that, and I felt Him leading me to..."

Make it a family practice. Set aside time once a week (or daily, if you can) for listening prayer together. Read a passage. Pray. Sit in silence. Then share: "What did God bring to mind for you?"

Don't create false expectations. The Spirit doesn't always speak in dramatic terms. Sometimes listening prayer is just a quiet, restful time with God. That's okay. **The practice itself is forming you, even when you don't "hear" anything specific.**

Watch for this: Kids who never learn to listen in prayer often develop one-sided relationships with God. They talk *to* Him but never expect Him to respond. Teaching them to listen transforms prayer from duty into dialogue.

Important reminder: Listening prayer isn't about waiting for audible voices or mystical experiences. It's about **creating space to be attentive to the Spirit's gentle leading through Scripture, conviction, and inner witness.**

ACTION STEP

Tonight, practice listening to each other's prayers together as a family.

1. Read a short passage of Scripture (Psalm 23, John 15:1–11, or Philippians 4:4–7).
2. Each person shares briefly: "What stands out to me?"
3. Sit in silence for 3–5 minutes. Invite the Spirit to speak.
4. Share: "What did God bring to mind? What is He saying to me?"

Commit to doing this daily this week—individually or as a family.

> ### ONE-SENTENCE ANCHOR
>
> **Listening prayer creates space for the Spirit to speak—transforming prayer from monologue to conversation.**
> *"Speak, LORD, for your servant hears." — 1 Samuel 3:9*

SCRIPTURE READING

1 Samuel 3:9–10
Psalm 46:10
John 10:27
Revelation 3:20
Isaiah 30:21

DAY 8 BIG QUESTION—HOW DOES GOD GUIDE DECISIONS?

OPENING SCENARIO

Your son is staring at two college brochures, looking overwhelmed. "How am I supposed to know which one God wants me to choose? I've prayed. I've asked for a sign. I don't feel anything. What if I pick the wrong one and mess up my whole life?"

Your daughter is dealing with a friendship conflict and doesn't know whether to confront it or let it go. "I keep asking God to show me what to do, but I don't feel like He's answering. How do I know if I'm supposed to say something or stay quiet?"

You sit down with both of them, and you realize: **they're paralyzed by the fear of making the "wrong" decision.** They've been taught to "seek God's will," but they don't have a clear framework for what that actually means. **And they're waiting for a level of certainty that God rarely gives.**

CONVERSATION STARTER

Let's wrestle with this: Do you think God has one specific, perfect plan for every decision—and if you miss it, everything falls apart? Or is there freedom in how you make decisions?

SHORT TEACHING

Here's a question that plagues many Christians: **How does God guide my decisions?** And underneath it is a deeper fear: *What if I choose wrong and ruin everything?*

Let's start with some clarity. **God does have a will for your life.** He cares about your decisions, and He's involved in guiding you. But here's what many people misunderstand: **God's will is less like a tightrope you have to find and more like a wide path you walk on.**

Think about it this way. God has a **moral will**—the things He's clearly revealed in Scripture. Don't lie. Love your neighbor. Forgive. Pursue holiness. **These aren't up for debate.** You don't need to pray about whether lying is okay—God already said no.

God also has a **sovereign will**—His ultimate plan for history, which He's working out behind the scenes. You can trust that God is in control and working all things for His purposes. **You're not going to derail His sovereign plan accidentally.**

And then there's **personal decision-making.** Most of life falls into this category: which school to attend, which job to take, which friendships to invest in. And here's the freeing truth: **God often gives you freedom to choose wisely within His moral will.** You're not trying to guess one perfect answer. You're making a wise, prayerful decision and trusting God to guide your steps.

So how do you make decisions? **Pray. Study Scripture. Seek wisdom. Get godly counsel. Consider circumstances. And then make a thoughtful decision.** Trust that God is guiding you—not by hiding one perfect answer and making you guess, but by working through the wisdom and discernment He's already given you.

And here's the best part: **even if you make a less-than-ideal decision, God can still use it.** He's bigger than your mistakes. He redeems, redirects, and works all things for good. **You're not going to accidentally fall out of His will because you chose the wrong major or took the wrong job.**

Walk in wisdom. Trust God's sovereignty. And rest in His grace.

DISCUSSION PROMPTS

1. **Understanding:** What's the difference between God's moral will (revealed in Scripture) and personal decision-making (where you have freedom to choose wisely)?

2. **Personal Response:** Have you ever been paralyzed by fear of making the "wrong" decision? How does it feel to know God gives you freedom to choose wisely?

3. **Lived Practice:** This week, when you're facing a decision, use this process: Pray. Study Scripture. Seek wisdom. Get counsel. Then make a thoughtful choice and trust God to guide you.

PARENT NOTE

This is a **huge source of anxiety for many Christians,** and your kids need clarity. They've been taught to "find God's will," but often that creates paralyzing fear: *What if I miss it?*

Your job: Help them see that **God's will isn't a hidden treasure you have to find. It's a path you walk on with wisdom, prayer, and trust.** Most decisions don't have one "right" answer. They have several good options, and God gives you freedom to choose wisely.

Model decision-making yourself. Let your kids hear you say: "I've prayed about this. I've sought wisdom. I've gotten counsel. I don't have 100% certainty, but I'm making the best decision I can and trusting God to guide me." Show them that **faith involves trust, not perfect certainty.**

Watch for this: Kids who think God's will is a tightrope often become paralyzed by indecision (afraid to move without absolute certainty). Kids who think God doesn't care about decisions often become careless or self-reliant. The biblical balance: **God cares, He guides, and He gives you freedom to choose wisely.**

Important clarification: Saying "God gives you freedom" doesn't mean all choices are equal or that wisdom doesn't matter. Some decisions are wiser than others. But **within the boundaries of wisdom and Scripture, you often have genuine freedom.**

ACTION STEP

Tonight, talk about a decision someone in the family is facing. Walk through the process together:

1. What does Scripture say (moral will)?
2. What does wisdom suggest?
3. What do godly people advise?
4. What are the circumstances?
5. What are the options, and which seems wisest?

Then pray together: "God, we're making the best decision we can with the wisdom You've given us. We trust You to guide us."

ONE-SENTENCE ANCHOR

God guides your decisions through Scripture, wisdom, counsel, and circumstances—and He gives you freedom to choose wisely within His will.

"The heart of man plans his way, but the LORD establishes his steps."
— Proverbs 16:9

SCRIPTURE READING

Proverbs 16:9
James 1:5
Psalm 37:23–24
Proverbs 3:5–6
Romans 12:2

DAY 9 REFLECTION ANCHOR—REAL CHANGE IS EMPOWERED, NOT FORCED

OPENING SCENARIO

It's the end of the week, and you're reflecting with your kids over dinner. Your son says, "I think I get it now. Like, I can't just try harder and expect to change. I actually need God's help."

Your daughter nods. "Yeah. And I've been realizing that when I try to force myself to be different, it doesn't last. But when I ask the Spirit to help me, it actually feels... possible."

You smile because **they're connecting the dots.** They're learning that transformation isn't about willpower or self-effort. **It's about dependence on the Holy Spirit.** And that's the difference between exhausting religion and Spirit-empowered growth.

CONVERSATION STARTER

Let's reflect: What's one thing you've learned this week about the Holy Spirit and how real change happens?

SHORT TEACHING

Here's the anchor truth of this entire unit: **Real change is empowered, not forced.** You can't transform yourself through sheer effort, willpower, or trying harder. **Lasting transformation is a work of the Holy Spirit.**

Think about the difference. **Forced change** looks like this: "I'm going to stop losing my temper. I'm going to white-knuckle it, grit my teeth, and not do it anymore." And for a while, it might work. But eventually, you crack. Because **you're trying to change from the outside in, and it's exhausting.**

Empowered change looks like this: "I struggle with anger. I can't fix this on my own. Holy Spirit, I need Your help. Change my heart. Give me patience. Empower me to respond differently." And over time, with the Spirit's help, **you change from the inside out.** It's not instant. It's not easy. But it's sustainable, because it's not dependent on your strength—it's dependent on God's.

This is the difference between religion and relationship. Religion says, "Try harder. Do better. Be good enough." **Relationship says, "Depend on Me. I'll change you. Trust My power, not yours."**

And here's what's so freeing: **when you stop trying to force change and start depending on the Spirit, the pressure lifts.** You're not carrying the weight of transformation on your shoulders. You're cooperating with what God is already doing. You're not manufacturing growth—you're receiving it.

But here's the tension: **dependence doesn't mean passivity.** You still make choices. You still obey. You still practice disciplines. But **you do it in the Spirit's strength, not your own.** You're not the hero of your transformation story. The Spirit is.

Real change is empowered, not forced. And that changes everything.

DISCUSSION PROMPTS

1. **Understanding:** What's the difference between trying to force change (in your own strength) and depending on the Spirit to empower change?

2. **Personal Response:** Think about an area where you've been trying to change. Have you been forcing it, or have you been depending on the Spirit? What needs to shift?

3. **Lived Practice:** How can we keep depending on the Spirit for transformation—not just this week, but as a lifelong rhythm?

PARENT NOTE

This is the culmination of everything you've been teaching about the Spirit. **Your kids need to walk away with this truth burned into their hearts: transformation is the Spirit's work, not theirs.**

Keep reinforcing it. When they're struggling to change, don't just say "try harder." Say, "This is hard. You can't do it on your own. Let's ask the Spirit for help." Point them to dependence, not self-effort.

Model it yourself. Let your kids hear you pray: "Spirit, I can't do this. I need your power." Let them see that *you're* depending on the same Spirit they have access to.

Celebrate the journey. Your family has spent nine days learning about the Spirit—who He is, how He works, how to listen to Him, and how to depend on Him. That's significant. Don't rush past it. Thank God for what He's teaching you. And commit to walking in the Spirit's power—together.

ACTION STEP

Tonight, go around the table and finish this sentence:
"One area where I need to stop forcing change and start depending on the Spirit is..."

Then pray together, asking the Spirit to empower the transformation only He can do.

ONE-SENTENCE ANCHOR

Real change is empowered by the Spirit, not forced by effort—and that frees us to grow in His strength, not ours.
"And we all, with unveiled face, beholding the glory of the Lord, are being transformed into the same image from one degree of glory to another. For this comes from the Lord who is the Spirit." — 2 Corinthians 3:18

SCRIPTURE READING

2 Corinthians 3:18
Galatians 5:16–25
Philippians 2:12–13
Romans 8:13–14
Ezekiel 36:26–27

UNIT
7

GROWTH AND CHARACTER FORMATION

(SANCTIFICATION)

DAY 1 WHY GROWTH IS GRADUAL, NOT INSTANT

OPENING SCENARIO

Your daughter is sitting at the kitchen table, frustrated. "I've been working on being more patient for months now, and I still snapped at my brother today. I feel like I'm not getting anywhere. When is this going actually to change?"

Your son overhears and adds, "Yeah, I thought when I became a Christian, things would be different. But I still struggle with the same stuff. I still get jealous. I still lie sometimes. What's the point if nothing's changing?"

You sit down with them, and your heart aches—because **they expected transformation to be instant.** They thought salvation meant immediate perfection. And now they're discouraged because **growth is taking longer than they expected.**

CONVERSATION STARTER

Let's be honest: Have you ever expected growth to happen faster than it does? What made you think it should be instant?

SHORT TEACHING

Here's a truth that's both humbling and freeing: **growth is gradual, not instant.** When you trust in Jesus, you're declared righteous immediately—that's justification. But the process of actually becoming like Jesus—that's sanctification—takes a lifetime.

Think about it. **You didn't become who you are overnight.** Your habits, patterns, fears, and desires have been forming for years.

Some of them are deeply ingrained. So when the Spirit begins the work of transformation, He's not just tweaking surface behavior—He's **reordering your loves, reshaping your character, and renewing your mind.** And that doesn't happen in a week.

The Bible uses agricultural metaphors for this reason. Growth is like a seed becoming a tree. It's slow. It's seasonal. It's imperceptible day to day, but undeniable over time. **You don't see a tree growing in real-time, but if you look back a year later, the change is obvious.**

Here's why this matters: **if you expect instant transformation, you'll be constantly discouraged.** Every setback will feel like failure. Every struggle will seem like proof that you're not really changing. But if you understand that growth is gradual, **you can celebrate small steps, learn from setbacks, and trust that God is at work—even when progress feels slow.**

And here's the hope: **God is patient with your process.** He's not frustrated that you're not there yet. He's not disappointed by how long it's taking. He knows exactly where you are, and He's committed to finishing what He started. **He who began a good work in you will complete it.**

So don't despair when growth feels slow. **Keep showing up. Keep depending on the Spirit. Keep taking small steps.** And trust that over time—slowly, steadily, faithfully—God is making you new.

DISCUSSION PROMPTS

1. **Understanding:** Why is growth gradual instead of instant? What does that tell us about how transformation works?
2. **Personal Response:** What's one area where you've been discouraged because growth feels slow? How does it help to know that gradual change is normal?
3. **Lived Practice:** This week, instead of expecting instant transformation, commit to one small step of growth. What's one habit, choice, or practice you can start?

PARENT NOTE

This conversation is critical because **unrealistic expectations about growth are crushing your kids.** They've been told (or assumed) that becoming a Christian means life gets easier, and sin goes away quickly. When that doesn't happen, they feel like failures—or worse, like frauds.

Your job: Reset expectations. Help them see that **sanctification is a lifelong journey, not a one-time event.** Growth is real, but it's slow. And that's okay. God is patient with the process.

Model honesty about your own slow growth. Let your kids hear you say: "I've been working on this area for years, and I still mess up. But I can see that God is changing me over time. I'm not who I used to be." Show them that **maturity isn't perfection—it's faithfulness over the long haul.**

Celebrate small steps. When your child shows even a little growth—pausing before reacting, confessing sin quickly, choosing kindness when it's hard—name it and celebrate it. "I see God at work in you. That's growth." Help them see progress they might be missing.

Watch for this: Kids who expect instant transformation often become either discouraged quitters (convinced they'll never change) or self-deceived perfectionists (pretending they're better than they are). Teaching them that growth is gradual produces **humble, patient, persevering disciples.**

Important reminder: Gradual doesn't mean optional. You're still responsible for pursuing growth. But **you pursue it with patience, not panic. With hope, not despair.**

ACTION STEP

Tonight, each person shares one area where they've seen slow but real growth over the past year.

It might be small—more patient, kinder, more honest, quicker to apologize. But name it. Celebrate it. Thank God for it.

Then ask: "What's one area where we want to keep growing, even if it takes time?"

ONE-SENTENCE ANCHOR

Growth is gradual, not instant—and God is patient with your process, faithfully completing what He started.

"But we all, with unveiled face, beholding as in a mirror the glory of the Lord, are being transformed into the same image from glory to glory, just as from the Lord, the Spirit. "— 2 Corinthians 3:18

SCRIPTURE READING

Philippians 1:6
2 Corinthians 3:18
Proverbs 4:18
2 Peter 3:18
1 Thessalonians 5:23–24

DAY 2 HOW TRANSFORMATION WORKS—HABITS AND RENEWED THINKING

OPENING SCENARIO

Your son is lying on the couch, frustrated. "I keep asking God to make me more disciplined, but nothing changes. I still sleep in. I still procrastinate. I still waste time on my phone. If God is supposed to be transforming me, why isn't it working?"

Your daughter overhears and says, "Yeah, I've been praying to be less anxious, but I still worry about everything. I thought the Holy Spirit was supposed to change us."

You sit down with both of them and realize: **they think transformation is something that happens to them—like magic.** They're waiting for God to zap them into maturity while they remain passive. **They don't understand that transformation involves cooperation, not just passivity.**

CONVERSATION STARTER

Let's talk: Do you think transformation is something God does *to* you while you wait? Or is it something God does *with* you as you cooperate?

SHORT TEACHING

Here's how transformation actually works: **God empowers it, but you participate in it.** It's not magic. It's not passive. It's a partnership between the Spirit's power and your willing cooperation.

The Bible gives us two clear pathways for transformation:

1. Renewed thinking.

Romans 12:2 says, "Be transformed by the renewing of your mind." **The way you think shapes the way you live.** If your mind is filled with lies—about God, about yourself, about what will satisfy you—you'll live accordingly. But when your mind is renewed by truth—by Scripture, by the Spirit's conviction—your life begins to change.

This is why Bible reading, memorization, and meditation matter. You're not just gaining information. **You're reprogramming the way you think.** You're replacing lies with truth. And over time, as your thinking changes, so do your desires, choices, and character.

2. Intentional habits.

You become what you repeatedly do. **Habits form character.** If you practice patience in small moments—pausing before reacting, choosing kindness when you're frustrated—you're forming the habit of patience. Do it enough times, and it becomes part of who you are.

But the opposite is also true. If you practice impatience, snapping, reacting, venting—you're forming the habit. **Every choice is training you toward something.**

So here's the practical takeaway: **You can't just pray for change and do nothing.** You have to cooperate with what God is doing. You study Scripture to renew your mind. You practice new habits to form new character. You depend on the Spirit for power, **but you also take action.**

God transforms you. **But He does it through the ordinary, repeated, Spirit-empowered work of renewing your thinking and forming godly habits.**

DISCUSSION PROMPTS

1. **Understanding:** What does it mean that transformation involves both God's power *and* your cooperation? How do those two work together?

2. **Personal Response:** Think about an area where you want to grow. What lies do you need to replace with truth? What habits do you need to start practicing?

3. **Lived Practice:** This week, pick one small habit that aligns with who you want to become. Practice it daily and ask the Spirit to empower it.

PARENT NOTE

This is **profoundly practical theology**—and your kids need it. Many Christians grow up thinking transformation is mystical or passive: "Just pray more and God will change you." But the Bible teaches that **transformation involves cooperation.** God empowers, but you participate.

Your job: Help your kids see the connection between daily choices and long-term character. Every time they choose patience, they're forming patience. Every time they practice gratitude, they're forming gratitude. **Small, repeated choices shape who they're becoming.**

Model this yourself. Let your kids see you intentionally forming habits. "I'm working on being less reactive, so I'm practicing pausing before I respond." "I want to grow in gratitude, so I'm writing down three things I'm thankful for each day." Show them that **transformation is intentional, not accidental.**

Don't let them off the hook with passivity. If your child says, "I'm just waiting for God to change me," gently push back: "God will empower you, but He's also calling you to participate. What's one step you can take?"

Watch for this: Kids who think transformation is passive often become spiritually lazy—waiting for change that never comes. Kids who think transformation is all effort often burn out—the biblical balance: **Spirit-empowered, habit-forming, mind-renewing cooperation with God.**

Important reminder: This isn't about earning transformation through effort. It's about **cooperating with the Spirit's work through intentional practices.** Grace is still the foundation. But grace produces action, not passivity.

ACTION STEP

Tonight, each person identifies one area they want to grow in. Then answer two questions:

1. **What lies do I believe that I need to replace with truth?** (Write it down.)
2. **What's one small habit I can practice this week to form new character?** (Be specific.)

Commit to doing it daily and checking in at the end of the week.

ONE-SENTENCE ANCHOR

Transformation happens through renewed thinking and intentional habits—Spirit-empowered cooperation, not passive waiting.
"Do not be conformed to this world, but be transformed by the renewal of your mind." — Romans 12:2

SCRIPTURE READING

Romans 12:2
Philippians 4:8–9
Colossians 3:1–10
2 Peter 1:5–8
James 1:22–25

DAY 3 MISUNDERSTANDINGS—PASSIVITY VS. PERFECTIONISM

OPENING SCENARIO

You're having a conversation with two friends, and your kids are listening.

One friend says, "I just trust God to work in my kids. I don't push them too hard about spiritual stuff. If God wants to change them, He will. I don't want to force it."

The other friend responds, "I'm the opposite. I have clear expectations. My kids know what's required—Bible reading, prayer, and good behavior. If they're not meeting the standard, I'm on them. You have to hold the line."

On the drive home, your daughter asks, "Which one is right?" And you realize: **both are extremes.** One is passive, assuming God does everything and we do nothing. The other is perfectionistic, assuming transformation is all about human effort and rule-keeping. **And neither reflects the biblical balance.**

CONVERSATION STARTER

Let's talk: Which extreme are you more tempted toward—being too passive ("God will do it, so I don't need to try") or too perfectionistic ("I have to get this right or I'm failing")?

SHORT TEACHING

When it comes to spiritual growth, there are two common extremes—**passivity and perfectionism**—and both are misunderstandings of how transformation works.

Passivity says: "God is sovereign. He'll change me when He's ready. I don't need to do anything. I trust Him and wait." This sounds spiritual, but it's actually **lazy.** Yes, God is sovereign. Yes, He empowers transformation. But **He also calls you to cooperate.** Passivity ignores the biblical commands to "work out your salvation," "put off the old self," "renew your mind," and "practice godliness." **God works, *and* you work. Both are true.**

Perfectionism says, "I have to get this right. I have to perform. I have to meet the standard. If I mess up, I've failed." This sounds disciplined, but it's actually **exhausting.** Perfectionism turns growth into a performance, where every failure feels like proof you're not good enough. It replaces grace with law and produces anxiety rather than transformation. **You can't perfect yourself. That's not how sanctification works.**

Here's the biblical balance: **You are responsible to pursue growth—but you depend on God's power to produce it.** You don't sit back and wait for God to do everything (that's passivity). And you don't try to manufacture transformation through sheer effort (that's perfectionism). **You cooperate with the Spirit—taking intentional steps while trusting His power to change you.**

Think of it like gardening. **You plant, water, and weed, but God makes it grow.** You can't force a plant to grow faster by pulling on it. But you also can't just throw seeds on the ground and ignore them. **You participate, but you depend on something beyond yourself.**

This is the rhythm of sanctification: **Effort empowered by grace, obedience rooted in trust. Growth pursued with patience, not panic.**

DISCUSSION PROMPTS

1. **Understanding:** What's wrong with passivity (just waiting for God to change you)? What's wrong with perfectionism (trying to change yourself through effort)? What's the biblical balance?

2. **Personal Response:** Which extreme are you more tempted toward? What would it look like to shift toward the biblical balance?

3. **Lived Practice:** This week, practice Spirit-dependent effort: take one intentional step toward growth *and* pray for God's power to sustain it.

PARENT NOTE

This is a critical conversation because **both extremes are toxic**—and your kids are likely being pulled toward one or the other.

Passivity is common in grace-emphasizing environments. Kids hear "God does it all" and assume they don't need to do anything. They become spiritually lazy, waiting for a change that never comes.

Perfectionism is common in performance-driven environments. Kids hear "you need to do better" and assume their worth depends on their performance. They burn out trying to earn what grace already gives.

Your job: Teach the biblical balance. **God empowers transformation, but you cooperate with it.** Grace is the foundation, but grace produces action.

Model this yourself. Let your kids see you taking intentional steps (practicing habits, renewing your mind) while also depending on God's power. "I'm working on this, *and* I'm asking God to help me because I can't do it on my own."

Watch for this:

- Passive kids often lack discipline, consistency, or spiritual engagement.

- Perfectionistic kids often struggle with anxiety, burnout, or shame.
  The biblical balance produces **humble, disciplined, grace-dependent disciples.**

Important reminder: This isn't about finding a perfect 50/50 balance. It's about holding two truths together: **You can't do this on your own (grace),** ***and*** **you›re not passive (responsibility).**

ACTION STEP

Tonight, talk about where your family tends to lean—passivity or perfectionism.
Then ask: "How can we shift toward the biblical balance? What would it look like to pursue growth intentionally *and* depend on God's power?"

Commit to one specific practice this week that reflects both: Spirit-dependent effort.

ONE-SENTENCE ANCHOR

Transformation isn't passive waiting or perfectionistic striving—it's Spirit-dependent cooperation, rooted in grace and expressed through intentional growth.
"Therefore, my beloved, as you have always obeyed, so now, not only as in my presence but much more in my absence, work out your own salvation with fear and trembling, for it is God who works in you, both to will and to work for his good pleasure." — Philippians 2:12-13

SCRIPTURE READING

Philippians 2:12–13
2 Peter 1:3–11
Hebrews 12:14
1 Timothy 4:7–8
Colossians 1:28–29

DAY 4 IDENTITY AND CONSISTENCY

OPENING SCENARIO

Your daughter comes home from school frustrated. "I try to be kind at school, but sometimes I'm not. I try to be honest, but sometimes I lie. I try to be patient with my friends, but sometimes I snap at them. It's like... I'm two different people. Who even am I?"

Your son overhears and nods. "Yeah, I feel like that too. Like, at church I'm one person, but with my friends I'm different. And at home I'm different again. Which one is the real me?"

And you realize: **they're struggling with identity and consistency.** They don't know who they're becoming, and they're discouraged by the gap between who they want to be and who they actually are. **They need to understand that consistency doesn't come from trying harder to be the same—it comes from becoming someone new.**

CONVERSATION STARTER

Let's be honest: Do you ever feel like you're a different person in different situations? How does that make you feel about who you really are?

SHORT TEACHING

Here's a truth that will anchor you: **identity shapes consistency.** You don't become consistent by trying really hard to act the same in every situation. You become consistent by **becoming someone who naturally acts a certain way because of who you are.**

Think about it. If your identity is constantly shifting—based on who you're with, how you're feeling, or what you think people expect—then of course you'll be inconsistent. **You're trying to be different versions of yourself depending on the context.** And that's exhausting.

But when your identity is rooted in Christ, you know who you are no matter where you are. You're a child of God. You're loved. You're being transformed into the image of Jesus. And that identity doesn't change based on your audience. You're the same person at church, at school, at home, and with friends because your core identity is secure.

Now, here's the tension: you won't be perfectly consistent. You'll still struggle. You'll still have moments where you act out of character. That's normal. You're not fully sanctified yet. **But over time, as the Spirit transforms you, the gap between who you are and how you act begins to close.**

This is what character formation is all about. Character is who you are when no one's watching. It's the consistency between your public and private selves. It's acting the same way at home as you do at church, not because you're performing, but because you're becoming someone who naturally lives that way.

So here's the takeaway: Don't just try to act more consistently. Instead, become someone whose identity is so deeply rooted in Christ that consistency flows naturally. And over time, with the Spirit's help, **you'll find that who you are and how you act increasingly align not perfectly, but meaningfully.**

DISCUSSION PROMPTS

1. **Understanding:** What does it mean that identity shapes consistency? How is that different from just trying to act the same everywhere?

2. **Personal Response:** Do you struggle with feeling like different people in different situations? What do you think is driving that?

3. **Lived Practice:** This week, when you're tempted to be one person at church and another at school, pause and ask: "Who am I in Christ? And how would that person act in this situation?"

PARENT NOTE

This conversation is critical because **adolescence is a peak time for identity formation**—and your kids are trying to figure out who they are. The cultural pressure is to perform different versions of themselves depending on the context. The gospel offers something better: **an identity so secure that it produces consistency.**

Your job: Help them see that inconsistency is often an identity issue, not just a behavior issue. When they act differently in different situations, gently ask, "Why? What are you trying to prove? Who are you trying to be?" Help them trace it back to identity.

Model consistency yourself. Are you the same person at church and at home? Do your kids see integrity as a clear alignment between who you say you are and how you actually live? Your consistency (or lack of it) teaches them more than your words.

Don't shame them for inconsistency. Growth takes time. Instead, point them to their identity in Christ: "You're a child of God. That's who you are everywhere. Let that identity shape how you live."

Watch for this: Kids who struggle with identity often become chameleons, constantly shifting to fit in. Kids who are rooted in Christ often develop integrity and a steady consistency between who they are and how they act, no matter the context.

Important reminder: Consistency doesn't mean you act the same in every situation. You can be appropriately different (playful with friends, respectful with adults) without compromising your core character. **The goal is integrity, not rigidity.**

ACTION STEP

Tonight, each person answers these questions:

1. "Is there an area where I act differently depending on who's around? Why?"
2. "What does my identity in Christ say about who I actually am?"
3. "How would that identity shape how I act—consistently—in every situation?"

Talk it through together. Pray for the Spirit to form consistency rooted in identity.

ONE-SENTENCE ANCHOR

Consistency flows from identity—when you know who you are in Christ, you become the same person everywhere.
"Therefore, if anyone is in Christ, he is a new creation. The old has passed away; behold, the new has come." — 2 Corinthians 5:17

SCRIPTURE READING

2 Corinthians 5:17
Colossians 3:1–17
Ephesians 4:22–24
1 Peter 2:9–12
Galatians 2:20

GROWTH THROUGH ENCOURAGEMENT AND CORRECTION

OPENING SCENARIO

Your son messes up, he's been dishonest about something, and you find out. You sit him down and correct him firmly. He nods, says he understands, but later you find him sulking in his room, defeated. "I can't do anything right," he mutters. "You're always disappointed in me."

Meanwhile, your daughter has been working really hard on being kinder to her siblings, and you haven't said anything. She's discouraged. "Does anyone even notice? What's the point of trying if no one sees it?"

And you realize: **both kids need something you're not consistently giving them. One needs encouragement to balance the correction.** The other needs affirmation to sustain her growth. **They need both, and you haven't been providing the full picture.**

CONVERSATION STARTER

Let's talk: Do you feel like you get more correction or more encouragement in this family? What would it feel like to have both?

SHORT TEACHING

Here's a truth about growth: **You need both encouragement and correction.** One without the other produces either complacency or despair.

Encouragement fuels growth. When someone notices your progress, affirms your effort, and celebrates your growth, **it motivates you to**

keep going. Encouragement says, "I see you trying. I see God at work in you. Keep it up." It doesn't ignore sin or pretend everything's perfect, but it recognizes and celebrates movement toward Christlikeness.

Correction redirects growth. When someone lovingly and firmly points out where you're off course, it protects you from destructive patterns. Correction says, "This isn't who you're meant to be. This is hurting you and others. Let's get back on track." It's not about tearing you down, it's about guiding you toward the truth.

But here's the problem: most people only get one or the other. Some families are heavy on correction and light on encouragement, and kids grow up feeling like they're never good enough. Other families are heavy on encouragement and light on correction, and kids grow up with no accountability or awareness of their sin.

The biblical model is both. Hebrews 10:24 says, "Let us consider how to stir up one another to love and good works." That's encouragement. And Hebrews 3:13 says, "Exhort one another every day... that the deceitfulness of sin may harden none of you." That's correct.

So here's the practice: Encourage often. Correct when necessary. And always do both in love. Notice growth and name it. Celebrate progress, even when it's small. And when sin shows up, address it clearly and redemptively. Don't just critique, also affirm. Don't just affirm, also guide.

When encouragement and correction work together, they create a culture where growth is both celebrated and protected.

DISCUSSION PROMPTS

1. **Understanding:** Why do we need both encouragement *and* correction? What happens when we only get one?

2. **Personal Response:** Do you tend to hear more correction or more encouragement in this family? How does that affect your motivation to grow?

3. **Lived Practice:** This week, let's practice both. Each person commits to encouraging someone *and* lovingly correcting (or self-correcting) when needed.

PARENT NOTE

This is one of the most practical, high-impact conversations you'll have because **the ratio of encouragement to correction in your home shapes your kids' entire view of growth.**

If correction dominates, your kids will internalize that they're never good enough. They'll become discouraged, performance-driven, or avoidant. They'll stop trying because they're convinced they'll always fail.

If encouragement dominates without correction, your kids will become complacent, entitled, or blind to their sin. They'll assume they're fine when they're not, and they'll miss the sanctifying work of conviction.

Your job: Provide both, generously and consistently. Encourage far more than you correct. Some say the ratio should be 5:1, five affirmations for every correction. That doesn't mean ignoring sin. It means creating a culture where encouragement is so consistent that correction feels redemptive rather than crushing.

Model receiving both. Let your kids see you respond well to encouragement ("Thank you. That means a lot.") and to correction ("You're right. I need to work on that. Thanks for pointing it out."). Show them what humility and teachability look like.

Watch for this: Kids who only receive correction often become defensive, anxious, or rebellious—kids who only receive encouragement often become entitled or self-deceived. But kids who consistently receive both tend to become humble, motivated, and resilient disciples.

Important reminder: Correction is most effective when it's specific, redemptive, and rooted in a relationship. Don't just say, "Do better." Instead, say, "Here's what happened. Here's why it matters. **Here's what it should look like instead. And I believe God is going to help you grow in this."**

ACTION STEP

Tonight, practice both encouragement and correction:

1. Each person shares one way they've seen someone else grow at this table (encouragement).
2. If there's an area where correction is needed, address it lovingly: "I care about you, and I need to point this out. Here's what I've noticed. Let's work on this together."

Let this become a regular rhythm—both/and, not either/or.

ONE-SENTENCE ANCHOR

Growth thrives in a culture of both encouragement and correction—celebrating progress and lovingly guiding toward truth.

"Therefore, encourage one another and build one another up, just as you are doing." — 1 Thessalonians 5:11

SCRIPTURE READING

1 Thessalonians 5:11, 14
Hebrews 10:24–25
Proverbs 27:17
Galatians 6:1–2
Ephesians 4:15, 29

DAY 6 CULTURE LENS—QUICK FIXES AND INSTANT GRATIFICATION

OPENING SCENARIO

Your daughter is scrolling through her phone, and you notice she's watching videos promising "10 easy hacks to be happier," "3 steps to fix your anxiety," and "How to transform your life in 30 days." Later, she's frustrated. "I tried all these things, and nothing worked. I'm still the same. What's wrong with me?"

Your son is obsessed with a fitness influencer who went from out of shape to ripped in three months. "If I just follow his program, I can do it too." But two weeks in, he's already discouraged. "This is taking forever. Why isn't it working faster?"

And you realize: **they've been conditioned to expect instant results.** The culture has trained them to believe that transformation should be quick, easy, and painless. **And when it's not, they assume something's wrong with them—or they give up entirely.**

CONVERSATION STARTER

Let's talk: Do you ever get frustrated when growth takes longer than you expected? Where does that expectation of quick results come from?

SHORT TEACHING

Here's one of the most toxic lies of our culture: **transformation should be instant.** You should be able to fix yourself quickly, easily, and painlessly. Just follow the right hack, buy the right product, watch the right video—and boom, you're changed.

This shows up everywhere. **Quick fixes for complex problems.** Instant gratification instead of long-term investment. Shortcuts instead of steady work. And when real transformation takes time, effort, and struggle, people assume it's not working or that they're doing it wrong.

But here's the reality: real transformation is slow, hard, and costly. It's not a life hack. It's not a 30-day challenge. It's a lifelong process of becoming who God is shaping you to be.

Think about the things that matter most in life: deep relationships, strong character, spiritual maturity, physical health, and wisdom. None of them happens quickly. They require time, repetition, setbacks, and perseverance. You can't rush them. You can't skip the process.

But the culture hates that. The culture worships speed and convenience. And so it promises shortcuts that don't exist. It sells you the illusion that if you find the right formula, you can bypass the hard work of growth. **And when those shortcuts don't deliver, you're left feeling like a failure.**

Here's **the truth: there are no shortcuts to sanctification**. God transforms you slowly, steadily, and deeply. He's not interested in quick fixes that don't last. He's after big, lasting, root-level change. **And that takes time.**

So reject the lie of instant transformation. Embrace the slow, faithful work of cooperating with the Spirit. Trust that growth is happening even when it feels imperceptible. And remind yourself: **you're not behind, you're exactly where God has you right now. Keep walking.**

DISCUSSION PROMPTS

1. **Understanding:** Why does our culture promise quick fixes and instant transformation? What's wrong with that approach?

2. **Personal Response:** Where have you been frustrated by slow growth? How does it feel to know that real transformation is meant to be gradual?

3. **Lived Practice:** This week, when you're tempted to look for a shortcut or quick fix, pause and ask: "Am I willing to do the slow, faithful work of real growth?"

PARENT NOTE

This conversation is urgent because a culture of instant gratification is shaping your kids' expectations and weakening their capacity for perseverance. **They've been conditioned to expect immediate** results in everything: entertainment, information, relationships, and even success. And when spiritual growth takes time, they assume it's not working.

Your job: Reset expectations. Help them see that slow growth is real growth. The most valuable things in life take time. There are no shortcuts.

Model patience with your own growth. Let your kids hear you say: "I've been working on this for years, and I'm still not where I want to be. But I can see progress. God is faithful." **Show them that maturity is about long, steady obedience in the same direction, not instant transformation.**

Celebrate incremental progress. When your child shows even a small step of growth, name it: "I see change. God is at work." Help them see that small, steady steps over time lead to lasting transformation.

Watch for this: Kids raised in an instant gratification culture often become either impatient (giving up when growth is slow) or disillusioned (convinced transformation isn't real). **But teaching them to embrace slow growth helps form patient, resilient, and faithful disciples.**

Important reminder: Rejecting quick fixes doesn't mean you can't use tools, resources, or helpful practices. It just means you don't expect them to be magic. Instead, you use them as part of the slow, steady work of cooperating with the Spirit.

ACTION STEP

Tonight, talk about one area where you've been looking for a quick fix or instant result.
Ask together: "What would slow, faithful growth look like in this area instead?"

Then commit: "We're going to reject the lie of instant transformation and embrace the slow, Spirit-empowered work of real change."

ONE-SENTENCE ANCHOR

Real transformation isn't instant or easy—it's slow, faithful, Spirit-empowered growth over time.
"And let us not grow weary of doing good, for in due season we will reap, if we do not give up." — Galatians 6:9

SCRIPTURE READING

Galatians 6:9
Proverbs 13:11
James 1:2–4
Hebrews 12:1–2
2 Peter 1:5–8

DAY 7 PRACTICE—ONE SMALL FAMILY HABIT FOR THE WEEK

OPENING SCENARIO

It's Sunday evening, and you're reflecting on the week. You realize: **life has been chaotic.** You had good intentions—pray together, read Scripture as a family, encourage each other—but none of it happened. Everyone was busy. Everyone was distracted. And now another week is starting, and you're wondering: *How do we actually make spiritual growth part of our everyday rhythm?*

Your daughter overhears your frustration and says, "Maybe we're trying to do too much. What if we just picked one thing—something small—and actually did it this week?"

And you realize: **she's right.** You don't need a massive overhaul. You need **one small, sustainable habit that you can actually practice.**

CONVERSATION STARTER

Let's talk: If we could only practice one small habit this week—something simple and doable—what would make the most difference?

SHORT TEACHING

Here's a truth about habit formation: small, consistent practices beat big, inconsistent efforts every time. You don't transform your family's spiritual life through grand plans and dramatic overhauls. You transform it through small, sustainable rhythms that you actually practice day after day.

Think about it. What's more effective: trying to do family devotions for an hour every day and burning out by Wednesday, or reading one verse together at dinner every night for a year? The second one. Because over time, consistency matters more than intensity

This is how habits form character. Every small, repeated action shapes who you are. If you practice gratitude at the table each night, you're forming a family culture of gratitude. If you practice confession and forgiveness when conflict happens, you're forming a family culture of grace. Over time, these small habits shape who you're becoming.

Here's this week's practice: Pick one small habit. Just one. Not five. Not a complete spiritual makeover. Choose one simple, sustainable practice that your family can actually follow through on each day.

Examples:

- Read one verse at dinner and talk about it.
- Share one thing you're grateful for before bed.
- Pray together for two minutes in the morning.
- Confess one thing and receive forgiveness before the day ends.
- Encourage one family member each day.

Pick one. Do it daily. And at the end of the week, evaluate: Did it stick? Did it help? Do we want to keep it?

Over time, these small habits compound. **They become the rhythms that shape your family's spiritual life.** And the beauty is this: you're not trying to be perfect. You're just trying to be faithful—one small habit at a time.

DISCUSSION PROMPTS

1. **Understanding:** Why are small, consistent habits more effective than big, inconsistent efforts?

2. **Personal Response:** What's one small habit you think would actually make a difference in our family's spiritual life this week?

3. **Lived Practice:** Let's pick one habit together right now and commit to doing it daily this week. What will it be?

PARENT NOTE

This is **profoundly practical,** and it's how real transformation happens in families. Not through grand spiritual plans that last three days, but through **small, sustainable rhythms that become part of your family's DNA.**

Your job: Help your family choose wisely. Don't pick something overwhelming. Instead, choose something small, specific, and achievable and commit to it together.

Model consistency yourself. If the family commits to a habit, you lead the way. Show up for it. Remind the family. Follow through. Your consistency sets the tone.

Don't give up if you miss a day. If you forget one night, start the next day again. Habit formation isn't about perfection; it's about getting back on track when you fall off.

Celebrate at the end of the week. If you practiced the habit most days, celebrate it. **If it didn't stick, talk about why: Was it too hard? Too vague? Was the timing off?** Adjust and try again.

Watch for this: Families who never establish small, consistent habits often drift into sporadic, inconsistent spiritual lives. But families who build sustainable rhythms tend to experience deep, lasting spiritual growth.

Important reminder: Start small. You can always add more habits later. But if you try to do too much, you'll end up doing nothing. One habit practiced consistently is far more powerful than ten habits practiced sporadically.

ACTION STEP

Tonight, choose one small habit your family will practice every day this week.

Write it down. Be specific about when and how you'll do it. Then commit together: "This is our habit for the week. Let's help each other stick to it."

At the end of the week, evaluate and decide whether to keep it.

> **ONE-SENTENCE ANCHOR**
>
> **Small, consistent habits practiced over time form deep, lasting character—one faithful step at a time.**
> *"Whoever is faithful in very little is also faithful in much." — Luke 16:10*

SCRIPTURE READING

Luke 16:10
Proverbs 13:11
1 Corinthians 15:58
Hebrews 10:23–25
Deuteronomy 6:6–9

DAY 8 BIG QUESTION—WHY DO WE REPEAT THE SAME STRUGGLES?

OPENING SCENARIO

Your son is sitting at the table, head in his hands. "I keep doing the same thing over and over. I promise myself I won't lose my temper, and then I do. I promise I won't be lazy, and then I am. I feel like I'm stuck in a loop. Why can't I change?"

Your daughter overhears and sighs. "Me too. I keep falling into the same patterns: saying yes when I should say no, trying to please everyone, and avoiding conflict. I know what I should do differently, but I keep doing the same thing. What's wrong with me?"

You pause, because you've asked yourself the same question. You've struggled with the same sins for years. You've confessed them, prayed about them, and tried to change, yet they keep showing up. **And you wonder: Why do we keep repeating the same struggles? Is there any real hope for change?**

CONVERSATION STARTER

Let's be honest: What's one struggle you keep dealing with over and over? Why do you think it keeps coming back?

SHORT TEACHING

This is one of the most frustrating realities of the Christian life: **you keep struggling with the same sins.** And it's easy to spiral into despair: *Maybe I'm not really saved. Maybe God's given up on me. Maybe I'll never change.*

But here's the truth: **repeating struggles doesn't mean you're not growing. It means you're human.** And there are reasons you keep falling into the same patterns.

1. **Sin runs deep.**
   You're not just fighting surface behavior. You're fighting deeply ingrained patterns, disordered desires, and spiritual strongholds. These things don't disappear overnight. **You're in a lifelong battle, not a quick skirmish.**

2. **You haven't addressed the root.**
   Often, the sin you keep repeating is a symptom of something deeper. You lose your temper—but underneath is fear of losing control. You people-please—but underneath is insecurity and fear of rejection. **If you only address the behavior without addressing the root, the behavior will keep coming back.**

3. **You're trying to change in your own strength.**
   You make resolutions, set goals, try harder—but you're not depending on the Spirit. And **transformation doesn't happen through willpower. It happens through Spirit-empowered renewal.**

4. **You're not practicing new habits.**
   Breaking a bad habit isn't enough. You have to replace it with a good one. Otherwise, you'll find yourself slipping back into the same old patterns. You need to form new grooves through repetition.

Here's the hope: **Just because you keep struggling doesn't mean you're not growing. Growth isn't linear; it's often slow and messy.** You take steps forward, then fall back, and then move forward again. But over time, the Spirit is at work helping you see your sin more clearly, softening your heart, and producing real, lasting change.

So don't despair. **Keep confessing. Keep repenting. Keep depending on the Spirit. And trust that God is faithful to finish what He has begun in you.**

Discussion Prompts

1. **Understanding:** Why do we keep repeating the same struggles? What are some of the reasons sin keeps showing up?

2. **Personal Response:** Think about a struggle you keep facing. What might be the root underneath it? What would it take to address that root instead of just the symptom?

3. **Lived Practice:** This week, when you fall into an old pattern, don't just confess the behavior. Ask: "What's the root? And what does the Spirit want to change in me?"

PARENT NOTE

This conversation is critical because **your kids are likely discouraged by repeated failures.** They think, "I keep messing up. I must not really be a Christian. God must be so disappointed in me."

Your job: Help them see that **repeated struggles don't mean they're not saved or that they're beyond hope.** They mean they're in a battle. And battles take time.

Model honesty about your own struggles. Let your kids hear you say: "I've been struggling with this for years. I still mess up. But I can see that God is changing me over time. I'm not who I used to be." **Show them that growth is messy, but real.**

Help them trace sin to the root. When they confess a repeated struggle, don't just say, "Try harder next time." Ask, "What do you think is underneath this? What are you afraid of? What are you trying to get?" Help them see the deeper issue.

Point them to the Spirit. Remind them that transformation is the Spirit's work, not theirs. They can't change themselves, but they can respond to and cooperate with what God is doing.

Pay attention to this pattern: Kids who don't understand why they repeat struggles often become either hopeless (convinced they'll

never change) or self-deceived (pretending the struggle doesn't exist). Teaching them to address the root and depend on the Spirit produces humble, hopeful, and growing disciples.

An important reminder: Repeating struggles don't mean you're not saved. But if there's no growth over time, no conviction, no repentance, no desire to change, it's something worth prayerfully examining.

ACTION STEP

Tonight, each person shares one struggle they keep repeating. Then ask together: "What might be the root underneath this? What is the Spirit inviting us to address?"

Pray together, asking God to reveal the root and empower the change only He can produce.

ONE-SENTENCE ANCHOR

Repeating struggles don't mean you're not growing—they mean you're in a battle, and God is faithful to complete what He started.
"And I am sure of this, that he who began a good work in you will bring it to completion at the day of Jesus Christ." — *Philippians 1:6*

SCRIPTURE READING

Philippians 1:6
Romans 7:15–25
Galatians 5:16–17
2 Corinthians 12:9–10
Hebrews 12:1–2

DAY 9 REFLECTION ANCHOR—SMALL FAITHFUL CHOICES SHAPE CHARACTER

OPENING SCENARIO

It's the end of the week, and you're reflecting over dinner. Your daughter says, "You know, I think I'm starting to see it. **The little things I do every day, how I talk to my brother, whether I complain or choose gratitude, whether I scroll or pray, those things are actually shaping who I'm becoming."**

Your son nods. "Yeah. I used to think character was about big moments. But it's actually about what I do when no one's watching the small stuff."

You smile, because they're getting it. They're starting to see that transformation isn't about dramatic moments or massive overhauls. It's about small, faithful choices repeated over time that shape you into the image of Christ.

CONVERSATION STARTER

Let's reflect: What's one small, faithful choice you've made this week that's shaping who you're becoming?

SHORT TEACHING

Here's the anchor truth of this entire unit: small, faithful choices shape character. Not big, dramatic moments. Not overnight transformations. **But small, everyday, seemingly insignificant decisions repeated consistently over time form who you are.**

Think about it. Character isn't built in crisis. It's built in the mundane. It's built when you choose patience in traffic, when you pause before reacting, when you tell the truth even when lying would be easier, when you serve without being asked, and when you forgive when it's hard. **These are the moments that shape you.**

And the beautiful part? **You get these moments every single day.** You don't have to wait for some big opportunity to grow. Every interaction, every decision, and every thought is an opportunity to be formed toward Christlikeness or away from it.

This is why habits matter so much. Habits are just small choices repeated. And over time, those repeated choices become part of who you are. You don't wake up one day as a patient person. You become a patient person by choosing patience again and again.

Here's the hope: you don't have to change everything at once. You have to make one faithful choice today, and then another tomorrow, and another the day after that. And slowly, steadily, faithfully, God shapes you into someone new.

This is the rhythm of sanctification. Not perfection. Not instant transformation. But steady, faithful obedience over time. **And God honors that. He turns your small steps into big, lasting change.**

So don't despise small beginnings. Don't dismiss the everyday moments as insignificant. Every choice matters. Every moment is forming you**, and God is at work in all of it.

DISCUSSION PROMPTS

1. **Understanding:** How do small, faithful choices shape character over time? Why are they more important than we think?

2. **Personal Response:** What's one small choice you've been making consistently this week? How is it shaping you?

3. **Lived Practice:** How can we keep making small, faithful choices as a family—not just this week, but for the long haul?

PARENT NOTE

This is the culmination of everything you've been teaching about growth and character formation. If your kids walk away with one truth, let it be this: **transformation happens through small, faithful choices repeated consistently over time.**

Keep reinforcing this. When your kids make a good choice, even a small one, name it: "That was a small, faithful choice. That's how character is formed." Help them see that the ordinary moments matter.

Model it yourself. Let your kids see you making small, faithful choices: pausing before reacting, choosing kindness, practicing gratitude, and confessing quickly. Show them that maturity is built in the mundane.

Celebrate the journey. Your family has spent these past nine days learning about growth, habits, identity, and perseverance. That's significant. Take time to thank God for what He's teaching you. **And commit to the long, slow, faithful work of becoming like Christ together.**

ACTION STEP

Tonight, go around the table and finish this sentence:
"One small, faithful choice I want to keep making is..."

Then pray together, asking God to help you be faithful in the small things—trusting that over time, those small things shape you into the image of Christ.

ONE-SENTENCE ANCHOR

Small, faithful choices repeated over time shape deep, lasting character—and God honors every step of obedience.
"Let us not lose heart in doing good, for in due time we will reap if we do not grow weary. "— Galatians 6:9

SCRIPTURE READING

Luke 16:10
Proverbs 4:23
2 Peter 1:5–8
Colossians 3:23–24
Galatians 6:9

UNIT

8

COMMUNITY, CHURCH, AND FAMILY

(ECCLESIOLOGY APPLIED)

DAY 1 WHY FAITH WAS NEVER MEANT TO BE SOLO

OPENING SCENARIO

Your son is in his room, door closed, earbuds in. When you ask him about the youth group, he shrugs. "It's fine. I don't really connect with anyone. I'd rather do my own thing."

Your daughter seems similar. She reads her Bible, prays, and goes to church, but she doesn't have any close Christian friends. When you ask if she's talked to anyone about what she's learning or struggling with, she says, "Not really. I mean, my faith is personal. It's between God and me."

And you realize: **they think faith is meant to be a solo journey.** They've absorbed the cultural message that spirituality is private, individualistic, and self-sufficient. They don't understand that they were never meant to follow Jesus alone.

CONVERSATION STARTER

Let's talk: Do you think faith is mostly a private, personal thing between you and God? Or is it meant to be shared with others?

SHORT TEACHING

Here's a truth that cuts against the grain of modern culture: **faith was never meant to be solo. From the very beginning,** God designed His people to live, grow, worship, and follow Him together. Not in isolation. Not as independent spiritual free agents. Together.

Think about the Bible's story. God didn't just save individuals; He formed a people. Israel wasn't a collection of isolated believers. It was a community bound together by covenant. **The early church wasn't a group of solo Christians doing their own thing. It was a family sharing life, resources, struggles, and worship.**

Why does this matter? Because you can't become who God made you to be on your own. You need other believers to encourage you when you're weary, correct you when you're off course, carry you when you're struggling, and celebrate with you when you grow. **You need the body of Christ.**

Hebrews 10:24–25 says it clearly: "Let us consider how to stir up one another to love and good works, not neglecting to meet together… but encouraging one another." Faith grows in community. It withers in isolation.

Here's the reality: when you try to follow Jesus alone, you become vulnerable to deception (no one to correct you), vulnerable to discouragement (no one to encourage you), vulnerable to sin (no one to hold you accountable), and vulnerable to burnout (no one to carry you when you're weak).

But when you're connected to other believers, really connected, not just showing up on Sundays, you have a support system, a source of wisdom, a place of belonging, and a context for growth. **You're not just surviving, you're thriving.**

Faith is personal, yes. But it's not private. God invites you into a relationship with Him and with His people. **Both matter. Both are essential.**

DISCUSSION PROMPTS

1. **Understanding:** Why was faith never meant to be solo? What are we missing when we try to follow Jesus alone?

2. **Personal Response:** Do you feel like your faith is mostly solo right now, or are you connected to other believers? What would it take to go deeper in community?

3. **Lived Practice:** This week, take one step toward deeper community—reach out to a Christian friend, join a small group, or have an honest conversation with someone about your faith.

PARENT NOTE

This conversation is urgent because your kids are growing up in one of the most isolated, disconnected generations in history. They've been conditioned to believe that faith is private, spirituality is individualistic, and community is optional. And it's deeply harmful.

Your role is to help them see this clearly: community isn't a nice add-on to faith, it's essential. They need the body of Christ, and the body of Christ needs them.**

Model this yourself. Do you have a Christian community? Do your kids see you in meaningful relationships with other believers being encouraged, corrected, and cared for? **If your faith looks isolated, theirs will too.**

Create opportunities for connection. Don't just assume your kids will naturally find Christian community. Help them: invite families over, connect them with healthy youth groups, and encourage Christian friendships. Make the community both accessible and normal.

Pay attention to this pattern: Kids who try to do faith solo often become either spiritually proud (convinced they don't need anyone) or spiritually isolated (drifting away because they have no support). Kids who are rooted in community become resilient, accountable, and growing disciples.

An important clarification: Community doesn't mean you're never alone with God. Personal time with God is essential, too. But private faith and isolated faith are different. You can have a deep personal walk with God and be deeply connected to His people.

ACTION STEP

Tonight, talk honestly as a family:
"Do we feel connected to the Christian community, or are we doing faith mostly on our own?"

Then ask: "What's one step we can take this week to grow in community, either as individuals or as a family?"

ONE-SENTENCE ANCHOR

Faith was never meant to be solo—we need the body of Christ to encourage, correct, and carry us as we follow Jesus together.
"And let us consider how to stir up one another to love and good works, not neglecting to meet together, as is the habit of some, but encouraging one another." — Hebrews 10:24-25

SCRIPTURE READING

Hebrews 10:24–25
Ecclesiastes 4:9–12
Acts 2:42–47
1 Corinthians 12:12–27
Proverbs 27:17

DAY 2 PURPOSE OF CHURCH AND SHARED FAITH PRACTICES

OPENING SCENARIO

Your daughter asks a question at breakfast: "Why do we have to go to church every week? I mean, I can worship God at home. I can read my Bible by myself. What's the point of sitting in a building with a bunch of people I barely know?"

Your son nods. "Yeah, and half the time it's boring. The music feels outdated, the sermons are long, and I don't feel like I get anything out of it. Can't we skip it?"

You pause, realizing: they don't understand what church is for. They see it as an event to attend, a religious obligation, or a performance to consume. **They don't see it as the gathered people of God practicing their faith together in ways they can't experience on their own.**

CONVERSATION STARTER

Let's talk: What do you think church is actually *for*? Why do we gather as God's people?

SHORT TEACHING

Here's a truth that will reshape how you think about church: **church isn't primarily a building, an event, or a service you attend. It's the people of God gathering to worship, learn, encourage, and practice faith together.**

Let's break down what that means practically.

1. Church is where we worship together.
Yes, you can worship God alone. But there's something powerful about joining your voice with other believers and declaring God's goodness together. **Corporate worship reminds you that you're part of something bigger than yourself.** You're part of a global, multi-generational family that has been worshiping Jesus for thousands of years.

2. Church is where we learn together.
When you hear God's Word taught, you're not just gaining information. **You're being formed.** The preaching of Scripture shapes your thinking, challenges your assumptions, and points you to Christ. And you're learning alongside others—hearing insights, asking questions, and growing together.

3. Church is where we encourage one another.
When you gather with other believers, you get to speak life into each other. **You encourage the weary, pray for the struggling, and celebrate growth.** You're reminded that you're not the only one fighting the fight. You belong to a family.

4. Church is where we practice the "one anothers."
The New Testament is full of commands like "love one another," "serve one another," "bear one another's burdens," "confess to one another," and "forgive one another." **You can't do any of that alone.** Church is where you practice what it means to live as the body of Christ.

5. Church is where we receive the sacraments.
Baptism and Communion aren't just rituals. They're **visible reminders of the gospel**—tangible ways to remember who you are and what Jesus has done. And they're meant to be practiced in the community.

Here's the point: **You can do some of these things on your own. But you can't do all of them.** Church isn't optional. It's **essential for your spiritual health and growth.**

Is every church perfect? No. Is every service going to be amazing? No. But **the church is Christ's body, and He's committed to it.** So if you're a Christian, you should be too.

DISCUSSION PROMPTS

1. **Understanding:** What's the difference between *attending* church (showing up to an event) and *being* the Church (part of the gathered people of God)?

2. **Personal Response:** What's one way you've experienced the value of gathering with other believers—even if it wasn't always comfortable or exciting?

3. **Lived Practice:** This week, instead of just showing up to church, engage intentionally. Worship fully. Listen actively. Talk to someone. Serve in some way. What would that look like?

PARENT NOTE

This conversation is critical because your kids are absorbing a consumer mentality toward church. They may begin to see it as a service to evaluate, an event to attend (or skip), or a product to consume. And that's harmful.

Your role is to help them see this clearly: **church isn't something you attend, it's something you are.** It's the people of God, and they are part of it.

Model engagement yourself. Do your kids see you actively participating in church worshiping, serving, building relationships, or do they see you passively consuming? **Your posture toward the church shapes theirs.**

Address legitimate concerns. If your kids find church boring or disconnected, don't just dismiss it. Ask, "What would make it more meaningful? How could you engage differently?" **Help them take ownership instead of just critiquing from the sidelines.**

Don't let them drift. Church attendance isn't optional. Yes, it should be meaningful. Yes, it should be engaged. But it's not something they can opt out of, because it's not always exciting. Consistency matters, even when it's hard.

Pay attention to this pattern: Kids who see church as optional often drift away entirely as young adults. Kids who are taught that church is essential and who see their parents living that out are far more likely to stay rooted in the body of Christ.

An important reminder: Church isn't perfect because it's full of broken people being sanctified. **But it's still Christ's bride, and He loves it.** Teach your kids to love what Jesus loves.

ACTION STEP

Tonight, talk as a family about your current relationship with the church.

Ask:

- "Are we just attending, or are we truly engaging?"
- "What's one way we could participate more meaningfully this week—serving, connecting, encouraging someone, etc.?"

Commit to one specific way to engage, not just attend.

ONE-SENTENCE ANCHOR

Church isn't an event to attend—it's the people of God gathering to worship, learn, encourage, and practice faith together.
"And they devoted themselves to the apostles' teaching and the fellowship, to the breaking of bread and the prayers." — Acts 2:42

SCRIPTURE READING

Acts 2:42–47
Ephesians 4:11–16
Hebrews 10:24–25
1 Corinthians 12:12–27
Colossians 3:16

DAY 3 MISUNDERSTANDINGS—INSTITUTION VS. LIVING COMMUNITY

OPENING SCENARIO

You're at a gathering, and two conversations are happening simultaneously.

One parent is venting: "Church is just an institution. It's all about buildings, budgets, and programs. It's lost the heart of what faith is supposed to be. We stopped going, and honestly, we're better off."

Another parent responds: "But you still need structure, teaching, and accountability. You can't just do faith on your own terms. The church exists for a reason."

Later, your kids ask, "So which one is right? Is church an institution we're supposed to submit to, or is it just about relationships and community?"

And you realize: both extremes miss the point. Church is neither a cold, lifeless institution nor an unstructured free-for-all. **It's a living community with structure, leadership, and shared practices all designed to help us follow Jesus together.**

CONVERSATION STARTER

Let's talk: Do you think of church more as an institution (with rules, structure, and authority) or as a community (with relationships and shared life)? Which feels more right to you?

SHORT TEACHING

When it comes to church, there are two common distortions, and both miss the biblical vision.

The first distortion: the church as an institution only.

This view sees the church primarily as an organization with buildings, programs, budgets, hierarchy, and rules. It emphasizes structure and authority but often loses warmth, relationship, and life. It becomes about compliance, not community. People show up, check the boxes, and leave. **There's little real connection or shared life.**

Here's the problem: Jesus didn't die to create just an institution. He died to create a family. Yes, structure matters. Yes, leadership matters. **But if all you have is an institution, you've missed the heart of what the church is supposed to be.**

The second distortion: the church as an unstructured community only.

This view rejects all structure, authority, and organized practice. It says, "We don't need buildings or formal gatherings. We need authentic relationships. Church is wherever two or three believers are spending time together." It sounds appealing, relational, organic, and free from religious baggage.

Here's the problem: the Bible doesn't support that model. The New Testament church had structured elders, deacons, teaching, sacraments, discipline, and shared rhythms. Structure isn't the enemy of community. **It's what protects and sustains it. Without it, the community becomes shallow, untethered, and vulnerable to error.**

The biblical vision is both/and. The church is a living community with God-given structure. It's a family (warm, relational, and life-sharing) with leadership, teaching, sacraments, and accountability. **Both matter. Both are biblical.**

So here's the balance: Reject cold institutionalism that loses the heart of community, and reject chaotic individualism that dismisses structure and authority. Embrace the church as Jesus designed it, a living body with a healthy skeleton.

DISCUSSION PROMPTS

1. **Understanding:** What's wrong with seeing the church as *only* an institution? What's wrong with seeing it as *only* informal relationships? What's the biblical balance?
2. **Personal Response:** Which extreme are you more tempted toward—over-emphasizing structure or dismissing it entirely?
3. **Lived Practice:** This week, how can we appreciate both the structure (teaching, leadership, gathered worship) *and* the community (relationships, shared life) of our church?

PARENT NOTE

This conversation is important because your kids are being influenced by one of these extremes, and both can be harmful.

Some kids grow up in overly institutional churches and come to associate faith with rules, performance, and religious duty. **They often walk away as young adults, convinced that the church is lifeless and irrelevant.**

Other kids grow up with no structure or accountability, and their faith becomes shallow, untethered, and individualistic. They drift because there's no solid foundation holding them.

Your role is to help them see this clearly: the church is both a living community and a structured body. It's not either/or. It's both/and.

Model balance in your own life. Are you engaged in both the formal and informal aspects of the church? Do you participate in gathered worship and build relationships? Do you respect leadership and invest in community? Your example teaches more than your words.

Address your children's frustrations honestly. If your kids are frustrated by the institutional aspects of church (boring services, irrelevant programs), validate their feelings, but don't let them dismiss the need for structure. If they're frustrated by a lack of connection, help them take ownership: **"How could you invest more in relationships?"**

Pay attention to this pattern: Kids who only experience church as an institution often become cynical or apathetic. Kids who experience church only as an unstructured community often lack depth and drift theologically. Kids who experience both develop a healthy, rooted, and relational faith.

ACTION STEP

Tonight, talk about your current church experience:

- "Do we appreciate both the structure (teaching, worship, sacraments) *and* the community (relationships, shared life)?"
- "Are we leaning too far in one direction?"
- "What's one way we could grow in the area we're neglecting?"

ONE-SENTENCE ANCHOR

The Church is a living community with God-given structure—both family and body, both relational and ordered.
"And he gave the apostles, the prophets, the evangelists, the shepherds and teachers, to equip the saints for the work of ministry, for building up the body of Christ." — Ephesians 4:11-12

SCRIPTURE READING

Ephesians 4:11–16
1 Timothy 3:14–15
Acts 2:42–47
1 Corinthians 14:40
Hebrews 13:17

DAY
4

IDENTITY THROUGH BELONGING

OPENING SCENARIO

Your daughter comes home from school looking deflated. "I don't really fit in anywhere. I'm not cool enough for the popular kids, not smart enough for the honors crowd, not athletic enough for the sports teams. I just... don't belong."

Your son overhears and mutters, "Same. Everyone has their group. I'm just floating."

Later, you're thinking about your own life. You've felt that same ache, the longing to belong somewhere, to be known and wanted. And you realize: **your kids are searching for identity through belonging. And if they don't find it in the right place, they'll find it somewhere else.**

CONVERSATION STARTER

Let's talk: Where do you feel like you belong? And where do you wish you belonged, but don't?

SHORT TEACHING

Here's a deep human need we all share: the need to belong. To be part of something. To be known, accepted, and wanted. This isn't a weakness; it's part of how God created you.

But here's the problem: most people try to find belonging in the wrong places. They look for it in popularity, success, relationships, activities, or social groups. And those things can provide a sense of belonging for a while. But it's fragile. It's conditional. **It depends on your performance, your status, or how useful you seem to others.**

Here's the gospel truth: If you're a Christian, you already belong. Not because you earned it. Not because you're cool, talented, or successful. But because God has adopted you into His family. You are a child of God. You are part of the body of Christ. You belong to a people who span the globe and stretch back thousands of years.

This is what it means to find your identity through belonging. Your worth isn't based on whether the popular kids accept you. It's based on the fact that the Creator of the universe knows you and calls you His own. You don't have to earn it. You don't have to maintain it. It is already yours.

And here's where the church comes in: The church is the visible expression of that belonging. It's where you get to experience, in real time, what it means to be part of God's family. You're not just welcomed, you are truly needed. Your gifts matter. Your presence matters. You have a place here.

Does this mean earthly belonging doesn't matter? No. It's still good to have friends, to be part of teams, to find your people. But those things are secondary. They're gifts, not foundations. Your core identity and belonging are secure in Christ and expressed in His church.

So when you feel like you don't fit in anywhere, remember where you truly belong. You're not floating. You're not unwanted. You are deeply loved, a beloved child of God and part of His forever family.

DISCUSSION PROMPTS

1. **Understanding:** What's the difference between trying to earn belonging (through performance or popularity) and receiving it as a gift (through Christ)?
2. **Personal Response:** Where have you been looking for belonging? And how does it feel to know you already belong in Christ and His church?

3. **Lived Practice:** This week, when you feel like you don't belong, remind yourself: "I am a child of God. I belong to His family. That's my foundation."

PARENT NOTE

This conversation is urgent because your kids are deeply longing to belong, and they are looking for it everywhere. **If they don't find a secure sense of belonging in Christ and the church, they will begin to chase it in peer groups, on social media, in romantic relationships, or through achievement.** And those things will ultimately fail them.

Your job: Help your children understand that their deepest need for belonging is already met in Christ. They don't have to earn it. They don't have to perform for it. It is a gift freely given.

Model this yourself. Do you live like your identity is secure in Christ? Or are you still striving for approval, chasing status, or looking for validation from earthly sources? Your kids will learn more from watching you than from anything you say.

Create belonging at home. Your family should be a place where your kids feel truly known, fully accepted, and deeply valued, not because of what they do, but because of who they are. Home is the training ground for the belonging they find in the church and in Christ.

Watch for this: Kids who don't find belonging in Christ often become either people-pleasers, constantly seeking acceptance, or withdrawn and isolated, believing they will never truly belong. Kids who are secure in their identity in Christ become confident, rooted, and free from the pressure to perform.

Important reminder: Earthly belonging is still good. It's a gift. But it's not ultimate. Teach your kids to enjoy friendships and community without making them the foundation of their lives.

ACTION STEP

Tonight, each person shares one place where they've been seeking belonging—and whether that source is stable or shaky.

Then say together: *"I already belong to God's family. That's my foundation. Everything else is a gift, not a need."*

ONE-SENTENCE ANCHOR

Your deepest need for belonging is already met in Christ—you are part of His family, known, loved, and wanted forever.

"But you are a chosen race, a royal priesthood, a holy nation, a people for his own possession." — 1 Peter 2:9

SCRIPTURE READING

1 Peter 2:9–10
Ephesians 2:19
Romans 8:14–17
1 John 3:1
Psalm 68:6

DAY 5 FAMILY AS FIRST DISCIPLESHIP SPACE

OPENING SCENARIO

You are driving home from church, and your kids are in the back seat. Your daughter says, "That was a good sermon. I liked what the pastor said about loving your neighbor."

Your son nods. "Yeah… too bad we do not actually live that out at home."

She laughs. "Right? We say all the right things at church, but then we are unkind to each other the rest of the week."

You wince **because you know there is truth in what they are saying.** You have been focused on getting them to church, signing them up for programs, and making sure they are learning theology. But you realize: **the most important place for discipleship is not the church building, it is your home. And you have not been treating it that way.**

CONVERSATION STARTER

Let's be honest: Do we live at home the way we talk about faith at church? Or is there a gap between what we say we believe and how we actually treat each other?

SHORT TEACHING

Here's a truth that is both convicting and hopeful: your family is the first and most important place for discipleship. **Not the church program. Not the youth group. Not the Christian school. Your home.**

Think about it. Where do you spend the most time? Where are you most yourself, unfiltered, unguarded, and real? At home. And that means your home is where your faith is tested, practiced, and formed. It is where faith becomes real.

The Bible is clear about this. Deuteronomy 6:6–7 says, "These words that I command you today shall be on your heart. You shall teach them diligently to your children, and shall talk of them when you sit in your house, and when you walk by the way, and when you lie down, and when you rise." **Faith is meant to be woven into everyday life, not just taught in formal settings.**

So here is the question: what does your home teach about Jesus? Not what you say about Him at church, but what your daily rhythms, interactions, and priorities reveal. Do your kids see patience, grace, and forgiveness at home? Or do they see inconsistency in people who talk about Jesus on Sunday but live as if He does not matter the rest of the week?

Here is the good news: you do not have to be perfect. In fact, your imperfections can become part of the discipleship process. When you mess up and apologize, you are teaching repentance and grace. When you are patient in hard moments, you are modeling dependence on the Holy Spirit. **When you confess your struggles, you are showing them that faith is honest and real, not something to pretend.**

Your home is the place where faith is practiced and lived out daily. **And the everyday moments, dinner conversations, resolving conflict, bedtime prayers**, how you talk about money, and how you treat your spouse, those are the moments that shape your kids' understanding of what it means to follow Jesus.

So do not outsource discipleship. Own it. Lead it. Live it out at home. The church supports you. But you are the primary discipler of your children.

DISCUSSION PROMPTS

1. **Understanding:** Why is home the most important space for discipleship? What makes it different from church or other programs?

2. **Personal Response:** What does our home actually teach about Jesus—through how we treat each other, resolve conflict, and live daily life?

3. **Lived Practice:** What's one way we could make discipleship more intentional at home this week, not just in formal moments, but in everyday interactions?

PARENT NOTE

This is convicting for most parents because many have unintentionally outsourced discipleship. We assume that church programs, Christian schools, or youth groups will do the heavy lifting. **And while those things are valuable, they are supplements, not substitutes.**

Your job: own the responsibility that you are the primary discipler of your children. Not the church. Not the youth pastor. You are. And discipleship happens primarily at home, in the small, everyday moments.

Model faith daily. Let your kids see you reading Scripture, praying, repenting, extending grace, and trusting God in hard moments. Your life becomes the curriculum.

Create intentional rhythms, such as dinner table conversations, bedtime prayers, weekly family devotions, and even spontaneous theological discussions. Make faith a natural part of everyday life, not something reserved only for formal settings.

Do not panic if you feel unqualified. You do not have to be a theologian. You have to be faithful. **Keep pointing your kids to Jesus, depend on the Holy Spirit, and keep showing up consistently.**

Watch for this: kids whose primary discipleship happens at church often develop a compartmentalized faith, religious on Sundays, but disconnected from everyday life during the week. But kids whose primary discipleship happens at home develop an integrated, everyday, lived-out faith.

Important reminder: this does not mean you do it alone. You need the church. But the church supports and strengthens what you are already doing at home. It is not either/or. It is both/and.

ACTION STEP

Tonight, talk as a family:
"What does our home actually teach about Jesus—through how we treat each other, what we prioritize, and how we live?"

Then ask: "What's one thing we want to change or improve about how we practice faith at home?"

Commit to one specific, sustainable change.

ONE-SENTENCE ANCHOR

Your family is the first and most important discipleship space—faith is formed in everyday life, not just formal teaching.
"You shall teach them diligently to your children, and shall talk of them when you sit in your house, and when you walk by the way, and when you lie down, and when you rise." — Deuteronomy 6:7

SCRIPTURE READING

Deuteronomy 6:4–9
Psalm 78:1–7
Ephesians 6:4
Proverbs 22:6
2 Timothy 1:5

DAY 6 CULTURE LENS—RADICAL INDIVIDUALISM

OPENING SCENARIO

Your daughter is scrolling through social media, and you notice a pattern: every post, every video, every message is centered on self. "Find yourself." "Trust yourself." "You do not need anyone." "Your truth is all that matters." "Live your best life for you."

Later, your son talks about his plans for the future, and everything he says focuses on himself. "I am going to do what makes me happy. I am going to live where I want. I am going to follow my dreams." There is no mention of community, responsibility to others, or how his life might fit into something bigger than himself.

And you realize: **they have absorbed one of the most dominant ideologies of our time, radical individualism.** It is the belief that you are the center of your own universe, that autonomy is the highest good, and that commitment to others is a burden rather than a blessing. **And this way of thinking is completely incompatible with the gospel.**

CONVERSATION STARTER

Let's talk: Do you think life is mostly about pursuing your own happiness and freedom? Or is it about something bigger than yourself?

SHORT TEACHING

Here's one of the most pervasive lies of our culture: **radical individualism, the belief that you are autonomous, self-sufficient, and the ultimate authority over your own life**. You define your own truth. You pursue your own happiness. You owe nothing to anyone else. You become the center of your own universe.

This shows up everywhere: "Follow your heart." "Do what makes you happy." "You do you." "Do not let anyone tell you who to be." It sounds empowering. It sounds like freedom. But in reality, it leads to a different kind of bondage.

Here's why: **Radical individualism is incompatible with reality**. You are not self-sufficient. You are not autonomous. You were created for a relationship with God and with others. You need community. You need accountability. **You need people to correct you when you are wrong lovingly, support you when you are weak, and challenge you to grow.** You were never meant to live life alone.

And radical individualism is incompatible with the gospel. Jesus did not die so you could pursue your own happiness. He died to reconcile you to God and to bring you into His family. The Christian life is not about autonomy; it is about surrender. It is not about self-fulfillment; it is about self-sacrifice. **It is not about doing what makes you happy; it is about loving God and loving others, even when it is difficult.**

Here's the irony: **radical individualism promises freedom, but it produces isolation.** When you make yourself the center of your universe, you end up alone. You have no deep relationships because true relationships require sacrifice, commitment, and putting others first. You have no purpose beyond yourself because there is nothing bigger than your own desires. **And over time, you begin to discover that a life centered on self is empty.**

The gospel offers something better: **a life centered on God and lived in community. You find freedom not in autonomy, but in surrendering to Him.** You find purpose not in self-fulfillment, but in serving something greater than yourself. You find joy not in isolation, but in deep, committed, and sacrificial love for God and others.

Radical individualism is a lie, and if you believe it, it will ultimately lead to destruction.

DISCUSSION PROMPTS

1. **Understanding:** What is radical individualism, and why is it incompatible with the gospel?

2. **Personal Response:** Where do you feel the pull toward individualism—thinking life is mostly about *your* happiness, *your* freedom, *your* self-fulfillment?

3. **Lived Practice:** This week, when you're tempted to make everything about yourself, pause and ask: "How can I serve someone else? How can I prioritize community over autonomy?"

PARENT NOTE

This is one of the most important cultural conversations you'll have because **radical individualism is the air your kids breathe.** It's in every song, every show, every influencer, every message they absorb. And unless you actively counter it, they'll internalize it as truth.

Your job: help them see that individualism is a lie that ultimately leads to emptiness. True freedom, purpose, and joy come from surrendering to God and committing to others.

Model counter-cultural living. Let your kids see you sacrificing for the community. Let them watch you prioritize relationships over convenience. Let them hear you say, "I am doing this not because it makes me happy, but because it is the right thing to do."

Challenge the messaging. When your kids absorb individualistic ideas, gently name and question them: **"That sounds appealing, but is it true? Does it align with Scripture?** What would Jesus say about that?"

Watch for this: kids raised in radical individualism often become either lonely or isolated because they have prioritized autonomy or entitlement, believing the world revolves around them. But kids who embrace gospel-centered community become connected, purposeful, and others-centered disciples.

Important clarification: Rejecting individualism does not mean you lose your personal identity or autonomy. It means your identity and freedom are rooted in Christ and lived out in community, not in isolation.

ACTION STEP

Tonight, talk about one area where individualism has influenced your thinking:
"Am I making decisions based only on what makes *me* happy, or am I considering how my life fits into God's purposes and His people?"

Then ask: "What would it look like to choose community over autonomy this week?"

ONE-SENTENCE ANCHOR

Radical individualism promises freedom but produces isolation—true life is found in surrender to God and commitment to His people.
"For none of us lives to himself, and none of us dies to himself. For if we live, we live to the Lord, and if we die, we die to the Lord." — Romans 14:7-8

SCRIPTURE READING

Romans 14:7–8
Philippians 2:3–4
1 Corinthians 12:12–27
Galatians 6:2
Ecclesiastes 4:9–12

DAY 7 PRACTICE—ENCOURAGEMENT NIGHT AT THE TABLE

OPENING SCENARIO

It has been a hard week for everyone. Your son is discouraged about school. Your daughter is frustrated with friendships. You are exhausted from work. And your spouse is carrying their own burdens.

Everyone is struggling, but no one is talking about it. You are all just… existing, going through the motions. And you realize: **this family needs encouragement, not someday, not when things get better, but tonight.**

So you decide to do something different. You gather everyone at the table and say, "Tonight, we are going to encourage each other. We are going to speak life into one another. And we are going to do it intentionally."

CONVERSATION STARTER

Before we start: When was the last time someone in this family genuinely encouraged you? How did it make you feel?

SHORT TEACHING

Here's a simple but transformative practice: Encouragement Night. One night a week (or even once a month), you gather as a family to speak life into one another. Not correcting, not critiquing. Just intentionally encouraging.

Why does this matter? Because everyone in your family is carrying something: school stress, friendship struggles, insecurity, fear, or exhaustion. And often, the people closest to you have no idea. Or worse, they may see you struggling but do not know how to respond.

Encouragement changes that. It creates space to notice, name, and affirm what God is doing in each person's life. It says, "I see you. I see you trying. I see growth. I see your gifts. I see God at work in you."

Here's how it works:

1. Each person takes a turn being encouraged.
Go around the table. When it's your turn, everyone else shares one specific way they've seen growth, character, or God's work in you.

2. Be specific, not generic.
Don't just say, "You're great." Say, "I saw you choose patience with your brother this week, even when you were frustrated. That's growth."

3. Name character, not just achievements.
Encouragement isn't just about what someone *did*. It's about who they're *becoming*. "I see kindness in you." "I see courage." "I see faithfulness."

4. Point to God.
Ultimately, encouragement points people to Jesus. "I see the Spirit at work in you." "That's evidence of God's grace."

5. Receive it humbly.
When it's your turn, don't deflect or minimize. Just say, "Thank you." **Let the encouragement sink in.**

This practice does something powerful: **it builds a culture where affirmation is normal, growth is celebrated, and people feel seen.** And over time, it trains your family to notice and name the good in each other—not just at the table, but in everyday life.

DISCUSSION PROMPTS

1. **Understanding:** Why is it important to encourage each other regularly, not just when someone does something impressive?
2. **Personal Response:** Who in this family do you think needs encouragement most right now? What would you want to say to them?

3. **Lived Practice:** How can we make encouragement a regular rhythm in our home—not just tonight, but ongoing?

PARENT NOTE

This is **one of the most high-impact practices you can establish**—and it's simple, sustainable, and immediately effective.

Your job: lead it intentionally. Do not assume it will happen organically. Set the time. Gather the family. Model it first by showing them what specific, character-based, gospel-centered encouragement looks like.

Make it regular. Once a week is ideal. Once a month is better than nothing. The key is consistency, make it a rhythm your family can count on.

Do not skip yourself. Parents need encouragement, too. Let your kids speak life into you. Receive it humbly. Model what it looks like to both give and receive encouragement.

Watch for resistance. Some kids will find this awkward at first. That is normal. Keep doing it. Over time, it will become more natural, and they may even begin to look forward to it.

Important reminder: encouragement does not mean you ignore correction. Both are necessary. But encouragement should far outweigh correction. Make affirmation the norm, not the exception.

ACTION STEP

Tonight, practice Encouragement Night.
Go around the table. Each person gets a turn. Everyone else shares one specific way they've seen growth, character, or God at work in that person.

Be specific. Be sincere. Point to God. And commit to doing this regularly.

ONE-SENTENCE ANCHOR

Encouragement builds a culture where growth is celebrated, people feel seen, and God's work is recognized.
"Therefore, encourage one another and build one another up, just as you are doing." — 1 Thessalonians 5:11

SCRIPTURE READING

1 Thessalonians 5:11
Hebrews 10:24–25
Proverbs 16:24
Ephesians 4:29
Colossians 3:16

DAY 8 WHY OUR VIEW OF GOD SHAPES EVERYTHING

OPENING SCENARIO

Your daughter comes home from church frustrated. "I am so tired of this. The worship leader was off-key. The sermon felt boring. Half the people seem hypocritical. And no one even talked to me. Why do we keep going?"

Your son nods. "Yeah, I mean, I get that church is supposed to be important. But if it is this broken, what is the point? Can't we worship God at home?"

You pause, because you have felt the same frustration. Church is imperfect. People are flawed. Leadership makes mistakes. Programs can feel irrelevant. And you may have asked yourself the same question: **why stay connected when the church feels so broken?**

CONVERSATION STARTER

Let's wrestle with this: If church is full of imperfect, broken people—and it is—why should we stay? What's the point of committing to something so flawed?

SHORT TEACHING

Here's the truth: **church is messy, imperfect, and sometimes frustrating.** There will be bad sermons. Off-key worship. Hypocrites. Disagreements. Hurt. Disappointment. **And that's because the church is full of sinners being sanctified—including you.**

So why stay? Here are a few reasons:

1. Because Jesus loves the church.
Ephesians 5:25 says, "Christ loved the church and gave himself up for her." **The church is His bride.** And if Jesus is committed to it—despite all its flaws—then we should be too. You don't get to love Jesus and dismiss His people.

2. Because you need the church.
You can't grow in isolation. You can't obey the "one another" commands alone. You can't receive the sacraments, teaching, encouragement, and accountability you need without the gathered body of Christ. **You need the church, even when it's imperfect.**

3. Because the church needs you.
The body of Christ isn't complete without every member. Your gifts matter. Your presence matters. Your faithfulness matters. **If you leave, the body is diminished.**

4. Because commitment is formative.
When you commit to something imperfect and stay anyway, **you grow in patience, humility, grace, and perseverance.** Running from imperfection doesn't make you mature—it makes you a consumer. Staying and serving make you a disciple.

5. Because no church is perfect.
If you leave this church because it's flawed, you'll end up at another flawed church. **There is no perfect church.** And if you find one, don't join it—because you'll ruin it.

Here's the bottom line: **Yes, the Church is imperfect. But it's still Christ's body, and He's committed to it.** So stay. Serve. Love. Be patient. Extend grace. And trust that God is at work—in the church, and in you through the church.

DISCUSSION PROMPTS

1. **Understanding:** Why should we stay connected to church even when it's imperfect and frustrating?

2. **Personal Response:** What's one frustration you have with the church? And how could staying and serving help you grow instead of just walking away?

3. **Lived Practice:** This week, instead of critiquing from the sidelines, ask: "How can I serve, encourage, or contribute to the health of my church?"

PARENT NOTE

This conversation is critical because your kids will face disillusionment with the church. That is inevitable. And how you respond will shape whether they stay connected or walk away.

Your job: validate their frustrations without feeding cynicism. Yes, the church is imperfect. Yes, it is messy. And it is still Christ's body, and you are called to remain committed to it.

Model commitment to yourself. Do your kids see you staying through hard seasons, serving faithfully, and extending grace to imperfect leaders and members? Or do they see you jumping from church to church, constantly criticizing, or disengaging when things are not ideal?

Help them distinguish between legitimate concerns and consumer preferences. Some issues are serious false teaching, abuse, or unrepentant sin. Others are preferences for worship style, preaching length, or programming. Teach them discernment.

Watch for this: kids who walk away from church when it is imperfect often become spiritual nomads, drifting, isolated, and untethered. But kids who learn to stay, serve, and extend grace become mature, committed, and resilient disciples.

Important reminder: staying connected does not mean staying in an abusive or heretical church. There are legitimate reasons to leave. But discomfort, disappointment, and imperfection alone are not among them.

ACTION STEP

Tonight, talk honestly as a family:
"What frustrates us about the church right now?"

Then ask: "How could we respond with grace, patience, and service instead of cynicism or withdrawal?"

Commit to one way you can contribute to the health of your church this week.

ONE-SENTENCE ANCHOR

The Church is imperfect because it's full of sinners being sanctified—but it's still Christ's bride, and He's committed to it.
"Christ loved the church and gave himself up for her, that he might sanctify her." — Ephesians 5:25-26

SCRIPTURE READING

Ephesians 5:25–27
1 Corinthians 12:12–27
Hebrews 10:24–25
Romans 12:4–5
1 Peter 4:10

DAY 9 REFLECTION ANCHOR—FAITH GROWS STRONGEST IN COMMUNITY

OPENING SCENARIO

It is the end of the week, and you are sitting around the table, reflecting on the past nine days. Your son says, "I think I get it now. I cannot do this alone. I need other people to encourage me, to call me out, and to remind me who I am when I forget."

Your daughter nods. **"Yeah, I used to think faith was just between God and me.** But now I see God uses people. The church is not optional. It is where I actually grow."

You smile **because they are connecting the dots.** They are beginning to see that faith is not meant to be a solo journey; it is meant to be lived, practiced, and deepened in community.

CONVERSATION STARTER

Let's reflect: What's one thing you've learned this week about why community and the church matter for your faith?

SHORT TEACHING

Here's the anchor truth of this entire unit: faith grows strongest in community, not in isolation, not in independence, but in community.

Think about why that is true: Community encourages when you are weary. When you are ready to give up, someone speaks life into you. When you are discouraged, someone reminds you of God's faithfulness. **You do not have to carry that weight alone.**

Community corrects when you are off course. When you are blind to your sin, someone lovingly points it out. **When you believe lies,**

someone speaks truth. You need people who love you enough to tell you the hard things.

Community provides accountability when you are struggling. When temptation feels overwhelming, you have people to call. When you slip into old patterns, people notice and ask hard questions. **You are not left to fight alone.**

Community provides a sense of belonging when you feel lost. When you do not know who you are, the body of Christ reminds you: you are a child of God. You are loved. **You are wanted. You belong.**

Community provides a witness to the world. When the church loves each other well, the world notices. Jesus said, "By this all people will know that you are my disciples, if you have love for one another." **Your community is a testimony to the gospel.**

Here's the bottom line: you can survive spiritually on your own for a while, but you cannot thrive. Thriving requires a messy, imperfect, committed, and grace-filled community.

So do not isolate. Do not try to go it alone. Stay connected. Serve faithfully. Love generously. **Trust that God grows your faith strongest when you are rooted in His people.**

DISCUSSION PROMPTS

1. **Understanding:** Why does faith grow strongest in community? What are we missing when we try to go it alone?
2. **Personal Response:** How have you experienced the value of community this week—or over your life?
3. **Lived Practice:** How can we keep prioritizing community as a family—not just attending church, but truly engaging and investing in relationships?

PARENT NOTE

This is the culmination of everything you have been teaching about church, community, and belonging. If your kids walk away with one truth, let it be this: faith is meant to be lived in community.

Keep reinforcing this. When your kids are tempted to isolate, remind them: "You need people." When they are frustrated with church, remind them: "This is where you grow." When they are struggling, remind them: **"You do not have to carry this alone."**

Model it yourself. Let your kids see you investing in Christian community, not just attending church, but actively building relationships, serving others, being vulnerable, and receiving care. **Your example teaches more than your words.**

Celebrate the journey. Your family has spent nine days intentionally learning about community, church, belonging, and family discipleship. That is significant. Thank God for what He is teaching you. **And commit to living as the body of Christ together, in unity and love.**

ACTION STEP

Tonight, go around the table and finish this sentence:
"One way community has strengthened my faith is..."

Then pray together, thanking God for His people and asking Him to help you stay rooted, connected, and committed to the body of Christ.

ONE-SENTENCE ANCHOR

Faith grows strongest in community—where we encourage, correct, carry, and belong to one another as the body of Christ.
"And let us consider how to stir up one another to love and good works, not neglecting to meet together, as is the habit of some, but encouraging one another." — Hebrews 10:24-25

SCRIPTURE READING

Hebrews 10:24–25
Ecclesiastes 4:9–12
1 Corinthians 12:12–27
Ephesians 4:11–16
Acts 2:42–47

UNIT

9

Purpose, Work, and Responsibility

DAY 1 THE PRESSURE OF FINDING PURPOSE

OPENING SCENARIO

Your daughter is sitting at the kitchen table, staring at a blank college application essay. The prompt asks, "What is your purpose? What unique contribution will you make to the world?" She looks up at you, anxious. "I do not know what my purpose is. I am 16. How am I supposed to know what I am meant to do with my entire life?"

Your son overhears and mutters, "At least you are thinking about it. I have no idea what I want to do. Everyone keeps asking, 'What are you going to be?' and I just… do not know. What if I never figure it out?"

Later, you scroll through social media and see post after post of people who seem to have it all figured out, launching businesses, pursuing dreams, and "living their purpose." **And you feel that familiar twinge of anxiety: "Am I doing what I am supposed to be doing? Have I missed my calling?"**

And you realize: **the pressure to find purpose is not just affecting your kids, it is weighing on all of you.**

CONVERSATION STARTER

Let's be honest: Do you ever feel pressure to figure out your purpose like you're supposed to know exactly what you're meant to do with your life? Where does that pressure come from?

SHORT TEACHING

Here's one of the heaviest burdens our culture places on people, especially young people: finding your purpose. You have to discover your unique calling, your one true passion, and your special contribution to the world. **And if you do not figure it out, or worse, if you choose wrong, you will waste your life.**

This sounds inspiring, but in reality, it is often paralyzing. Because how are you supposed to know at 16, or 18, or even 30, what you are "meant" to do for the rest of your life? And what if you choose a path and it turns out to be the wrong one? **What if you feel like you have missed your calling?**

Here's the truth the world will not tell you: the pressure to find one perfect, unique purpose is a myth. It is not biblical, and it is not how God works.

Yes, God has a purpose for your life. But His primary purpose for you is the same as it is for every believer: to know Him, love Him, and make Him known. Everything else in your career, your talents, and your opportunities flow from that. Your purpose is not something you discover; **it is something you grow into as you follow Jesus.**

Think about it this way: God does not have one secret plan you have to guess. He has general purposes for all believers to love God, love others, make disciples, use your gifts, steward what He has given you, and live faithfully where you are. And then He provides specific opportunities and assignments that unfold as you walk with Him.

So instead of agonizing over "finding your purpose," ask better questions:

- How can I love God and love others *today*?
- What has God given me to steward *right now*—time, relationships, resources, opportunities?
- What needs do I see around me that I'm equipped to meet?

Purpose isn't a destination you arrive at. It's a direction you walk in. And the direction is simple: Follow Jesus. Serve faithfully. Use what He's given you. And trust Him to unfold the rest.

DISCUSSION PROMPTS

1. **Understanding:** What's the difference between "finding your one perfect purpose" and "living faithfully in the purpose God has for all believers"?

2. **Personal Response:** Do you feel pressure to figure out your purpose? What would change if you focused less on finding it and more on being faithful where you are?

3. **Lived Practice:** This week, instead of stressing about your future purpose, ask: "How can I love God, serve others, and steward what I have *today*?"

PARENT NOTE

This conversation is critical because purpose anxiety has become widespread, and many of your kids are feeling overwhelmed by it. The culture tells them they have to find their passion, discover their calling, and live their best life. And if they do not, they begin to feel like failures.

Your job: relieve that pressure. Help them see that God's primary purpose for them is the same as it is for every Christian to know Him, love Him, and reflect Him. Everything else is secondary.

Model this yourself. Do you live as if your worth depends on achieving some grand purpose? Or do you live faithfully in the mundane, loving your family, serving your neighbors, and **stewarding your work while trusting that God is at work in the ordinary**?

Do not add to the pressure. Resist the urge to constantly ask, "What do you want to be when you grow up?" Instead, ask: "How are you seeing God use you right now? What are you learning about Him? How can you serve faithfully today?"

Watch for this: kids who feel intense pressure to find purpose often become either paralyzed, unable to make decisions for fear of choosing the wrong one, or restless, constantly chasing new passions without discernment. But kids who understand that purpose is lived, not found, are free to serve faithfully wherever God has them.

Important clarification: saying "purpose is not found" does not mean careers, callings, and specific assignments do not matter. It means they flow from faithfulness rather than anxiety. Trust God, walk obediently, and He will open doors in His timing.

ACTION STEP

Tonight, each person shares:
"What's one way I can live out God's purpose *today*—loving Him, loving others, or stewarding what He's given me?"

Then pray together, asking God to free you from the pressure to find purpose and help you walk faithfully in the purpose He's already revealed.

ONE-SENTENCE ANCHOR

Purpose isn't something you discover—it's something you live into by faithfully following Jesus wherever He leads.
"And whatever you do, in word or deed, do everything in the name of the Lord Jesus, giving thanks to God the Father through him." —Colossians 3:17

SCRIPTURE READING

Colossians 3:17
Micah 6:8
Matthew 22:37–40
Ephesians 2:10
Proverbs 3:5–6

DAY 2

WORK AND CALLING AS STEWARDSHIP

OPENING SCENARIO

Your son is complaining about his homework. "This is pointless. When am I ever going to use algebra in real life? I want to do something that actually matters."

Your daughter is stressing about a part-time job application. "It is just retail. It is not like it is my calling or anything. I am just doing it for money."

You pause and realize: they do not see work as meaningful unless it feels significant, impactful, or connected to some larger purpose. They think that if it is not their "calling," then it does not really matter. And in doing so, they miss the biblical vision of work as stewardship, **faithfully using what God has given them right where He has placed them.**

CONVERSATION STARTER

Let's talk: Do you think some work is more important or meaningful than others? Or does God care about all work—even the ordinary, everyday stuff?

SHORT TEACHING

Here's a truth that will transform how you think about work: all work done faithfully for God's glory is meaningful, not just "ministry" or a specific "calling." God cares about the cashier, the accountant, the teacher, the mechanic, and the student doing homework. **All of it matters when it is done as an act of stewardship.**

Let's define stewardship: it is faithfully managing what God has entrusted to you, your time, your talents, your opportunities, and your responsibilities. Stewardship says: God has given me something to do, and I am going to do it well, not to earn His approval, but to honor Him.

This changes everything. Your job is not just about making money. Your homework is not just a hoop to jump through. Your chores are not just obligations. They are opportunities to steward what God has given you: your time, your ability, and your responsibility.

Colossians 3:23 says, "Whatever you do, work heartily, as for the Lord and not for men." Whatever. Not just pastors or missionaries. Not just jobs that feel significant. Whatever you do, mowing the lawn, bagging groceries, studying for a test, or changing diapers can be done for God's glory.

Here's the shift: stop asking, "Is this my calling?" and start asking, "Am I stewarding this faithfully?" You do not have to know your life's grand purpose to honor God today. You need to do what is in front of you with excellence, integrity, and a heart of worship.

And here's the hope: God often reveals calling through faithful stewardship. When you serve well in small, ordinary tasks, He opens doors to bigger opportunities. **But even if He does not, and even if you never do something the world calls significant, your faithfulness still matters. It is worship.**

Every job becomes kingdom work when it is done for God's glory.

DISCUSSION PROMPTS

1. **Understanding:** What's the difference between thinking of work as "finding your calling" and thinking of it as "stewarding what God has given you"?

2. **Personal Response:** What's one responsibility you have right now that feels meaningless or mundane? How would it change if you saw it as stewarding what God has entrusted to you?

3. **Lived Practice:** This week, pick one ordinary task and do it "heartily, as for the Lord." What does that look like practically?

PARENT NOTE

This conversation is foundational because your kids are absorbing a toxic view of work that only "significant" work matters, that anything outside of their passion is wasted time, and that work is primarily about **self-fulfillment rather than service or stewardship.**

Your job: help them see that all work, when done faithfully, is an act of worship. God does not rank jobs. He cares about faithfulness.

Model this yourself. Do you complain about mundane tasks? Do you treat some work as beneath you? Or do you honor God in the ordinary doing laundry, working your job, and serving your family with excellence and gratitude? Your kids are watching.

Affirm all kinds of work. Do not just celebrate the impressive things. Also, celebrate the ordinary. When your child finishes homework, cleans their room, or helps with chores, say: **"You just stewarded what God has given you. That honors Him."**

Watch for this: kids who think only "significant" work matters often become either entitled, dismissing ordinary responsibilities as beneath them, or anxious, paralyzed by the pressure to find the "right" calling. But kids who embrace stewardship become faithful, humble, and committed to excellence in whatever they do.

Important reminder: Stewardship does not mean you are stuck in a job you hate forever. It means you honor God where you are while trusting Him to lead you forward in His timing.

ACTION STEP

Tonight, each person shares one responsibility they have right now—school, work, chores, etc.—that feels ordinary or mundane.

Then ask: "How can I steward this faithfully this week, doing it as for the Lord?"

Commit to excellence in one ordinary task this week—not to earn approval, but as worship.

> **ONE-SENTENCE ANCHOR**
>
> **All work done faithfully for God's glory is meaningful—not just "callings," but every act of stewardship.**
> *"Whatever you do, work heartily, as for the Lord and not for men."*
> *— Colossians 3:23*

SCRIPTURE READING

Colossians 3:23–24
1 Corinthians 10:31
Ephesians 6:5–8
Proverbs 22:29
Luke 16:10

DAY 3 MISUNDERSTANDINGS—ONE PERFECT CALLING MYTH

OPENING SCENARIO

Your daughter is anxious about choosing a major. "What if I pick the wrong one? What if I am supposed to be a doctor, but I choose business and miss God's plan for my life? What if I spend years doing the wrong thing?"

Your son is paralyzed by indecision about his summer plans. "I do not know if I should get a job, volunteer, or take a class. What if I choose wrong and miss an opportunity God had for me?"

You see the pattern: **they believe there is one perfect path, one divinely ordained calling, and if they miss it, everything will fall apart. And that pressure is crushing them.**

CONVERSATION STARTER

Let's wrestle with this: Do you think God has one specific, perfect plan for every decision—and if you miss it, you've blown it? Or is there more freedom than that?

SHORT TEACHING

Here's one of the most damaging myths in Christian culture: the belief in one perfect calling. The idea that God has one specific, predetermined plan for your life, one job, one major, one city, one spouse, and your job is to figure it out. And if you choose wrong, you miss God's will and ruin your entire life. **This sounds spiritual, but it is neither biblical nor deeply paralyzing.**

Here's the truth: God does have purposes for your life. But most of life does not come with a detailed roadmap. Instead, God gives you wisdom and freedom to make choices within His will.

Think about it this way: God has a moral will, clear commands revealed in Scripture. Do not lie. Love your neighbor. Forgive. Honor Him in all you do. Those are not negotiable.

God also has a sovereign will, His ultimate plan for history, which He is working out. You are not going to accidentally derail that plan. **God is bigger than your choices.**

And then there is a category of wisdom and freedom. Most decisions in life fall into this category: which school to attend, which job to take, and where to live. God does not have one secret answer you have to guess. He gives you wisdom through Scripture, counsel, and circumstances, and then invites you to make a thoughtful decision and trust Him.

Here's the freedom in this: you are not going to accidentally fall out of God's will by choosing the "wrong" major. You can serve God as a doctor, a teacher, or a plumber. You can honor Him wherever you live. What matters is that you walk faithfully, trust Him, and steward what He gives you.

And here's the grace: even when you make less-than-ideal choices, God is still at work. He redeems. He redirects. He works all things together for good. You cannot out-mess God's plan.

So stop agonizing over finding the one perfect calling. **Make wise, prayerful decisions. Trust God to guide you and walk faithfully wherever He leads.**

DISCUSSION PROMPTS

1. **Understanding:** What's wrong with the "one perfect calling" myth? How does it create anxiety instead of freedom?

2. **Personal Response:** Where have you felt paralyzed by the fear of choosing the "wrong" path? How does it feel to know you have more freedom than you thought?

3. **Lived Practice:** This week, when you're facing a decision, ask: "What does wisdom say? What aligns with God's moral will? What opportunities has He given me?" Then choose and trust Him.

PARENT NOTE

This conversation is urgent because the myth of one perfect calling is quietly crushing your kids. They are terrified of making the wrong choice and missing God's will, and that fear often leaves them paralyzed.

Your job: free them from that fear. Help them see that God gives wisdom and freedom, not a hidden blueprint they have to decode. They do not have to guess the one perfect answer. They are free to make wise, faithful choices and trust God with the outcome.

Model freedom yourself. Do you agonize over every decision, terrified of making the wrong choice? Or do you pray, seek wisdom, and make thoughtful choices, trusting that God will guide and redirect as needed? Your kids will mirror your approach.

Teach them decision-making skills. Help them evaluate options using Scripture, wisdom, counsel, and circumstances. Then encourage them to choose and trust that God is sovereign over those choices.

Watch for this: kids who believe the one-perfect-calling myth often become either paralyzed, unable to make decisions, or reckless, making impulsive choices to escape the pressure. But kids who understand wisdom and freedom become confident, prayerful, and discerning decision-makers.

Important clarification: freedom does not mean all choices are equal. Some choices are wiser than others. But within the bounds of wisdom and Scripture, there is often genuine freedom.

ACTION STEP

Tonight, talk about one area where someone in the family feels stuck or anxious about making the "right" choice.
Walk through it together: What does Scripture say? What does wisdom suggest? What are the options, and which seems best?

Then pray: "God, we're making the best decision we can. We trust You to guide us and work all things for good."

ONE-SENTENCE ANCHOR

God doesn't have one secret calling you have to guess—He gives you wisdom, freedom, and the promise that He's sovereign over all your choices.
"The heart of man plans his way, but the LORD establishes his steps."
— Proverbs 16:9

SCRIPTURE READING

Proverbs 16:9
James 1:5
Psalm 37:23–24
Romans 8:28
Philippians 2:13

DAY 4 IDENTITY BEYOND OUTCOMES AND ACHIEVEMENT

OPENING SCENARIO

Your son just got his test back. He failed. And he's devastated, not just disappointed, but crushed. "I'm so stupid. I'm such a failure. I'll never get into a good college. My life is over."

You try to comfort him, but he will not listen, because in his mind, this grade defines him. It is not just a test. It feels like proof of his worth or his lack of it.

Later, your daughter is scrolling through social media, comparing herself to classmates who just won awards, got accepted into prestigious programs, and posted about their accomplishments. **She sighs. "Everyone else is succeeding.** I'm not special at anything. What's the point?"

And you realize: both of them are tying their identity to outcomes and achievements. **And when those things fail, as they inevitably will, their sense of self begins to crumble.**

CONVERSATION STARTER

Let's be honest: Do you ever feel like your worth depends on what you achieve—grades, awards, success, recognition? What happens when you don't measure up?

SHORT TEACHING

Here's one of the most toxic lies in our culture: you are what you achieve. Your grades, awards, success, and productivity measure your worth. If you accomplish great things, you are valuable. If you do not, you are not.

And the result? Your identity becomes fragile, unstable, and exhausting because achievement is never enough. You get the A, but now you have to maintain it. You make the team, but now you have to perform. You get into college, but now you have to prove you belong. The bar keeps rising, and you are never quite enough.

Here's the gospel truth that cuts through all of it: your identity is not based on what you achieve, it is based on whose you are. **You are a child of God, made in His image, loved unconditionally, and redeemed by Jesus. Your worth is settled, not earned.**

Think about what that means practically:

- When you fail a test, **it doesn't change who you are.** You're still loved. You're still valuable. You're still God's.
- When you don't make the team, **it doesn't diminish your worth.** You're still gifted. You're still purposeful. God is still forming you.
- When you don't get the recognition you hoped for, **it doesn't mean you don't matter.** God sees. God knows. And His approval is all that ultimately counts.

This does not mean outcomes do not matter. **Excellence, effort, and responsibility still matter, but they flow from security, not insecurity.** You work hard because you are faithfully stewarding what God has given you, not because your worth is on the line.

And here's the freedom: when your identity is anchored in Christ, failure is no longer final. You can try, fall short, learn, and try again because your value is not contingent on success. You are free to grow without the constant pressure to prove yourself.

DISCUSSION PROMPTS

1. **Understanding:** What's the difference between working hard because you're stewarding your gifts (secure identity) and working hard because your worth depends on success (insecure identity)?

2. **Personal Response:** Where do you feel the most pressure to achieve to prove your worth? What would change if you really believed your identity is secure in Christ?

3. **Lived Practice:** This week, when you face success or failure, practice saying: "This doesn't define me. I am loved and valuable because I'm God's—not because of what I achieve."

PARENT NOTE

This is one of the most critical conversations you will have because an achievement-based identity can quietly shape and damage your kids. They are being taught, explicitly and implicitly, that their worth depends on what they accomplish. And that pressure can be crushing.

Your job: relentlessly anchor their identity in Christ, not in outcomes. When they succeed, celebrate it, but do not tie their worth to it. When they fail, comfort them and remind them that their value has not changed.

Watch your own language. Do you primarily praise your kids for their achievements? "I am so proud you got an A!" Or do you also affirm character, effort, and identity? "I am proud of how hard you worked. I see perseverance in you. And I love you no matter what the grade is."

Model identity security for yourself. Do you spiral when you fail? Do you define yourself by your productivity or success? Or do you rest securely in your identity in Christ, regardless of outcomes? Your kids will mirror what they see in you.

Watch for this: kids with an achievement-based identity often become either perfectionists, constantly afraid of failure, or disengaged, convinced they will never measure up. But kids with a Christ-anchored identity become resilient, humble, and free to try, fail, and grow.

Important reminder: anchoring identity in Christ does not mean you stop caring about excellence or effort. It means you pursue them from a place of security rather than desperation.

ACTION STEP

Tonight, each person shares one recent success or failure.
Then say together: *"This doesn't define me. My identity is secure in Christ—loved, valued, and purposeful, no matter what I achieve."*

Let this become a regular practice, untethering worth from outcomes.

> ### ONE-SENTENCE ANCHOR
>
> **Your identity is not based on what you achieve it's anchored in who you are, loved and secure in Christ.**
> *"For you have died and your life is hidden with Christ in God."* —
> *Colossians 3:3*

SCRIPTURE READING

1 Peter 2:9
Ephesians 2:10
Romans 8:38–39
Colossians 3:3
Psalm 139:13–16

DAY 5 RESPONSIBILITY AT HOME AND IN RELATIONSHIPS

OPENING SCENARIO

Your daughter is sitting on the couch watching tv, while the kitchen is a disaster after dinner. You ask her to help clean up, and she sighs. "I didn't even eat that much. Why do I always have to help with everything?"

Your son leaves his backpack in the hallway, his shoes by the door, and his dishes on the table. When you point it out, he says, "I was going to get it later." But later never comes.

And you realize: they are avoiding responsibility not because they are bad kids, but because they do not see small, everyday responsibilities as meaningful. They think responsibility is about big, important things, not about cleaning up after themselves, contributing at home, or being reliable in the small, everyday moments.

CONVERSATION STARTER

Let's talk: Do you think responsibility is mostly about big, important things? Or does it also include the small, everyday stuff—like cleaning up, following through, and being reliable at home?

SHORT TEACHING

Here's a truth that will shape your character: responsibility starts at home. Not in your career. Not in some future calling, but in the small, everyday tasks of contributing to your household and honoring your relationships.

Think about Luke 16:10: "Whoever is faithful in very little is also faithful in much." You do not prove you are ready for big responsibilities by avoiding small ones. You prove it by being faithful in the things no one notices, doing your chores without being asked, **cleaning up after yourself, keeping your word, and showing up on time.**

Here's why this matters: responsibility is formative. Every time you take ownership, whether it is cleaning the kitchen, finishing your homework, or being reliable with your siblings, you are forming the habit of faithfulness. **And over time, those small habits shape who you become.**

But when you avoid responsibility by leaving messes for others, making excuses, or being unreliable, you begin forming the opposite habits. You are training yourself toward laziness, entitlement, and irresponsibility. And that will show up later in bigger ways in your job, your marriage, and your friendships.

And here's the relational side: responsibility at home is how you love others. When you clean up after yourself, you are serving your family. When you follow through on your commitments, you honor others. When you contribute without being asked, you reflect Jesus, who came not to be served but to serve.

So stop thinking of chores as beneath you or responsibilities as burdens. They are opportunities to steward what God has given you, opportunities to love the people around you, and opportunities to form the character that will carry you through life.

Faithfulness in the small things is what prepares you for the big things.

DISCUSSION PROMPTS

1. **Understanding:** Why does responsibility start with small, everyday tasks at home? How does faithfulness in little things prepare you for bigger things?

2. **Personal Response:** What's one small responsibility you've been avoiding or treating as unimportant? How could you steward that faithfully this week?

3. **Lived Practice:** This week, pick one household responsibility and do it without being asked, without complaining, as an act of service and stewardship.

PARENT NOTE

This conversation is critical because your kids are growing up in a culture that often dismisses everyday responsibility. **They are told to chase their dreams, find their passion, and do what makes them happy,** but they are rarely taught to clean up after themselves, contribute to the household, or be reliable in the mundane.

Your job: teach them that responsibility matters, especially the small, unglamorous kind. Do not lower the bar. Do not do everything for them. Instead, give them age-appropriate responsibility and hold them accountable.

Model this yourself. Do you treat household tasks as beneath you? Do you complain about everyday responsibilities? Or do you serve your family faithfully, stewarding what God has entrusted to you? Your kids will mirror what they see.

Do not enable irresponsibility. If your child avoids chores, makes excuses, or leaves messes for others to clean up, resist the urge to step in and fix it for them. Let them experience the consequences. Often, natural consequences teach responsibility more effectively than lectures.

Watch for this: kids who avoid everyday responsibility often become entitled and unreliable adults. But kids who learn to be faithful in small things grow into dependable, humble, and servant-hearted disciples.

Important reminder: responsibility is not about perfection. It is about ownership, follow-through, and learning from failure.

ACTION STEP

Tonight, each person commits to one small responsibility they'll take ownership of this week—without being reminded.
Examples: cleaning up after meals, doing laundry, taking out trash, and completing homework on time.

At the end of the week, check in: "Did I follow through? What did I learn about faithfulness?"

ONE-SENTENCE ANCHOR

Responsibility starts in the small, everyday tasks at home—faithfulness in little things prepares you for much.
"Whoever is faithful in very little is also faithful in much, and whoever is dishonest in very little is also dishonest in much."
—Luke 16:10

SCRIPTURE READING

Luke 16:10
Colossians 3:23–24
Proverbs 6:6–11
Galatians 6:4–5
1 Corinthians 4:2

DAY 6 CULTURE LENS—SUCCESS METRICS AND MEANING

OPENING SCENARIO

Your daughter comes home from school and announces, "Everyone is posting their college acceptance letters. **It feels like a competition to see who got into the best school."**

Your son is scrolling through videos of teenage entrepreneurs who have made millions, young athletes going pro, and influencers with massive followings. He sighs. "I feel like if I am not doing something big by the time I am 20, I am already behind."

And you realize: the culture is shaping how they define success. They are measuring it by unbiblical, unsustainable, and ultimately empty standards. They think success means wealth, fame, achievement, status, and getting ahead early. And if they do not measure up, they begin to feel like failures.

CONVERSATION STARTER

Let's talk: How does the world define success? And do you think that's the same as how God defines it?

SHORT TEACHING

Here's one of the most toxic lies in our culture: success is measured by wealth, fame, achievement, and status. **The more you have, the more you accomplish, and the more people know your name, the more successful you are.**

And the result? A generation of people chasing standards that never truly satisfy. They climb the ladder of success only to discover it's leaning against the wrong wall. **They achieve everything the world says matters and still feel empty.**

Here's what the Bible says about success: it's not about outcomes; it's about faithfulness. It's not about how much you have; it's about how you steward what you've been given. It's not about recognition; it's about obedience to God.

Jesus didn't measure success by worldly standards. He didn't own property, accumulate wealth, build an empire, or seek fame. Instead, He served, loved, obeyed, and sacrificed. **And He calls us to do the same: "Whoever wants to be great among you must be your servant."** Think about what that means practically:

- **Success isn't making a lot of money.** It's stewarding your resources generously and wisely.
- **Success isn't achieving fame.** It's using your influence—whatever size—to point people to Jesus.
- **Success isn't climbing the career ladder.** It's honoring God in whatever work He's given you.
- **Success isn't an early accomplishment.** It's long obedience in the same direction.

And here's the freedom: **you don't have to compete.** You don't have to be the richest, the most accomplished, or the most recognized. You have to be faithful. And God measures faithfulness differently from the world.

So stop chasing the world's standards. **They don't satisfy.** Instead, ask: Am I loving God well? Am I loving others well? Am I faithfully stewarding what He has given me? Am I walking in obedience? **That is what success looks like.**

DISCUSSION PROMPTS

1. **Understanding:** How does the world define success? How does God define it? What's the difference?

2. **Personal Response:** Where do you feel pressure to measure up to the world's success metrics? What would change if you pursued God's definition instead?

3. **Lived Practice:** This week, when you're tempted to compare yourself to others' achievements, pause and ask: "Am I being faithful? That's what matters."

PARENT NOTE

This conversation is urgent because the world's definition of success is crushing your kids. They're comparing themselves to outliers, teenage millionaires, early achievers, and viral sensations, and beginning to feel like failures.

Your role: reset their understanding of success. Help them see that God doesn't measure success by wealth, fame, or achievement. **He measures it by faithfulness.**

Model this yourself. Do you chase status, recognition, or wealth? Do you compare yourself to others? Or do you pursue faithfulness, loving God, **serving your family, and stewarding your work regardless of outcomes? Your kids will mirror what they see.**

Celebrate faithfulness, not just achievement. When your child does something impressive, celebrate it—but also celebrate faithfulness in the small, unseen things. "You were patient with your sibling, that's success." "You kept your word, that's success."

Watch for this: Kids who chase worldly definitions of success often become either burned out (exhausted by constant striving) or despairing (convinced they'll never measure up). But kids who pursue biblical faithfulness grow into content, generous, and obedient disciples.

Important reminder: Rejecting worldly success metrics doesn't mean avoiding hard work or excellence. **It means your worth is not tied to outcomes.**

ACTION STEP

Tonight, talk as a family:
"What metrics does the world use to measure success? What metrics does God use?"

Then ask: "What's one way we've been chasing the world's metrics? How can we shift toward God's definition of success—faithfulness?"

ONE-SENTENCE ANCHOR

Success isn't measured by wealth, fame, or achievement—it's measured by faithfulness to God in whatever He's called you to.
"His master said to him, 'Well done, good and faithful servant. You have been faithful over a little; I will set you over much.'" — *Matthew 25:21*

SCRIPTURE READING

Matthew 25:14–30
Mark 10:42–45
1 Timothy 6:6–10
Philippians 3:7–8
Proverbs 11:28

DAY 7 PRACTICE—PURPOSE INVENTORY (GIFTS AND OPPORTUNITIES)

OPENING SCENARIO

Your daughter is lying on her bed, staring at the ceiling. **You ask what she's thinking about, and she says,** "I just don't know what I'm supposed to do. I don't feel like I'm good at anything. I don't see how God could use me."

Your son overhears and says, "Same. I mean, I'm okay at some things, but nothing really stands out. How am I supposed to know what God wants me to do?"

And you realize: they're waiting for a dramatic revelation of purpose. They think God will send a sign, a voice, or a clear calling. Meanwhile, they're overlooking what's already right in front of them, the gifts **God has already given them and the opportunities He has already provided.**

CONVERSATION STARTER

Let's talk: What are you actually good at? What do you enjoy? What needs do you see around you that you're equipped to meet?

SHORT TEACHING

Here's a practical way to discern purpose: take inventory of what God has already given you. Not what you wish you had. Not what others have. What has God placed in your hands right now?

This isn't about finding some mystical, hidden calling. It's about faithful stewardship and growing awareness. **God has already equipped you with gifts, interests, relationships, and opportunities.** And often, your purpose unfolds as you faithfully use what He has already given you.

Here's a simple framework: three questions to guide you.

1. What has God given me? (Gifts)
What are you good at? What do you enjoy? What comes naturally to you? These aren't random—**God gave you these abilities for a reason.** There are clues to how He might use you.

2. What needs do I see? (Opportunities)
Look around. Where do you see needs in your family, church, school, or community? What problems do you notice? What burdens do you carry? **Often, God gives you a burden for something because He's calling you to be part of the solution.**

3. What am I positioned to do? (Access)
What unique opportunities or relationships has God given you? Who do you have access to that others don't? Where has He placed you strategically?

Your position isn't accidental, it's purposeful.

When you answer these three questions, you begin to see where God may be leading **you, not through a mystical sign, but through faithful, practical stewardship.** You take what He's given you, use it to meet the needs around you, and trust Him to unfold the rest.

Purpose isn't something you wait to discover. **It's something you actively live out by faithfully stewarding what God has already placed in your hands.**

DISCUSSION PROMPTS

1. **Understanding:** What's the difference between waiting for God to reveal your purpose and stewarding the gifts and opportunities He's already given you?
2. **Personal Response:** What gifts has God given you? What needs do you see? What opportunities are in front of you right now?
3. **Lived Practice:** This week, use what God has already given you to meet one need you see around you. What would that look like?

PARENT NOTE

This is deeply practical, and it helps your kids move from paralysis to action. Instead of waiting for some dramatic revelation of purpose, they begin stewarding what God has already placed in their hands.

Your role: help them recognize what God has already given them. **Ask questions that draw it out: "What are you good at? What do you enjoy? What needs do you notice?** Where has God uniquely positioned you?"

Affirm their gifts. Don't wait until those gifts seem impressive before you affirm them. **Notice and name the gifts, interests, and strengths you see in them now**. "You're really good at encouraging people." "You notice when others are struggling." "You're great at solving problems."

Create opportunities for stewardship. Don't just talk about gifts; help them put them into practice. If they're good at teaching, let them help a younger sibling. If they're compassionate, connect them with meaningful opportunities to serve. **As they practice, their sense of purpose becomes clearer.**

Watch for this: Kids who don't recognize their gifts often underestimate themselves or wait passively for a sense of calling. But kids who faithfully steward what they have **grow into confident, purposeful, and active servants of God wherever He has placed them.**

ACTION STEP

Tonight, each person does a purpose inventory using the three questions:

1. **What has God given me?** (List 2-3 gifts, strengths, or interests.)
2. **What needs do I see?** (Name 1-2 needs around you.)
3. **What am I positioned to do?** (Identify opportunities or relationships God has given you.)

Then ask: "How can I use what God has given me to meet a need I see this week?"

> ### ONE-SENTENCE ANCHOR
>
> **Purpose unfolds as you faithfully steward the gifts and opportunities God has already placed in your hands.**
> *"As each has received a gift, use it to serve one another, as good stewards of God's varied grace." — 1 Peter 4:10*

SCRIPTURE READING

1 Peter 4:10–11
Romans 12:6–8
Ephesians 2:10
Matthew 25:14–30
1 Corinthians 12:4–7

DAY 8 BIG QUESTION—HOW DO WE MAKE WISE DECISIONS?

OPENING SCENARIO

Your son is staring at two summer opportunities, both of which are good options. One is a paid internship. The other is a ministry trip. He's paralyzed. "I don't know which one to choose. **What if I choose wrong? How do I know what God wants?**"

Your daughter is facing a similar dilemma with friendships. She's being pulled in two directions and is unsure which group to invest in. "I've prayed about it, but I don't feel like God is giving me a clear answer. How am I supposed to decide?"

And you realize: they don't yet have a clear framework for making wise decisions. They think every choice requires a clear sign from God. **And when they don't get one, they feel** stuck.

CONVERSATION STARTER

Let's wrestle with this: When you're facing a decision, and you don't feel like God is giving you a clear answer, how do you know what to choose?

SHORT TEACHING

Here's a question that comes up constantly: **How do I make wise decisions?** And underneath it is usually fear: *What if I choose wrong?*

Let's build a simple, biblical framework for decision-making:

1. Start with Scripture.
Does the Bible address your decision? If so, **that's your answer.** You don't need to pray about whether to lie, cheat, or dishonor your parents. God already said no. Start with what He's already revealed.

2. Seek wisdom.
Pray for wisdom (James 1:5). Gather information. Consider consequences. Think it through. **God gave you a mind, use it.** Wisdom isn't mystical. It's a prayerful, thoughtful evaluation.

3. Get counsel.
Seek input from mature, godly people who know you and love Jesus. That may include parents, mentors, or trusted friends. Proverbs says, "Plans fail for lack of counsel, but with many advisers they succeed." **So don't make major decisions in isolation.**

4. Consider circumstances.
What doors are open? What doors are closed? What resources, opportunities, and limitations do you have? **God often guides through practical realities.**

5. Pay attention to your heart.
Not just feelings, but a deep, settled conviction. As you pray and seek God, do you sense a growing peace about one option? Does one align more clearly with your gifts and the burdens God has placed on your heart? **The Spirit can guide through an inner witness, but it must always be tested against Scripture and godly wisdom.**

6. Choose and trust God.
After seeking God through prayer, wisdom, counsel, and careful evaluation, **make a decision and trust Him with it.** You don't need complete certainty. **You need to take a step of faith and trust that God is sovereign over your choices.**

Here's the freedom: most decisions don't have just one "right" answer. God gives you wisdom and freedom. And even when you choose poorly, He is still at work. He redeems, redirects, and works all things together for good.

Make wise, prayerful decisions and then trust God with the outcome.

DISCUSSION PROMPTS

1. **Understanding:** What's the difference between waiting for a divine sign and using the tools God has already given you (Scripture, wisdom, counsel, circumstances)?
2. **Personal Response:** Think about a decision you're facing. Walk through the six steps. What clarity does that bring?
3. **Lived Practice:** This week, when you face a decision, use this framework instead of waiting for a mystical sign. Pray, seek wisdom, get counsel, and then choose.

PARENT NOTE

This is deeply practical, and your kids desperately need it. Decisions often paralyze them because they think every choice requires a special sign from God. And when they don't get it, they feel stuck.

Your role: teach them a clear, biblical framework for decision-making. Help them see that God often guides through ordinary means, Scripture, wisdom, counsel, and circumstances. **They don't need to wait for a voice from heaven to move forward.**

Model decision-making yourself. Let your kids hear you walk through the process out loud: "I'm praying about this. I'm seeking wisdom. I'm asking for counsel. **Here's what I'm sensing. I'm going to make a decision and trust God.**"

Empower them to decide. Don't make every decision for them. Guide them through the process, then let them choose. They will make mistakes, and that's okay. **Mistakes are part of learning wisdom.**

Watch for this: Kids who expect a divine sign for every decision often become paralyzed or even superstitious. But kids who learn biblical decision-making grow into confident, prayerful, and **wise stewards of their choices.**

ACTION STEP

Tonight, someone in the family shares a decision they're currently facing. Walk through the six-step framework together:

1. What does Scripture say?
2. What does wisdom suggest?
3. What counsel have you received?
4. What do circumstances indicate?
5. What do you sense in your heart (tested against truth)?
6. What's the best choice—and how can you trust God with it?

Practice this as a family.

ONE-SENTENCE ANCHOR

Wise decisions come from Scripture, wisdom, counsel, and circumstances—not waiting for mystical signs, but trusting God as you steward what He's given.

"If any of you lacks wisdom, let him ask God, who gives generously to all without reproach, and it will be given him." —James 1:5

SCRIPTURE READING

James 1:5
Proverbs 15:22
Psalm 32:8
Proverbs 3:5–6
Philippians 4:6–7

DAY 9 REFLECTION ANCHOR— PURPOSE GROWS THROUGH FAITHFUL RESPONSIBILITY

OPENING SCENARIO

It's the end of the week, and you're reflecting over dinner. Your son says, "I think I've been waiting for purpose to just… appear. But this week I realized it's more about being faithful with what's right in front of me."

Your daughter nods. "Yeah. I don't have to know my whole life's purpose. I have to steward today well and trust God to unfold the rest."

You smile, **because they're getting it**. They're starting to see that purpose isn't a destination you arrive at. **It's a direction you walk in one faithful step at a time.**

CONVERSATION STARTER

Let's reflect: What's one thing you've learned this week about purpose, calling, or how to make wise decisions?

SHORT TEACHING

Here's the anchor truth of this entire unit: **Purpose grows through faithful responsibility.** Not through dramatic revelations. Not through finding the one perfect calling. **Through faithful stewardship of what God has already given you.**

Think about it:

- **You don't find purpose by waiting.** You find it by serving faithfully where God has placed you.

- **You don't discover your calling through mystical signs.** You discover it by stewarding your gifts and opportunities.
- **You don't become who you're meant to be overnight.** You become it through small, repeated acts of obedience over time.

This is the rhythm of a purposeful life: steward what you have, serve where you are, and trust God with the outcome. And over time, He unfolds something beautiful, not because you had it all figured out, but because you were faithful.

And here's the hope: you don't have to have your whole life mapped out. You don't have to know at 16 what you'll be doing at 40. You need to be faithful today. Love God. Love others. Steward your gifts. Work as though you are serving the Lord. And trust that God is weaving it all into a purpose greater than you can see.

So stop waiting for purpose to arrive. Start living it right here, right now, in the mundane, ordinary, everyday moments; that's where purpose grows.

DISCUSSION PROMPTS

1. **Understanding:** What does it mean that purpose grows through faithful responsibility? How is that different from waiting for purpose to reveal itself?
2. **Personal Response:** What's one area where you've been waiting for clarity about purpose instead of being faithful with what's in front of you?
3. **Lived Practice:** How can we keep prioritizing faithfulness—not just this week, but as a lifelong rhythm?

PARENT NOTE

This is the culmination of everything you have been teaching about purpose, calling, and stewardship. If your kids walk away with one truth, let it be this: purpose is lived, not found, and it grows through faithful responsibility.

Keep reinforcing this. When your kids are anxious about their future, remind them, "Be faithful today. God will take care of tomorrow." When big decisions paralyze them, remind them, **"Steward what you have. Trust God with the rest."**

Model it yourself. Let your kids see you living purposefully, not through grand achievements, but through faithful stewardship of your work, your family, your relationships, and your gifts. **Show them that purpose is ordinary faithfulness over time.**

Celebrate the journey. Your family has spent nine days learning about purpose, calling, stewardship, and decision-making. **That is significant.** Thank God for what He is teaching you. And commit to walking faithfully together.

ACTION STEP

Tonight, go around the table and finish this sentence:
"One way I want to be more faithful with what God has given me is..."

Then pray together, asking God to help you steward what you have, serve where you are, and trust Him to unfold purpose as you walk faithfully.

ONE-SENTENCE ANCHOR

Purpose grows through faithful responsibility—stewarding what God has given you, right where He's placed you, one obedient step at a time.
"His master said to him, 'Well done, good and faithful servant. You have been faithful over a little; I will set you over much.'" — Matthew 25:23

SCRIPTURE READING

Matthew 25:14–30
Luke 16:10
1 Corinthians 4:2
Colossians 3:23–24
Proverbs 3:5–6

UNIT

10

HOPE AND THE FUTURE

(ESCHATOLOGY)

DAY 1 WHY HOPE MATTERS NOW

OPENING SCENARIO

You are watching the news with your kids, and it is relentless: climate disasters, political division, violence, economic instability, and disease. Your daughter shakes her head. "The world is so messed up. It just keeps getting worse. What is even the point?"

Your son is scrolling through social media, and it is filled with doomscrolling people posting about how terrible everything is, how hopeless the future looks, and how nothing will ever get better. He mutters, "Everyone is so depressed. It is like no one thinks there is any hope."

Later, you are lying in bed thinking about your own anxieties, financial stress, health concerns, relational strain, and uncertainty about the future. And you feel it too: the weight of hopelessness, the fear that things will not get better, the gnawing sense that the world is spiraling out of control.

And you realize something urgent: **your family desperately needs hope. Not wishful thinking. Not toxic positivity. Real, biblical, life-sustaining hope.**

CONVERSATION STARTER

Let's be honest: When you think about the future—your own life, the world, everything—do you feel hopeful or hopeless? Why?

SHORT TEACHING

Here is why hope matters more than you think: **hope shapes how you live today**. If you believe the future is hopeless, you will live in fear, despair, or apathy. But if you believe the future is secure in God's hands, you can face today with courage, endurance, and purpose.

Our culture is saturated with hopelessness. Anxiety, depression, and despair are widespread, especially among young people. And it is not hard to see why. The news is relentless. The future feels uncertain. The problems feel too big to solve. And the narrative everywhere is: things are bad, and they are only getting worse.

But here is what the Bible says: the world is broken, yes. But it is not hopeless. God is still sovereign. He is still at work. And He has promised that this is not how the story ends.

Biblical hope is not naïve optimism. It is not pretending everything is fine. It is confident trust that God is in control and His promises are sure. It is the assurance that no matter how dark things get, God is faithful, and He will make all things new.

And here is why that matters now: hope sustains you in the present. When you know the ending is secure, you can endure the middle. When you trust that God is working all things for good, you can face hardship without collapsing. When you believe resurrection is coming, you can live faithfully even when the world feels like it is falling apart.

Romans 15:13 says, "May the God of hope fill you with all joy and peace in believing, so that by the power of the Holy Spirit you may abound in hope." Hope is not wishful thinking. **It is Spirit-empowered confidence in God's promises.**

So when the world feels hopeless, anchor yourself in hope, not in political change, not in human solutions, **but in the God who holds the future and has promised to finish what He started.**

DISCUSSION PROMPTS

1. **Understanding:** What's the difference between wishful thinking and biblical hope? Why does hope matter for how we live today?
2. **Personal Response:** When you think about the future, what makes you feel hopeless? What would it mean to anchor your hope in God instead?
3. **Lived Practice:** This week, when you feel overwhelmed by bad news or future anxiety, practice saying: "God is sovereign. His promises are sure. I can hope in Him."

PARENT NOTE

This conversation is urgent because your kids are growing up in a hopeless generation. Anxiety and despair are the dominant emotions of their peers. And unless you actively cultivate biblical hope, they will absorb the cultural narrative: the future is hopeless.

Your job: anchor them in hope, not denial, not toxic positivity, but confident trust in God's sovereignty and promises. **Help them see that the world is broken, yes, and God is still in control.**

Model hope for yourself. Do you live like the future is secure in God's hands, or do you spiral into anxiety, despair, or cynicism? **Your kids will mirror what they see in you.**

Do not dismiss their fears. When your kids express hopelessness, do not just say, "Just trust God." Validate their concerns: "Yes, the world is broken. Yes, it is hard. And here is why we still have hope." **Point them to Scripture, to God's character, and to His promises.**

Watch for this: Kids who grow up without hope often become either paralyzed (too anxious to move forward) or reckless (living for the moment because they see no future). Kids who are anchored in biblical hope become resilient, courageous, and purposeful disciples.

Important reminder: Biblical hope does not mean you ignore real problems or pretend everything is fine. **It means you face reality with confidence in God's sovereignty and promises.**

ACTION STEP

Tonight, each person shares one thing about the future that makes them feel anxious or hopeless.
Then, as a family, respond with this: *"That's real. That's hard. And here's why we still have hope: God is sovereign. His promises are sure. He will make all things new."*

Let this be the beginning of cultivating hope together.

ONE-SENTENCE ANCHOR

Hope matters now because it sustains us in the present—anchoring us in God's promises even when the world feels hopeless.
"May the God of hope fill you with all joy and peace in believing, so that by the power of the Holy Spirit you may abound in hope." — Romans 15:13

SCRIPTURE READING

Romans 15:13
Psalm 42:5
Romans 8:24–25
Hebrews 6:19–20
1 Peter 1:3–5

DAY 2 BIBLICAL HOPE—RESTORATION AND RENEWAL

OPENING SCENARIO

Your daughter asks a question at dinner: "If we go to heaven when we die, why does the world matter? If everything is going to burn anyway, why should we care about the environment, or justice, or making things better?"

Your son jumps in. "Yeah, I have heard people say, 'This world is temporary. Heaven is what matters.' So are we just supposed to wait around until we die?"

And you realize something important: **they have absorbed a distorted view of hope.** They think the Christian hope is escape, leaving this broken world behind and going to a disembodied heaven. And if that is the hope, then nothing here really matters.

But that's not what the Bible teaches.

CONVERSATION STARTER

Let's talk: What do you think happens in the end? Do we go to heaven and leave the earth behind? Or is there something more?

SHORT TEACHING

Here is one of the most misunderstood truths in Christianity: biblical hope is not about escaping the world; it is about the restoration and renewal of the world.

Yes, when believers die, they go to be with Jesus. That is real. But that is not the end of the story. **The Bible's ultimate hope is the**

resurrection—when Jesus returns, raises the dead, judges the world, and makes all things new.

Revelation 21:1 says, "Then I saw a new heaven and a new earth." Not no earth a new earth. **God does not destroy creation and replace it with some ethereal heaven**. He renews it. He restores it. He brings heaven to earth.

And that changes everything. Because if the hope is restoration, then this world matters. The work you do matters. **The relationships you build matter**. The justice you pursue matters. The creation you steward matters. None of it is wasted.

Romans 8:21 says that creation itself "will be set free from its bondage to corruption and obtain the freedom of the glory of the children of God." All of creation is groaning, waiting for redemption. And one day, **God will heal it, restore it, and make it what it was always meant to be.**

So here's the biblical hope:

- **Jesus will return.** Not to destroy the world, but to judge, heal, and restore it.
- **The dead will be raised, n**ot as disembodied souls, but with resurrected bodies in a restored creation.
- **God will dwell with His people.** Not in some distant heaven, but **here—on a renewed earth.**
- **All things will be made new.** Every tear wiped away. Every wrong made right. Every broken thing healed.

That is the hope: **restoration, renewal, and resurrection.** And it means that what you do now, how you love, how you serve, and how you steward truly matters for eternity.

DISCUSSION PROMPTS

1. **Understanding:** What's the difference between "escaping to heaven" and "the restoration of all things"? Why does that distinction matter?

2. **Personal Response:** How does it change the way you see your life now to know that the hope is restoration, not just escape?

3. **Lived Practice:** This week, when you're tempted to think "this world doesn't matter," remind yourself: "God is making all things new. What I do here matters for eternity."

PARENT NOTE

This is foundational theology, and most Christians get it wrong. They think the goal is to escape Earth and go to heaven. But that is Platonism, not Christianity. The biblical hope is bodily resurrection in a restored creation.

Your job: help your kids see that the world matters because God is redeeming it, not abandoning it. This changes how they steward creation, pursue justice, invest in relationships, and think about their work.

Model this yourself. Do you live like the world is temporary and meaningless, or do you live like what you do here matters for eternity? Your kids will mirror your theology.

Point them to Scripture. Show them passages about the new earth, the resurrection, and the restoration of all things. Let the Bible shape their eschatology, not pop culture Christianity.

Watch for this: Kids who think the hope is escape often become either apathetic (nothing here matters) or hyper-spiritual (only "ministry" matters). Kids who understand restoration become engaged, purposeful, and culture-shaping disciples.

Important clarification: Yes, when believers die, they go to be with Jesus. But that is an intermediate state. **The ultimate hope is resurrection and the new earth.**

ACTION STEP

Tonight, read Revelation 21:1–5 together.
Then talk: "What stands out to you? What does it mean that God is making all things new—not destroying everything, but restoring it?"

Ask: "How does this change the way we see our lives, our work, and our world now?"

> **ONE-SENTENCE ANCHOR**
>
> **Biblical hope is not escape from the world—it's the restoration and renewal of all things when Jesus returns.**
> *"Then I saw a new heaven and a new earth, for the first heaven and the first earth had passed away." — Revelation 21:1*

SCRIPTURE READING

Revelation 21:1–5
Romans 8:18–25
Isaiah 65:17–25
Acts 3:21
2 Peter 3:13

DAY 3 MISUNDERSTANDINGS—SPECULATION VS. FAITHFUL LIVING

OPENING SCENARIO

You're at a church event, and someone is giving a dramatic presentation about end-times prophecy—charts, timelines, predictions about who the Antichrist might be, speculation about when Jesus will return. Your kids are wide-eyed. Afterward, your son asks, "Is that really what the Bible says?"

Your daughter looks anxious. "Should we be worried? What if we are living in the end times right now?"

Meanwhile, you have noticed a pattern: some Christians obsess over end-times speculation, constantly looking for signs, predicting dates, and interpreting current events as prophetic fulfillment. Others dismiss eschatology entirely: "We cannot know anything, so why bother?"

And you realize something important: both extremes miss the point. The Bible does talk about the future, **but it is meant to shape how we live now, not fuel obsessive speculation or paralyzing fear.**

CONVERSATION STARTER

Let's talk: Have you ever heard people make predictions about the end times? What did you think about that? Did it help you or confuse you?

SHORT TEACHING

When it comes to the future and Jesus' return, there are two common extremes, both of which are unhealthy.

The first extreme: obsessive speculation.

This is the approach that turns end-times prophecy into a puzzle to solve. People create charts, decode symbols, predict dates, and identify current events as fulfilling prophecy. They become consumed with figuring out **the timeline instead of living faithfully.**

Here is the problem: Jesus explicitly said we do not know the day or hour of His return. Acts 1:7 says, "It is not for you to know times or seasons that the Father has fixed by His own authority." Trying to decode the exact timeline is not only fruitless, but it also misses the point entirely.

The second extreme: total dismissal.

This approach says, "We cannot know anything about the future, so why bother? Let's focus on the present." It treats eschatology as irrelevant or unimportant.

Here is the problem: the Bible speaks often about the future, and it is not just for curiosity; it is meant to shape how we live now. If you ignore what God has revealed about the future, you miss the **hope, urgency, and motivation to live faithfully.**

The biblical balance is this: God has revealed that Jesus will return, the dead will be raised, God will judge, and He will make all things new. We do not know when, and we are not supposed to obsess over the details. But we are called to live in light of this certain future.

So here's the takeaway:

- **Don't speculate obsessively.** You're not called to decode prophecy or predict the timeline.
- **Don't dismiss it entirely.** God revealed these truths for a reason—they matter.
- **Live faithfully.** Let the certainty of Jesus' return shape how you live today—with hope, urgency, and readiness.

Faithful living, not anxious speculation, is the point.

DISCUSSION PROMPTS

1. **Understanding:** What's wrong with obsessive speculation about end times? What's wrong with dismissing it entirely? What's the biblical balance?

2. **Personal Response:** Have you ever felt anxious or confused by end-times teaching? What would it mean to hold biblical hope without obsessing over details?

3. **Lived Practice:** This week, instead of speculating about when Jesus will return, ask: "How should the certainty that He *will* return shape how I live today?"

PARENT NOTE

This conversation is important because end-times teaching is often either sensationalized or ignored, and both approaches **harm your kids.** They need a balanced, biblical understanding.

Your job: teach them what Scripture clearly reveals: Jesus will return, the dead will be raised, God will judge, and He will make all things new. That is the hope. **But do not get drawn into speculation, date-setting, or conspiracy theories.**

Model healthy eschatology. Do you live with confident hope in Jesus' return, or do you either obsess **over prophecy charts or ignore the future entirely? Your** kids will mirror your approach.

Do not let fear-based teaching take root. Some end-times teaching is designed to scare people into a sense of urgency or obedience. That is manipulation, not discipleship. Biblical hope produces courage, not fear.

Watch for this: Kids raised on sensationalized end-times teaching often become either anxious (terrified of the future) or cynical (dismissive of all eschatology). Kids taught balanced, biblical eschatology become hopeful, urgent, and faithful disciples.

Important reminder: The point of eschatology is not to satisfy curiosity. It is to shape how you live now with hope, readiness, and faithfulness.

ACTION STEP

Tonight, talk as a family:
"What has God clearly revealed about the future in Scripture?"
"What hasn't He revealed—and what does that tell us about what we should focus on?"

Then ask: "How should the certainty of Jesus' return shape how we live today?"

> **ONE-SENTENCE ANCHOR**
>
> **God calls us to faithful living, not anxious speculation—trusting what He's revealed and living ready for Jesus' return.**
> *"But concerning that day and hour no one knows, not even the angels of heaven, nor the Son, but the Father only." — Matthew 24:36*

SCRIPTURE READING

Matthew 24:36–44
Acts 1:6–8
1 Thessalonians 5:1–11
2 Peter 3:8–13
Mark 13:32–37

DAY 4 IDENTITY SHAPED BY HOPE AND RESILIENCE

OPENING SCENARIO

Your daughter has been through a hard season, friendships have fractured, plans have fallen apart, and she is discouraged. She says quietly, "I feel like everything I try just fails. What is the point of hoping for anything if it is just going to fall apart?"

Your son is struggling too. He has faced rejection, disappointment, and setbacks. And instead of bouncing back, he has withdrawn. "I just do not want to get my hopes up anymore. It hurts too much when things do not work out."

And you realize something important: **they are losing hope.** And when hope fades, resilience fades with it. They are giving up not because they are weak, but because they do not believe there is anything worth hoping for.

CONVERSATION STARTER

Let's be honest: Have you ever been disappointed so many times that you stopped hoping for good things? What does that feel like?

SHORT TEACHING

Here is a truth that will sustain you through hardship: your identity is shaped by hope, and hope produces resilience. When you know the future is secure, you can endure the present. When you trust that God is at work, you can keep going even when things are hard.

Think about the connection. If you have no hope, you have no resilience. If you believe the future is hopeless, then every setback feels final. Every disappointment feels devastating. **Every failure feels like proof that nothing will ever get better, and eventually, you give up.**

But when you have real, biblical hope, you can endure. Not because life is easy, but because you know this is not the end of the story. You know God is at work. You know He is faithful. You know He will make all things new. **And that hope sustains you through the difficult middle.**

Romans 5:3–5 says, "We rejoice in our sufferings, knowing that suffering produces endurance, and endurance produces character, and **character produces hope, and hope does not put us to shame."**

Hope and resilience strengthen one another. Hope gives you the strength to endure, and endurance deepens and reinforces your hope.

Here's how this shapes identity:

- **Your setbacks do not define you.** You're defined by the God who holds your future.
- **Your failures do not shape you.** You're being shaped by the hope that sustains you through them.
- **You're not a victim of circumstances.** You're a child of God with an unshakable future.

So when life is hard—and it will be—**anchor your identity in hope.** Not wishful thinking. Not denial. **Biblical hope that says: God is faithful, and this is not the end.**

DISCUSSION PROMPTS

1. **Understanding:** How does hope produce resilience? What happens to you when you lose hope?
2. **Personal Response:** Think about a time when you faced disappointment or hardship. Did you have hope? How did it (or the lack of it) affect how you responded?

3. **Lived Practice:** This week, when you face setbacks, practice anchoring your identity in hope: "This is hard. But God is faithful. This isn't the end of my story."

PARENT NOTE

This conversation is critical because your kids will face disappointment, rejection, and hardship. And their ability to endure depends on whether they have hope.

Your job: cultivate hope in them, not false optimism, but deep, biblical confidence in God's faithfulness and promises. Help them see that setbacks are not the end of the story.

Model resilience yourself. When you face hardship, do you spiral into despair, or do you anchor yourself in hope and keep moving forward? **Your kids will learn resilience by watching you.**

Do not dismiss their pain. When your kids are disappointed, do not just say, "It will be fine" or "Look on the bright side." Validate their hurt, and then gently point them to hope: "This is hard. I am sorry. **And God is still faithful. This is not the end.**"

Watch for this: Kids without hope often become either defeated (giving up entirely) or cynical (refusing to hope to avoid disappointment). Kids with biblical hope become resilient, courageous, and enduring disciples.

Important reminder: Resilience does not mean you do not feel pain. It means you continue trusting God through the pain, believing He is at work even when you cannot see it.

ACTION STEP

Tonight, each person shares one area where they've been discouraged or tempted to give up hope.
Then, as a family, speak hope into it: *"This is hard. But God is faithful. He's not done with this yet. Keep trusting Him."*

Pray together, asking God to renew hope and strengthen resilience.

ONE-SENTENCE ANCHOR

Your identity is shaped by hope—and hope produces the resilience to endure, trust, and keep going when life is hard.
"And we rejoice in our sufferings, knowing that suffering produces endurance, and endurance produces character, and character produces hope." — Romans 5:3-4

SCRIPTURE READING

Romans 5:3–5
Psalm 42:5–11
Lamentations 3:21–26
Hebrews 6:19
Isaiah 40:28–31

DAY 5 RELATIONSHIPS WITH AN ETERNAL PERSPECTIVE

OPENING SCENARIO

Your daughter is frustrated with a friend. "She is so annoying. She keeps doing the same thing over and over, and I am just done. Why should I keep investing in this friendship?"

Your son is dismissive of an unkind classmate. "He is a jerk. I do not care what happens to him."

And you realize something important: they are treating people as disposable. They are evaluating relationships based on what they get out of them, not on eternal value. **They do not see people through the lens of eternity.**

CONVERSATION STARTER

Let's talk: How do you decide whether someone is worth investing in? What makes a relationship matter to you?

SHORT TEACHING

Here is a truth that will transform your relationships: people are eternal. Every person you encounter, friends, family, classmates, and strangers, will exist forever, either with God or separated from Him. **And that means every relationship matters.**

When you see people through the lens of eternity, everything changes.

It changes how you love. You do not love people just because they are easy, fun, or beneficial to you. You love them because they bear God's image and have an eternal destiny. Even the difficult people. **Even the ones who hurt you.** They matter to God, so they should matter to you.

It changes how you forgive. When someone wrongs you, you can hold a grudge, or you can release it, knowing that eternity is at stake. **Bitterness and unforgiveness do not just hurt you in this life; they can harden your heart toward the things of God.**

It changes how you share your faith. When you realize that the people around you will spend eternity somewhere, it creates a sense of urgency, not manipulative or fear-based, but compassionate urgency. **You care about their souls, not just their comfort.**

It changes how you prioritize. Eternal things matter more than temporary things. Relationships matter more than achievements. Souls matter more than status. **Loving people well matters more than accumulating possessions.**

1 Corinthians 13:13 says, "So now faith, hope, and love abide, these three; but the greatest of these is love." **Love is eternal.** Everything else fades. But how you love people, that is what echoes into eternity.

So do not treat people as disposable. Do not write off difficult relationships. **Do not prioritize temporary success over eternal souls.** Live with an eternal perspective. Invest in people. Love sacrificially. And trust that what you do for the sake of love will last forever.

DISCUSSION PROMPTS

1. **Understanding:** What does it mean to see people through the lens of eternity? How would that change the way you treat them?

2. **Personal Response:** Is there someone you've been dismissing, avoiding, or writing off? How would it change things if you saw them as an eternal soul who matters to God?

3. **Lived Practice:** This week, invest in one relationship you've been neglecting. Love someone difficult. Forgive someone who's wronged you. See them through the lens of eternity.

PARENT NOTE

This conversation is transformative because **it shifts focus from self-centered relationships to eternal investment.** Your kids are being trained by culture to evaluate relationships based on usefulness, pleasure, or benefit. This teaching challenges that entirely.

Your job: Help them see that **people are eternal, and how we love them matters forever.** Teach them to invest in difficult relationships, forgive when it's hard, and care about people's souls.

Model this yourself. Do you treat people as disposable? Do you write off difficult people, or do you invest in them, love them sacrificially, and care about their eternal destiny? Your kids will learn from and mirror what they see.

Watch for this: Kids who see people as disposable often become relationally shallow, using people, avoiding conflict, and prioritizing comfort. Kids who see people as eternal become sacrificially loving, forgiving, and mission-minded disciples.

Important reminder: An eternal perspective does not mean you stay in toxic or abusive relationships. **Boundaries are biblical and necessary.** But it does mean you do not dismiss people as worthless or beyond care.

ACTION STEP

Tonight, each person shares one relationship that has been difficult with someone hard to love, frustrating, or hurtful.

Then ask, "How would I treat this person differently if I truly saw them as an eternal soul who matters to God?"

Commit to one way to invest in that relationship this week with love, patience, or forgiveness.

ONE-SENTENCE ANCHOR

People are eternal—and how we love them now echoes into eternity.

"So now faith, hope, and love abide, these three; but the greatest of these is love." — 1 Corinthians 13:13

SCRIPTURE READING

1 Corinthians 13:13
Matthew 22:37–40
1 John 4:7–12
Colossians 3:12–14
Matthew 25:31–46

DAY 6 CULTURE LENS—FEAR-DRIVEN NARRATIVES ABOUT THE FUTURE

OPENING SCENARIO

Your daughter is scrolling through her phone, and you notice her expression growing darker. She is reading article after article about climate catastrophe, political collapse, economic disaster, pandemics, and societal breakdown. She looks up at you, genuinely scared. "What if the world just ends? What if we do not have a future?"

Your son has been consuming similar content videos predicting societal collapse, influencers talking about the futility of planning for the future, and memes about how "we are all doomed." He shrugs. "I mean, they are probably right. Everything is falling apart."

And you realize something important: fear-driven narratives about the future are everywhere. The culture is saturated with messages of doom, **catastrophizing, and hopelessness, shaping how your kids see the world.**

CONVERSATION STARTER

Let's talk: When you hear news about the future—climate, politics, economy, society—what do you usually feel? Hope or fear?

SHORT TEACHING

Here is one of the most destructive forces in our culture: fear-driven narratives about the future. Everywhere you look, someone is predicting disaster, collapse, or catastrophe. And the message is always the same: things are bad, they are getting worse, and there is no hope.

Now, let's be clear: the world is broken. There are real problems: injustice, suffering, environmental degradation, and conflict. **We do not deny reality or pretend everything is fine. But there is a difference between honest realism and fear-driven catastrophizing.**

Fear-driven narratives do two things:

1. **They paralyze you.** If the future is hopeless, why even try? Why pursue education, build relationships, and invest in the world? You either give up or live for the moment because "nothing matters anyway."

2. **They consume you.** Fear becomes a lens through which you see everything. Every news story confirms the narrative. Every setback feels like proof the world is ending. And you lose the ability to see hope, beauty, or God's faithfulness.

Here's the biblical truth: **Yes, the world is broken.** But God is sovereign. **He is not anxious or uncertain. He is not surprised.** He is still on the throne. And He has promised that this is not how the story ends.

So here's how to respond to fear-driven narratives:

1. **Acknowledge reality without catastrophizing.**
   Yes, there are problems. But **don't let fear magnify them beyond truth.**

2. **Limit your exposure to fear-based content.**
   You don't need to doomscroll. You don't need to consume every apocalyptic prediction. **Protect your mind.**

3. **Anchor yourself in God's sovereignty.**
   When fear rises, remind yourself: **God is in control. His promises are sure. I can trust Him.**

4. **Live with hope and purpose.**
   Do not let fear paralyze you. Live faithfully. Serve generously. Invest in the future, because God is making all things new.

Fear says the future is hopeless. Faith reminds us that God holds the future.

DISCUSSION PROMPTS

1. **Understanding:** What's the difference between honest realism (acknowledging real problems) and fear-driven catastrophizing (believing everything is hopeless)?
2. **Personal Response:** Where have you absorbed fear-driven narratives about the future? How has it affected the way you think or live?
3. **Lived Practice:** This week, when you encounter fear-based content or messages, pause and ask: "Is this truth, or is this fear? And how does God's sovereignty speak to this?"

PARENT NOTE

This conversation is urgent **because fear-driven narratives are everywhere**, and your kids are absorbing them. They are being taught that the future is hopeless, and it is producing anxiety, despair, and **even a sense of paralysis.**

Your job: disrupt the narrative. Help them see that while the world is broken, God is still sovereign, and His promises are sure. **Teach them to acknowledge real problems without falling into catastrophizing.**

Model hope for yourself. Do you consume fear-based content? Do you tend to catastrophize, or do you live with confident trust in God's sovereignty? **Your kids will often mirror your posture.**

Limit your exposure. You do not have to consume every news story, every social media panic, or every apocalyptic prediction. **Protect your family's mental and spiritual health by setting wise boundaries around media consumption.**

Watch for this: Kids who are shaped by fear-driven narratives often become either anxious (paralyzed by fear) or apathetic (giving up because they see no point). Kids who are shaped by biblical hope become courageous, purposeful, and faith-filled disciples.

Important reminder: Acknowledging problems and caring about justice is not fear-driven. **It becomes fear-driven when you begin to believe that the problems are bigger than God's power and His promises.**

ACTION STEP

Tonight, talk as a family:

"What fear-driven messages have we absorbed about the future?"

"How do God's sovereignty and His promises speak to those fears?"

Then commit: "This week, we will limit our exposure to fear-based content and anchor our hearts in truth and hope."

ONE-SENTENCE ANCHOR

Fear-driven narratives say the future is hopeless—but God's sovereignty and promises say He holds the future and will make all things new.
"For God gave us a spirit not of fear but of power and love and self-control." — 2 Timothy 1:7

SCRIPTURE READING

2 Timothy 1:7
Psalm 46:1–3
Isaiah 41:10
Matthew 6:25–34
Philippians 4:6–7

DAY 7 PRACTICE—HOPE-FOCUSED GRATITUDE EXERCISE

OPENING SCENARIO

It has been a heavy week. The news has been grim. Your kids are anxious about the future. You are carrying your own worries. **And the weight of it all feels overwhelming.**

But tonight, you decide: we need to shift the atmosphere. **We need to practice hope. One of the most powerful ways to cultivate hope is through gratitude, specifically gratitude that looks back at God's faithfulness and looks forward with trust.**

So you gather everyone around the table and say, "Tonight, we are going to practice hope. We are going to remember what **God has done, and we are going to trust Him with what is ahead."**

CONVERSATION STARTER

Before we start: When you think about the past year, what's one thing God has done that you're grateful for?

SHORT TEACHING

Here is a practice that will anchor you in hope: hope-filled gratitude. It is not just thanking God for good things. It is remembering His past faithfulness and letting that fuel trust for the future.

Think about it. Hope is not just wishful thinking about tomorrow. It is rooted in what God has already done. When you remember how He has been faithful in the past, **it strengthens your confidence that He will be faithful in the future.**

Psalm 77:11–12 says, "I will remember the deeds of the LORD; yes, I will remember your wonders of old. I will ponder all your work, and meditate on your mighty deeds."

Remembering is an act of worship, and it produces hope.

Here is how to practice hope-filled gratitude:

1. Look back.
What has God done in the past year? In your life? In your family? Name it. Be specific.

"God provided when we did not know how the bills would be paid."

"God sustained us through a hard season."

"God brought healing."

Remembering God's faithfulness builds confidence and strengthens your hope.

2. Give thanks.
Don't just mentally acknowledge it. **Thank Him out loud.** Gratitude shifts your focus from fear to faithfulness.

3. Look forward.
Now, with that remembrance fresh, **bring your future anxieties to God**. Name what you are worried about. Then say, "God, You were faithful then. I trust that you will be faithful now."

This practice does something powerful: **it anchors your hope in truth rather than wishful thinking**. You are not just hoping things will work out. You are trusting the God who has proven His faithfulness over and over again.

Over time, this rhythm of remembering, **thanking, and trusting trains your heart to live with hope.**

DISCUSSION PROMPTS

1. **Understanding:** Why does remembering God's past faithfulness help us trust Him for the future?

2. **Personal Response:** What's one way you've seen God be faithful in the past? How does that shape your hope for the future?

3. **Lived Practice:** How can we make this a regular rhythm—looking back with gratitude and looking forward with trust?

PARENT NOTE

This is deeply practical, and it is a practice you can return to again and again. When anxiety creeps in, when fear rises, and **when the future feels uncertain, pause and practice hope-filled gratitude.**

Your job: lead this practice tonight. Model it. Show your kids what it looks like to remember God's faithfulness and trust Him with the future.

Make it regular. This does not have to be a one-time thing. You can do this weekly, monthly, or whenever your family needs a reset in hope. Create a rhythm.

Do not force positivity. This is not about pretending everything is fine. It is about honestly bringing your fears to **God while remembering His proven faithfulness.**

Watch for this: Families who regularly practice gratitude and remembrance develop a **deep, resilient hope**; families who do not often spiral into anxiety and despair.

ACTION STEP

Tonight, practice hope-focused gratitude as a family:

Step 1: Look back.
Go around the table. Each person shares one way they've seen God be faithful in the past year.

Step 2: Give thanks.
Pray together, thanking God specifically for each thing that was shared.

Step 3: Look forward.
Each person shares one thing they feel anxious or uncertain about in the future. Then say together, "God, You were faithful then. We trust that You will be faithful now."

Commit to doing this regularly, whether weekly or monthly.

ONE-SENTENCE ANCHOR

Hope grows as we remember God's past faithfulness and trust Him with our future.
"I will remember the deeds of the LORD; yes, I will remember your wonders of old." — Psalm 77:11

SCRIPTURE READING

Psalm 77:11–15
Lamentations 3:21–24
Psalm 105:1–5
Deuteronomy 7:17–19
Hebrews 13:5–6

DAY 8 BIG QUESTION—HOW SHOULD HOPE CHANGE DAILY LIVING?

OPENING SCENARIO

Your son asks a question at breakfast:

"Okay, so we believe Jesus is coming back, and God is making all things new. That's great. But what does that actually change about today? I still have to go to school, do homework, and deal with annoying people. How does hope change any of that?"

Your daughter nods.

"Yeah. Sometimes it feels like hope is just a nice idea about the future, but it doesn't really help with the boring, hard parts of everyday life."

And you realize something important: they don't see the connection. They think hope is just an abstract idea, something you believe about the future, but not something that actually shapes how you live today.

CONVERSATION STARTER

Let's wrestle with this: If you really believed—deep down—that Jesus is coming back and God will make all things new, what would actually change about how you live today?

SHORT TEACHING

Here's the question at the heart of this entire unit: **How should hope change daily living?** Because if hope doesn't affect how you live *now*, it's not real biblical hope. It's just wishful thinking.

So let's get practical. Here's how hope changes everything:

1. Hope gives you courage in hard circumstances.
When you understand that your future is secure, you can face today's trials without losing hope. **You are not crushed by hardship because you know it is not the end.**

Romans 8:18 says, "I consider that the sufferings of this present time are not worth comparing with the glory that is to be revealed to us."

This hope sustains you, even in the midst of pain.

2. Hope gives you purpose in mundane work.
When you understand that what you do today matters for eternity, even the ordinary becomes meaningful. **Your homework, your job, and your chores are not pointless.** You are faithfully stewarding what God has given you in light of eternity.

Colossians 3:23–24 says, "Whatever you do, work wholeheartedly, as for the Lord… knowing that from the Lord you will receive the inheritance as your reward."

3. Hope gives you urgency in relationships.
When you realize people are eternal, you begin to care more about **their souls than their comfort. You invest in difficult relationships.** You share your faith. You love sacrificially, because eternity is at stake.

4. Hope gives you freedom from fear.
When you trust that God is sovereign and His promises are sure, **you do not need to live in anxiety about the future.** Instead, you can face uncertainty with confidence. As Hebrews 13:6 says, "The Lord is my helper; I will not fear."

5. Hope gives you endurance in suffering.
When you know resurrection is coming, **you can keep going even when life is hard.** You don't give up. You don't lose heart because this isn't the end of the story.

So here's the answer: Hope truly changes everything. It changes how you face hardship, how you work, how you love, how you respond to fear, and how you endure. **Hope is not just a theological idea; it is fuel for faithful living.**

DISCUSSION PROMPTS

1. **Understanding:** How does hope in Jesus' return and the restoration of all things actually change how you live today?
2. **Personal Response:** Which of these five areas—courage, purpose, urgency, freedom from fear, endurance—do you most need hope to shape right now?
3. **Lived Practice:** This week, when you face something hard, mundane, or uncertain, ask: "How does hope change how I respond to this?"

PARENT NOTE

This is the culmination of the entire unit and where theology becomes deeply practical. Your kids need to see that hope isn't abstract; it changes how you live every single day.

Your job: Help them connect the dots. When they're discouraged, point them to hope. **When they're anxious, point them to hope**. When they're struggling to see the point of everyday work, point them to hope. **Show them that hope isn't just future-focused; it empowers them in the present.**

Model this yourself. Do you live as if hope truly matters? Do you face hardship with courage, work with purpose, love with urgency, and endure with confidence? **Your kids will learn hope by watching you live it out.**

Make it concrete. Don't just talk about hope in the abstract; help your kids apply it. "You're anxious about this test. How does hope in God's sovereignty change that?"

"You're discouraged by this friendship. How does hope in eternity change how you invest in this person?"

Watch for this: Kids who don't connect hope to daily life often see faith as irrelevant. But kids who live in light of hope become **courageous, purposeful, faith-filled disciples.**

ACTION STEP

Tonight, go through the five ways hope changes daily living. Each person picks one and shares a specific example:

1. "Hope gives me courage to face [this hard thing]."
2. "Hope gives me purpose in [this mundane work]."
3. "Hope gives me urgency to invest in [this relationship]."
4. "Hope frees me from fear about [this uncertainty]."
5. "Hope gives me endurance through [this suffering]."

Then pray together, asking God to make hope real and active in your daily lives.

> **ONE-SENTENCE ANCHOR**
>
> **Hope isn't just theology—it's the fuel for courage, purpose, urgency, freedom, and endurance in everyday life.**
> *"Therefore, preparing your minds for action, and being sober-minded, set your hope fully on the grace that will be brought to you at the revelation of Jesus Christ." — 1 Peter 1:13*

SCRIPTURE READING

1 Peter 1:13
Romans 8:18–25
Colossians 3:1–4, 23–24
Titus 2:11–14
1 Corinthians 15:58

DAY 9

FINAL REFLECTION AND CELEBRATION—FAMILY TESTIMONY MOMENT

OPENING SCENARIO

It's the final day of your 90-day journey. You gather around the table one last time, and there's a sense of both completion and anticipation. Your daughter says, "I can't believe we actually did this, ninety days of talking about God, theology, and faith. I didn't think we'd make it."

Your son grins. "Yeah. And honestly? I feel like I understand so much more than I did three months ago. Faith actually makes sense now."

You look around the table and feel a deep gratitude. **You've spent 90 days building a foundation not just of knowledge, but of lived, practiced, and discussed faith.** And tonight, you're going to celebrate what God has done.

CONVERSATION STARTER

Let's celebrate: What's one thing you've learned over these 90 days that's changed the way you think about God, yourself, or how you live?

SHORT TEACHING

Here's what you've accomplished over the past 90 days: you've walked through the core doctrines of the Christian faith together. You've talked about who God is, who you are, why you're broken, how Jesus saves you, what grace means, how the Spirit empowers you, how growth happens, why community matters, what purpose looks like, and what hope sustains you.

But more than that, you've lived out your faith as a family. You've had hard conversations. You've asked honest questions. You've prayed together. You've confessed sin. You've encouraged each other. You've wrestled with doubt and anchored yourselves in the truth.

And here's what matters most: this isn't the end, it's the beginning. **You've laid a foundation. Now you get to keep building on it day by day, conversation** by conversation, and choice by choice.

So tonight, you're going to do two things:

1. Reflect.
Look back over the journey. What has God taught you? How have you grown? What truths have taken root?

2. Celebrate.
Thank God for His faithfulness. Celebrate what He has done in your family. And commit to keep walking in what you've learned.

Because here's the truth: **theology isn't just information, it's transformation.** And when you live it out together, faithfully and daily, **it changes everything.**

DISCUSSION PROMPTS

1. **Understanding:** What's one truth you've learned over the past 90 days that you want to hold onto for the rest of your life?
2. **Personal Response:** How have you seen God work in you—or in our family—over these three months?
3. **Lived Practice:** What's one thing you want to keep practicing as a family moving forward?

PARENT NOTE

You did it for ninety days of intentional, theological, formative conversation with your family. That's not small. That's significant. And it matters more than you know.

Your job tonight: celebrate, thank God, affirm your kids, and commit to keep going. This isn't a one-time thing. **It's a rhythm** you've established, one that can keep **shaping your family for years to come.**

Don't let it end here. You've built momentum. You've created a culture of conversation, so keep it going. Maybe you can do another unit. Maybe you revisit topics. Maybe you keep having intentional conversations at the table. **Whatever you do, don't stop.**

Model gratitude and humility. Let your kids hear you thank God for what He has taught you. **Let them see that you're still learning, still growing, still being shaped.**

Celebrate your kids. Affirm the growth you've seen, the questions they've asked, the honesty they've shown, and the faith they're walking in. Let them know you see **God at work in them.**

ACTION STEP

Tonight, do this as a family:

Step 1: Reflect.
Go around the table. Each person shares:

- One truth they've learned that changed them.
- One way they've seen God at work in themselves or the family.
- One thing they want to keep practicing.

Step 2: Celebrate.
Pray together, thank God for His faithfulness, for what He has taught you, and for the journey ahead.

Step 3: Commit.
Decide together how you will keep this going. Maybe it's weekly family devotions. Maybe it's monthly theological conversations. Maybe it's simply a commitment to staying intentional. Whatever it is, choose it together and **commit to it.**

ONE-SENTENCE ANCHOR

Ninety days of faith conversations laid a foundation—now we keep building, walking faithfully in what we've learned, trusting God to complete what He's started.

"Which we have heard and known, and our fathers have told us. We will not conceal them from their children, but tell to the generation to come the praises of the Lord, and His strentgth and His wondrous works that He has done." — Psalms 78:3-4

SCRIPTURE READING

Philippians 1:6
Deuteronomy 6:4–9
Psalm 78:1–7
2 Timothy 3:14–17
Colossians 2:6–7

CLOSING BLESSING

As you close this 90-day journey, receive this blessing:

May the God who made you continue to shape you.

May the Son who saved you continue to transform you.

May the Spirit who dwells in you continue to empower you.

And may you walk faithfully together as a family knowing Him, loving Him, and making Him known, not because you have it all figured out, but because He is faithful to complete what He has started

To God be the glory, forever and ever. Amen.

A SMALL FAVOR THAT MAKES A BIG DIFFERENCE

If this book has helped you or your family grow in understanding God's truth, build meaningful rhythms, or have deeper conversations about faith, I'd be grateful if you took a moment to leave a review on Amazon.

Reviews play an important role in helping this book reach other families who are seeking to be intentional about discipleship in their homes. Your words may be the encouragement someone else needs to begin.

It doesn't need to be long or polished—just a few honest sentences about your experience is more than enough.

Thank you for your time, your commitment to learning, and your desire to lead your family well in truth.

With gratitude,
Built to Stand Publishing

www.ingramcontent.com/pod-product-compliance
Lightning Source LLC
LaVergne TN
LVHW081322110826
845149LV00007B/1567

* 9 7 9 8 9 9 0 5 7 1 8 4 6 *